LET ME TELL YOU MY STORY

LET ME TELL YOU MY STORY

DENNIS SCHULZE

Book Design & Production:
Columbus Publishing Lab
www.ColumbusPublishingLab.com

Copyright © 2025 by
Dennis Schulze

All rights reserved.
This book, or parts thereof, may not be
reproduced in any form without permission.

Paperback ISBN: 978-1-63337-992-3
Hardcocer ISBN: 979-8-90183-003-1
E-Book ISBN: 978-1-63337-993-0

Printed in the United States of America
1 3 5 7 9 10 8 6 4 2

Dennis Schulze
Husband, father, grandfather, friend, soldier,
attorney, and lifelong storyteller

Let me tell you a story. It might stir an emotion. Perhaps it will stimulate action. Or maybe it will just make you think.

Storytelling is a timeless tradition that transcends disciplines and mediums, and the Arts & Sciences community continues to use the art form to explain, inspire, enlighten, and discover.

> The Ohio State University
> College of Arts & Sciences
> The Storytellers/Summer 2021

THE ANCIENT ART OF STORYTELLING

The art of storytelling began in the early days of human history. Since these early tales were oral, we do not have a resource to turn to where we can enjoy and learn from them.

As history progressed, storytellers would sometimes supplement their verbal tales with pictures (cave paintings for example) and eventually written words. These visual aids provide us with an insight into the content of the stories and thus a better understanding of what was happening in the lives of our ancestors.

The stories which were being told were sometimes true, sometimes fabricated, and sometimes a mixture of truth and fiction. In the ninth century, we find an example of fictional stories performed by Scheherazade in the epic story "One Thousand and One Nights." These fictional tales were told in order for the storyteller to save her life.

In the Middle Ages, storytellers were sometimes called minstrels or troubadours. They were often valued members of society. At times they were even part of the king's court. Their stories often mixed true happenings (news) with the traditional stories of the region (entertainment).

As I look back at my journey on this Earth, I now realize that I have been a storyteller for much of my life. I have recalled memories of actual life incidents which have shaped my view of the world and often guided my actions. I have always been willing to pass these stories along to others.

It is only recently that I have supplemented my oral stories with writings by publishing the book "Welcome to the Army" where I recount happenings during my 30 years in the United States Army. I have now written this book containing many more stories that happened throughout my life.

I hope you enjoy these tales and that you will tell your friends that a storyteller is in town.

LET ME TELL YOU MY STORY

Despite the title, this book is not just about me. When I reached my 75th birthday, I began to reflect on my life experiences and realized they were a series of happenings that shaped who I am. People have been telling stories of their lives for thousands of years. Most of these recollections are not written down. Over time, the details are forgotten and a rich history of a person is gone. I decided that I did not want my history to disappear so, I put it in writing.

I have been blessed with a wonderful family and friends, and God has given me just enough wisdom and strength to muddle through more than 80 years without destroying the creative being He made. Oh, I have made mistakes and sometimes bad choices have complicated things. But I have had a good life.

I hope that when you read this story, you will be inspired to sit down, reflect on, and write the story of your own life. If you feel overwhelmed by a project of such magnitude, pick a subject such as your childhood, your grandparents, your career, or whatever you would like to pass along to posterity.

When you do finish, you might decide to publish your creation, or you might give it to your children and grandchildren. Either way that's great! They will then have the opportunity to learn who you are and what is important to you. I am sure that it will have a positive impact on them as they travel thru life.

I won't give you advice on how to proceed with your endeavor because your experiences are distinctive to you. It is not important that you create a masterpiece; it is important that you memorialize some or all of your life.

I did find it helpful to identify various aspects of my life and randomly write down notes on what I could remember. Your list may be different, or you may choose to write chronologically.

For this book I selected the following areas of interest:

Chapter 1:   Early Life .... Page 1
Chapter 2:   Friends .... Page 69
Chapter 3:   Education .... Page 97
Chapter 4:   Dating & Marriage .... Page 119
Chapter 5:   Children & Grandchildren .... Page 149
Chapter 6:   Military Service .... Page 163
Chapter 7:   Legal Profession .... Page 211
Chapter 8:   Service to Others .... Page 235
Chapter 9:   Leisure Time .... Page 259
Chapter 10: Faith .... Page 287

Remember your life is unique! You must decide how you want to be remembered. <u>Try</u> to be truthful. You <u>are</u> allowed to leave out certain details. Have fun and send me a copy.

Throughout this book you will encounter life incidents which will help explain who I am. You will read about:
- a tornado, two fires, and a flood
- a manta ray and a pelican
- a prison riot
- LeBron James
- a helicopter and a mountain
- a heart attack
- gang fights and attempted armed robbery
- a stranger in paradise
- a stolen car in a police chase
- Archie Griffin, a luxury suite, and the Governor of Ohio
- how I became a singing star
- how I became an actor
- how I avoided trouble in a Panamanian bar

- an illegal slot machine
- the movie Psycho
- the soldier of the cycle
- laying a wreath at Arlington Cemetery
- my mother assisting President Ford
- a bus boycott in the sixth grade
- a supper club more than forty-five years old
- State football championship
- representing three killers
- the Last Supper, a play
- RBG and the United States Supreme Court
- 9/11 and the Pentagon
- a chicken in the jungle
- cedar tree smugglers in Panama
- a mad professor
- a 1930s movie theater
- the Energizer Bunny
- an angry taxi driver
- a golden anniversary
- a few good men
- a bet that changed my world
- the invasion of Normandy

Dennis Schulze at 8 Mos. Old

Chapter 1

EARLY LIFE

WHEN YOU ARE BORN, you usually become part of a group of individuals who look after you by providing you with food, water, information about life, and hopefully, love.

When you have lived long enough to form a self-identity, you may look back and evaluate your father, mother, siblings, and grandparents. How were they instrumental in your successes and your failures?

There are no perfect families. You may have been fortunate to have a stable, supportive family or you may have been dealt a hand where you needed to accomplish many life skills on your own.

I was one of the fortunate ones blessed with a family that gave me every opportunity to succeed. As we explore the first 21 years of my life, I believe you will agree that I was blessed with a good beginning and benefitted from that head start.

As I sat down to write this book, I began to remember incidents in my life from my early years (1940's) to the present. I soon realized that I would need to begin my story almost thirty years prior to my birth.

Events were happening before I was born that would have a profound influence on my life. My mother was born in 1921 and my father was born in 1917, but I realized that they, just like me, were impacted by events which changed their environment even before they were born.

I have chosen my early years to coincide with the time that I lived with my parents. For me, that would be from birth until I left home to attend law school at The Ohio State University.

As important as this formative stage of my development was, each of the succeeding chapters show the constant addition of influencing factors that impacted who I am.

THE EARLY YEARS

In the early 1940s, Mary Beth Akins and Wilbur Schulze fell in love and decided to get married. They knew that their families could not afford a big wedding, so they eloped to Indiana to be married by a "justice of the peace." About 18 months later, on February 17, 1943, I was born in Alliance, Ohio. Thus began my life's journey. I thank you for joining me and I hope that this story will evoke many memories of your own life.

In order to realize what life was going to be like for these new parents and their baby boy, we need to start by looking back to the beginning of World War One.

EARLY LIFE

1914 TO 1920

In 1914, my grandparents, Henry and Meta Schulze, were living in Bucyrus, Ohio. Their family was from Germany, and they still had family members living in Germany. They were integrated into the American culture but, this was not an easy time for them since their family's home country was at war with Great Britain and, in a few years, would be at war with the United States.

In the early years of the War, there was not a lot of popular support for the United States to get directly involved. This may have been because of the large number of central Europeans who immigrated to this country in the late 19th century. This was truly a "world" war and was often called the "war to end all wars." Before the conflict was over, millions of human lives were lost and loyalties were severely challenged.

After a number of incidents involving United States merchant ships being attacked and sunk by German submarines, President Thomas Woodrow Wilson finally declared war on Germany. This significant step occurred in April of 1917, the very month and year my father was born.

Unfortunately, the war raged on for over four years. During 1914 to 1918, many soldiers and civilians lost their lives. Despite the late entry into the war, the United States military suffered more than 117,000 casualties.

The war finally came to an end, and the world breathed a sigh of relief. Then, an enemy just as deadly began to ravage the world. The Spanish Flu pandemic began in early 1918 and continued into 1920. This deadly disease preceded the Covid disaster by about 100 years. Estimates of the number of United States citizens killed by the Spanish flu were over five times higher than the number of United States soldiers and sailors killed in combat during World War One.

1920 TO 1929

In 1920, Dad was turning three years old and the world was trying to recover from the suffering brought on by a major war and a deadly pandemic. A grateful nation began to celebrate the end of catastrophes and the apparent return of good times. The Roaring Twenties were about to begin.

On January 29, 1921, my mother was born in Alliance, Ohio. Her mother and father, Mary and Glen Akins, looked forward to an opportunity for a better life. Glen was a successful businessman and he and Mary were building a family of nine children (one of whom died in childbirth).

ROARING 20'S

A new style of dressing and dancing sprang up across the U.S., and flappers were dancing the Charleston with abandon. (Check out YouTube.) The concern over the evils of alcohol led to an amendment to the Constitution banning its sale. Prohibition made alcohol illegal, but by 1925 there were over 30,000 speakeasies in New York City alone! A speakeasy was a bar which was selling alcohol illegally.

These carefree times would not last. In 1929, the stock market crashed and banks began to run short of cash. The worst economic depression in the history of the United States was just beginning.

1929 TO 1941

Over the next decade, there would be no easy times for the Schulze and Akins families or for millions of other families in this country. The U.S. economy was in shambles and the number of people unemployed was massive.

EARLY LIFE

Just when it seemed that it couldn't get worse, my grandfather, Glen Akins, died at the age of 43 from complications with his gallbladder. If medical technology had been more advanced, a simple operation could have saved his life. My Grandma became a widow with eight children, the youngest just 15 months old. She and the children would need a deep resolve to survive, along with the help of God.

As the 1930s and the Great Depression began, so did the dust storms across much of the Midwest and West United States. Crops failed and topsoil was blown from its moorings. The government was facing not only massive unemployment, but the need to subsidize our food producers.

In an effort to deal with these national tragedies, people sought an escape from reality. A local movie theater was able to provide entertainment which many of them could afford. Talking motion pictures had begun in 1927, and complete color films instead of black and white became the way to go in the thirties.

As a part of the New Deal, the federal government offered grants and low-cost loans to businessmen to build and renovate theaters. The average cost of a movie ticket was twenty-five cents. Even in the 1950s I remember going to the Strand Theater in Alliance, Ohio, and watching movies for a quarter.

Some of the most popular movies of the time were Snow White, Gone With the Wind, and The Wizard of Oz. Shirley Temple and Clark Gable were major stars and Laurel and Hardy helped audiences laugh.

Superman and Batman were created and movie theaters were built in small towns across America. One of those theaters, called the "Avalon," was built in Marysville, Ohio, in 1936. Seventy-five years later, when Karen and I had moved to Marysville, I joined a group of local citizens to restore the Avalon Theatre to its glory days. It reopened in August 2022!

In the 30s, popular music was available on 78 RPM vinyl records and on the radio and included solo singers, groups, and big bands. Glenn Miller, Count Basie, Benny Goodman, Frank Sinatra, Patti Page, the

Andrews Sisters, and Bing Crosby were among the leading singers or musicians.

The 1930s sometimes brought out the best in people, such as Jesse Owens winning four gold medals at the 1936 summer Olympics. Sometimes it brought out the worst, including Adolf Hitler, Al Capone, Bonnie and Clyde, and John Dillinger.

The late 1930s showed promise of a stronger economy. Unfortunately, this renewed production was partly a result of the beginning of World War Two. It appears that World War One was not the "war to end all wars" after all. The Germans and the British were once again locked in combat, and the United States was again staying out of the war at that time.

During this time of turmoil my mother and father made their decision to get married. It was on April 14, 1941, that they exchanged their vows to live together as husband and wife. Eight months later on December 7, 1941, the Japanese bombed the United States Navy Base at Pearl Harbor. The United States declared war and began to draft young men for induction into the military service. My parents' vow to live together would not be possible for over two years.

1941 TO 1945

My father joined hundreds of thousands of other young men who received a draft notice, and he decided to join the United States Army. He trained as an infantry soldier and shipped off to England. From there, he prepared to take part in the invasion of Normandy.

Meanwhile, back in Ohio, my mother and I were living with my father's parents who, once again, saw their home country at war with the world. This time, their son would be joining in the fight against Germany.

I don't remember much about the first few years of my life other than what is recorded on a few photographs of that time. I do remember that

EARLY LIFE

my grandpa, Henry Schulze, was a retired tool and die maker who loved to smoke a pipe. He would spend much of his time pulling tobacco from a round silver container. He would then fill the pipe, tap it down with his finger, strike a wooden match and puff to catch the tobacco on fire. Sometimes he would repeat this procedure several times before settling down in his chair while sending clouds of white smoke billowing up into the air. I know now that secondhand smoke is a hazard, but I found a certain comfort in his bad habit.

Grandpa and Grandma Meta loved to play cards and to listen to polka music. Their favorite entertainer was Lawrence Welk whom they followed on the radio or record player and later on television. They also loved accordion music and Grandpa would slap his knee in time to the music. I don't remember any conversations about the war with Germany but I do know that they supported my dad as he helped fight the Axis powers.

Two of my aunts and their families lived within a block of my grandparents' house and we spent many happy hours with them. Both uncles and one of my aunts worked in local factories producing war supplies. My Aunt Edna was a social person who enjoyed traveling and parties. My Aunt Alma enjoyed her house and its gardens. I learned early on not to pick the flowers!

In addition to my dad's sisters, he had two brothers who were named Harry and George. Ironically, Harry was totally bald and George was 6' 7" inches tall. To a young me, he was a giant!

George loved to fish for carp using home-made dough balls. He also would get into the river and reach under the banks to catch snapping turtles with his bare hands! When I expressed concern, he would tell me that the turtles would always go head first into their hole. As far as I know, he never lost any fingers.

George also loved to play horseshoes and to bowl. On two occasions he bowled a perfect 300 game and was asked to bowl on television!

The Invasion of Normandy

MY FATHER GOES TO WAR

A major event in my father's life during his early years was his service in the United States Army during World War Two. When I was young, he never talked about these challenging times until I had graduated from college. I had heard from my mother and grandmother that he was wounded and still had shrapnel in his legs. He never really wanted to talk about the war, even after I found his Purple Heart and Bronze Star in a drawer.

After I graduated from college, I again asked him about his experiences in the war and he finally began to talk. He told me that after training in the United States he was sent to England on a boat. The threat of German submarines was very high and the soldiers on the ship were on constant lookout for periscopes.

One night, the troop transport was caught in a major storm and tossed about. The fear of being attacked by German submarines was

EARLY LIFE

suddenly not as menacing as the storm. At one point my dad was certain that the ship was going to roll over when it listed to its side and almost capsized! The next day, the storm had passed and the soldiers' attention returned to submarines.

When Dad reached England, there were a large number of Allied troops. The training increased in intensity, and everyone knew that a major campaign against the Germans, who were in France, was about to begin.

Hitler also knew that an invasion was likely, and he assigned one of his top generals, Rommel, to oversee building a defensive perimeter. This included the use of concrete bunkers, land mines, floating water mines, and beach and water obstacles. In addition, a large force of German soldiers was placed along 2400 miles of the French coastline. This became known as the Atlantic Wall.

On June 6, 1944, General Dwight David Eisenhower ordered my dad and 156,000 other allied soldiers to begin the invasion of Normandy. They were loaded onto ships with a mission to engage the Germans and retake France. The massive force soon neared its destination as airplanes buzzed overhead and large Navy battleships began to fire huge shells at the German fortifications.

Dad told me that there seemed to be confusion everywhere. Tens of thousands of armed soldiers were climbing down rope netting to board the landing crafts which would take them to the shoreline where the entrenched Germans waited for them! The beaches were well guarded, and rifle and machine gun rounds rained down on the invading troops. The sounds of mortars, artillery, mines, and hand grenades were deafening.

My dad had been ordered to carry a communications cable to shore along with his backpack and rifle and with that slung over his shoulder, he began to repel over the side of the ship to get into a landing craft. Even though his senses were being overwhelmed, my dad could see flashes of muzzle blasts coming from the German bunkers and could see that rifle and machine gun rounds were striking the landing crafts in front of them.

My dad was in the back of the landing craft near the pilot who was operating the craft. Next to the pilot was Dad's lieutenant. Dad heard the pilot tell the lieutenant that this was his first trip in and he didn't know what a safe direction was. The lieutenant told him to follow a landing craft in front of them and he did. A few minutes later a huge explosion from a floating mine tore apart the lead landing craft and many of the dead and wounded were thrown into the water.

The lieutenant, probably fearing the danger of the fortifications atop the beach, told the pilot to keep going. There was no time to try to save the wounded soldiers. A brief time later, the pilot told the lieutenant that this was where the men were to get out.

As my dad jumped off the landing craft, he realized that the water was over his head. The cable he was carrying was pulling him down as was his rifle and backpack. He dropped the cable and tried to swim but he was still underwater. Just then, his foot hit the ground and he began to climb toward the beach. He could hear bullets hitting the water and could see bodies floating around him as he tried to reach the shore.

As he was telling me his story, Dad paused. He then told me that he did not remember anything after that time until he was beyond the bunkers and in a vineyard. He then remembers that German snipers were firing down the grapevine rows. Later he discovered a bullet hole in his sleeve; a bullet had narrowly missed his body.

After silencing some of the hostile fire, the 175th Regiment gathered in a small town. They were going from building to building clearing out the Germans when airplanes flew overhead and began shooting at the soldiers. My dad took refuge in a dairy and hid behind a large metal milk container.

After the planes made several passes, they flew off and my dad noticed that there was milk flowing out of the can. He then realized that he had pieces of the shells, and the milk can, in his legs.

EARLY LIFE

My father was one of the lucky ones. He would have to live with shrapnel in his legs for the rest of his life, but he was still alive. He called for help and a medic ran to attend to him. According to the newspaper account, which appeared in the Alliance Review, Dad was wounded on the first day of the invasion. Army records indicate that he was wounded on the second day of the landing.

Somehow, the medic was able to acquire a flatbed truck and he loaded several wounded soldiers into the back of it. All the while, German and Allied planes battled in the sky and the big guns on the navy ships sent shells over their heads.

Medics were able to stop the bleeding. They began to transport Dad and the other wounded soldiers back toward a hospital ship which was in the harbor. Just then, German planes again screamed overhead. The driver stopped the truck and ran to hide in the ditch beside the road. Fortunately, the planes were more interested in getting to the beach and the battle ships than they were interested in a single truck. Dad watched all of this and then he did not remember much again until he was in an operating room on a ship and a doctor told him to count to backwards from ten.

After several operations, he began his recuperation in England. Approximately sixty days later, he returned to duty. He was assigned to a prisoner of war camp where he guarded prisoners until his reassignment back to the United States.

In Europe, the Allies were advancing on Germany and my mom received news that Dad had been wounded but was recovering from his wounds. As 1945 turned into 1946 we got the GREAT news that Dad was being sent back to the United States and would soon be discharged from the Army. He was coming home to his wife and son.

My father was a casualty of the war. Even though he survived, he lived with the consequences for over forty years of his life. He came home to us and we received that blessing that hundreds of thousands of his combat brothers and their families did not receive.

LET ME TELL YOU MY STORY

FRENCH COAST DEAD AHEAD June 6, 1944
Helmeted Yankee soldiers crouch, tightly packed, behind the bulwarks of a Coast Guard landing barge in the historic sweep across the English Channel to the shores of Normandy. These Coast Guard barges rode back and forth through D-day, bringing wave on wave of reinforcements to the beachhead.

The Official 175th After Action Report was published as follows:

AFTER ACTION REPORT

29th Infantry Division – June 1944 – Battle of Normandy
Phase 1 – Beach landing 7 June 1944 to capture of Isigny 9 June 1944.

June 7, 1944, D plus 1, the 175th Infantry landed on Omaha Beach, Normandy, France beginning at 1230 hours. Several of F Company's and one of L Company's landing craft were destroyed by under-water mines and machine gun fire as they approached the beach. The 1st and 2nd battalions landed abreast one mile East of Vierville sur Mer. Machine gun and small arms fire were encountered on the beach. Four hours later, the remainder of the regiment landed one mile East of Saint Laurent sur Mer. Once ashore, the leading battalions moved inland to Vierville, encountering occasional mortar and machine gun fire. The regiment, in a column of battalions, first, second and third, marched to Gruchy. During the march, detachments were deployed from time to time to wipe out small pockets of enemy resistance and snipers.

At 2330, in the vicinity of Gruchy, Company "F" and Regimental Headquarters Company were hit from the flank by enemy gun and artillery fire. Supporting tanks of the 747th Tank battalion moved up, supported the motion to clean up the opposition, and the advance continued.

From 0200 to 0400 8 June, a halt was made for reorganisation. Then turning West on the highway to Isigny, the 1st battalion passed through and captured La Cambe about 0900. Outside La Cambe, the column was attacked and strafed by aircraft bearing Allied insignia at 0930. Six men were killed, 10 wounded.

MY FATHER RETURNS

When Dad came home from the war, we moved into our own house. It was a modest duplex which was just right for us since one of Mom's brothers and his family moved into the other half. The presence of my cousins gave me friends to play with. Within a couple of years, I would get another playmate. Our new family member was a beautiful baby girl named Pamela. She became not only my sister but also a good friend to me and remained so for over 70 years.

The duplex was not ideal for a family of four and it was not in a good school district. My dad had returned to his job with the local newspaper and after a year or so, he began to look for a house with a larger lot so he could have a garden.

My uncle was also looking, and he told Dad about a neighborhood in a good school district which had reasonably priced houses. Soon, both Mom and Dad and my aunt and uncle bought homes across the street from each other.

MY DAD THE BUILDER

With my sister on the way, our home on Glenwood Drive was a bit small for us. When we moved there, it had two bedrooms and one bathroom. The size of the main floor was 1154 square feet. My father, being very talented with building, soon converted a large attic area into a third bedroom. That was a space that I would call home for the next 17 years.

EARLY LIFE

His next project was the basement. He constructed a workshop for himself complete with hand and power tools and a large assortment of nails, screws, nuts, and bolts. He then built an office for Mom where she could type on her typewriter and file important papers. In the front corner, he built a walk-in "fruit cellar" which housed many things including home-canned foods and a keg of wine which my parents made from grapes they had grown on an arbor in our back yard.

My parents' drinking of alcohol consisted of one or two drinks each New Year's Eve and a rare visit to the wine cellar for a sip of the homemade wine. I am not sure how long the mini keg lasted, but it had to be at least a decade. When I was a teen, a visit to the fruit cellar was an opportunity for my first taste of alcohol.

Dad was very talented in building things. He could work as a carpenter, an electrician, or a plumber with skill beyond his training. In addition to home projects, he made numerous set props for the local community theater, including a board which allowed knives to pop out of the back while appearing to be thrown from the front by an actor.

Another of his theater creations was "Mr. Hoskins." This was a full-size recreation of a person who had been poisoned by the little old ladies in the play "Arsenic and Old Lace." After the play concluded, Mr. Hoskins was invited into our home. Visitors were often shocked, but our family and friends made sure to say hello to him.

I did not inherit his skills as a tradesman. When I graduated from law school, he congratulated me but then he said, "Thank goodness you graduated from law school because if you had to make a living with your hands you would starve to death." I am going to assume that this was said in jest, but it was probably true.

He was not just skilled with his hands. He also was very creative, drawing original cartoons and drafting concepts for inventions. He never had the money to follow through on these creations, but his family and friends enjoyed them.

DAD'S GARDEN

Although the house was modestly sized, it had an empty lot next to the house. Dad planted some miniature fruit trees in the front part of the adjacent lot and had a very large garden in the back. The garden had grass walking paths which divided the garden into five sections. In the back section were raspberry bushes, cucumber vines, rhubarb plants, corn, potatoes, and a two-chamber compost holder.

The front of the garden contained a variety of vegetables including green beans, carrots, peas, lettuce, tomatoes, and whatever else that he had space for.

When the fruits and vegetables grew and ripened, Dad and I would harvest them and our family would have fresh and healthy meals. Any foods which were not immediately consumed would be frozen or canned and saved for later.

THE VALUE OF WORK

Work was important to my dad. He believed that everyone should actively use their God-given talents, both to support themselves and their family as well as to stay fit. As I grew older, the Glenwood house provided a lot of chores which were assigned to me. In addition to mowing the lawn, and shoveling snow, every spring I would take a shovel and turn over the dirt in the garden while adding compost to enrich the soil. We eventually had over eight inches of topsoil.

Another ongoing task was to trim the hedges that separated our driveway from the neighbor's property. I didn't have the benefit of electric clippers, so the long hedges were cut and shaped by hand.

We had a one-car garage and its paint began to flake and peel. According to my dad, this was the perfect opportunity to get my exercise by scraping and then painting the entire building. I spent many hot summer days converting this edifice into a structure of beauty.

PARENTING

As I said, Dad was big on keeping active. I had a large newspaper route and I would get exercise delivering over 80 papers each day. When I was not busy at home, he would volunteer me to go to Grandma and Grandpa's farm to pull wild mustard from the fields or help bale and store hay. I also got to clean out the chicken coop (my least favorite job of all time!).

On my wedding day, during his dance with Karen, Dad told her, "Don't let Denny become a couch potato." She has not been entirely successful, but has tried her best to follow Dad's advice.

Dad was also determined to set my moral compass on the right path. His many years in scouting guided this direction. He expected my sister and me to live up to the Scout Oath and Laws. That meant that we should try to be trustworthy, loyal, helpful, friendly, courteous, kind, obedient, cheerful, thrifty, brave, clean, and reverent. This was not just a saying to him; he valued the importance of every one of these attributes and expected us to understand and follow them throughout life.

My father was a special person! He always made time for my sister and me, and the example he set with his own life helped us learn the right way to live our lives. There were times when I deviated a bit and he would let me know that these actions or attitudes were not acceptable. I don't remember him raising his voice or striking me, but the admonition was clear.

He and Mom encouraged Pam and me to explore different interests. Some of mine included playing the saxophone, reading, learning about the law, Little League baseball, basketball, football, fishing, hiking, camping, and enjoying life!

When my dad was not working in his garden, he enjoyed playing board and card games with his family. He also enjoyed fishing, camping, hiking, and Boy Scouting. He was very active in providing a learning environment for the boys and his efforts were recognized. He was awarded the top honor in the district as a Boy Scout leader and he truly deserved it!

My father did not appear to be a radical person who would seek out ways to be different. He worked as a newspaper printer for decades, our family lived in a standard neighborhood, and his spare time was spent on gardening, fishing, and working with youth.

His interest in camping led him to activities on how to build a campfire like the Native Americans did thousands of years ago. He would find a gem rock called flint and create sparks by striking it with a piece of metal. Those sparks were then capable of setting wood on fire and creating a flaming campfire. He would often use this campfire for heat, light, and cooking something to eat.

Where he veered from the ordinary involved something he'd cook on his campfire. He would catch grasshoppers and roast them prior to enjoying them as a snack! He claimed that the grasshoppers provided high protein (it's true – Google it!) and they tasted a little like shrimp.

Although he offered to share this delicacy with me, I declined then and to this day, I have yet to pop one of those bugs into my mouth!

NEW YEAR'S EVE

My parents were not into drinking alcohol. Throughout the year they would occasionally sip on their homemade wine. New Year's Eve allowed them more flexibility. My mom would drink her annual piña colada at the New Year's party that they would host at our house.

A number of their friends were teachers. This was an era when teachers were held to a very strict standard of conduct. If they were seen drinking in public, rumors would fly, and at times, the school board members would discuss the need for discretion with the offending teacher.

My parents' party was attended by a number of teachers and others who could be counted on to not spread rumors. The party was designed for the attendees to have fun, not get drunk.

Each party had a theme, and my parents would send invitations informing regular guests of that year's theme in advance.

One year, a mock Kentucky Derby was held. Each guest had a horse that they "owned" and throughout the night miniature Styrofoam horses would race around a track that my dad had built. If you rolled the dice right, you would win significant "dollars." Mom and Dad printed the money with different attendees' pictures on the denominations.

They could also bet on other horses and could even negotiate the sale of their horse! My sister and I would run the races, complete with betting odds and disqualifications.

Another year, they hosted a hobo-themed party. My Uncle Bill showed up in costume and had not shaved for two weeks before the party. He really played the part.

As the evening got started, my dad said he had to go to the train station to pick up my grandma who had been visiting a daughter in California. Bill told my dad that he would go and pick her up and he would take me along.

We got to the station early and a train pulled in which was not the one we were waiting for. A well-dressed woman got off this train, looked at my uncle and firmly said, "You boy! Take these bags to my car." Uncle Bill did and she gave him a very small tip and we had a good laugh!

BOY SCOUTS

Scouting provided some very special occasions where I got to spend more time with my father. Each year our Boy Scout troop would camp for a week at Camp Tuscazoar. This 600-acre wilderness site is located near the historic Zoar village in north central Ohio. It was established in 1920 and has been used as a campsite by Boy Scouts for over 100 years. As a teenager, my father camped at Tuscazoar and, 25 to 30 years later, I spent many happy times with camp activities and earning the highest rank of Pipestone award, a camp honors recognition.

There are five levels of Pipestone, each with a different theme. For instance, the third year is devoted to brotherhood, where the recipients are counseled about equality and caring about people of different races, gender, and religions.

There is only one camp in the world where the Pipestone ceremony exists! Each recipient of the Pipestone wears it proudly.

Another memorable Scout activity was when we attended a National Jamboree at Valley Forge, Pennsylvania. There were 55,000 scouts and leaders at this memorable event. It was interesting to meet and talk to boys from many different states and even some foreign countries.

If you have never been involved in Boy Scouts, one of the strengths of the program is working to earn merit badges.

There are many different subject areas a Scout can explore. Each area has written insights to help the scout learn about them and eventually master the subject and be awarded a "merit badge."

I remember one major project I undertook was to learn about fingerprints. I learned about the history of fingerprints, the major groupings, and the unique characteristics that identify each and every one of us.

I then had to develop a finger print kit, complete with official cards, a glass surface to apply ink to, and the printer's ink to complete the cards in a recognizable manner. I eventually completed well over 100 prints from different people and then, with their consent, I forwarded them to the FBI in Washington D.C.

THE AUBURN

While we are reminiscing about the past, I am reminded of the opportunity I had to experience over 100 years of automobile manufacturing. I now drive a car that keeps track of approaching traffic and guides the car into the proper lane.

In the late 1950's my parents had some friends who owned twelve antique cars. These included a 1910 Oldsmobile Limited, a 1920 ReVere with a Duesenberg engine and a 1932 Auburn.

The Oldsmobile was often called a "horseless carriage." The ReVere was a touring car with running boards and the Auburn had a plaque on the dashboard which stated, "This automobile has been test driven at more than 100 miles per hour before it was shipped from the factory." It also had a V12 cylinder system. I was asked to drive the Auburn to several antique car shows.

These visits to the past gave me an appreciation of how far the automobile industry advanced in the 50 years following the turn of the century.

HOUSEHOLD PETS

With Dad's encouragement, we always seemed to have room for a pet or two. I believe it was expected that these pets would teach us children about responsibility and love.

We had the usual pets such as a cat, a dog, a hamster, and rabbits. We also had some rather unusual pets such as a chameleon, a praying mantis, and a snapping turtle.

The cat was named Katze which is German for cat. When she surprised us with kittens, Dad changed her name to Mrs. Katze. The 50s were a time to worry what the neighbors might think!

The praying mantis was kept in a screened-in portable cage that my dad made. We would catch grasshoppers and crickets to feed her. It may sound gross, but we were fascinated to watch her catch these insects and, holding them like an ear of corn, she would devour them in a most efficient manner.

We kept the mantis cage in the screened-in porch that Dad had built across the back of our house. One day, we noticed that there was something inside the cage attached to the screen. It was an egg case!

A praying mantis egg case can hatch as many as 300 mantises and when it did (45 to 60 days later) there were hundreds of the little ones running around. Unfortunately, they, and their mother, will eat each other if they are not separated. My sister and I tried to catch as many as we could and release them in Dad's garden where they could catch and eat many of the harmful insects that attack our plants.

The snapping turtle was a rather large one measuring about 12 to 14 inches across its shell. We kept it in a large metal container with an open top. My mother caught this monster with a regular fishing pole and the idea was that dad was going to make turtle soup. This didn't sound too good to me then, and it still doesn't!

Snapping turtles are not the cuddliest of animals. On their best day they will hiss at you and would be willing to take a finger off if you gave them a chance. When Dad would go out to feed this angry reptile, it would take an aggressive stance and hiss at him while exhibiting an angry glare. Dad would quietly talk to it and toss it chunks of meat for it to eat. The turtle never warmed up to Dad, but it must have made an impression on him, since he ended up taking Mr. Snapper to a local pond and releasing him.

EARLY LIFE

OUR NEIGHBORHOOD

Our house on Glenwood Drive was in a great location. It was not quite a block to the elementary school and there was a bus stop at a nearby corner. The neighborhood had many similar style homes. Below is a picture of our house as it looks today.

If you went a block up the street, there was a wooded area and the houses were somewhat bigger and mostly new. It was interesting that somehow, we thought of that area as the "rich" neighborhood even though it was middle class. It might be that we thought that because my cousins and I would occasionally go to that area to a friend's house to watch cartoons on a projector which his family owned. This same family would hire someone to work on their lawn and flower beds. They were obviously "very rich."

After we moved, our family settled into a routine. My mom always had dozens of projects going. Many of them were Girl Scout related. I began kindergarten at Parkway School, which was only a block away, and my dad would get up very early to go to work at the newspaper.

The Glenwood House (But we had trees and hedgerows)

DAD'S JOB

My father was a newspaper printer for 26 years. In that job, he would stand by a square metal table called a turtle. He would then take pieces of lead produced by a linotype machine and piece them together to create a lead page which could be inked and then the letters and images would be transferred to the paper pages.

I would go to visit him at work and there are two things I will always remember. One was the opportunity I had to preview the comics. Each month, the newspaper would receive the comics that would appear in that month's newspapers. I would get to see what happened to Dagwood, Beetle Bailey, and Donald Duck before my friends would.

The other thing I will remember, is the distinct presence of lead fumes which hung heavy in the air in the building. It also permeated the clothing of everyone who worked there. This was before the dangers of ingesting lead were known. The area that the printers worked in was ventilated by a single fan approximately 14"by 14".

Even though the significant long-term effects were not known, the workers demanded that the area have better ventilation systems. When no changes were made, they went on strike. The newspaper brought in new workers and all the veteran workers, including my dad, lost their jobs. At that time there was no requirement that retirement accounts be vested. That meant that my dad worked for 26 years in a lead-filled environment and did not receive a penny of his retirement pay!

Despite the financial setbacks which my father faced, neither he nor my mother ever discouraged me from planning to go to college and then to law school. At that time, I did not realize how much pressure that might have put on them.

My father was a gentle man. I can only remember two times that his emotions overcame the high standards he set for himself. He and I were fishing in Canada and he suddenly had a huge fish on his line right up by the boat. The fish dove beneath the boat pulling the tip of his pole under the boat and the line snapped!

He immediately began to try to break the line with his hands while shouting, "Damn! Damn! Damn!" I had never heard him swear before and I was surprised by this outburst. If I lost that big fish (and my dad wasn't there), I probably would have responded the same way.

The other incident was even more dramatic. My dad and I were working in the garden. This was his sanctuary. He would relax by pulling weeds, making compost, raking the dirt, and harvesting the crops. One day, a door-to-door salesman came to our house. When no one responded to the front doorbell, the salesman went to the garden behind our house where my dad was raking. The salesman began his sales pitch and my dad told him that he was not interested and that he wanted the salesman to leave his property now! The salesman tried to use a different approach and Dad's face started to get red.

As the persistent salesman advanced further into the garden, my dad raised the rake over his head and started toward the salesman shouting, "GET OUT – GET OUT!" The terrified salesman turned and ran down our driveway and into the street. My dad then began to rake the soil as though nothing had happened.

DAD'S CARTOONS

My dad was always thinking and creating. He never went commercial with his ideas, but our family enjoyed his efforts. On the next three pages, you will find a few of my dad's cartoons.

EARLY LIFE

DAD'S COMMUNITY INVOLVEMENT

Between his work and his family obligations, Dad never forgot his duty to serve the community. Not only did he volunteer for Boy Scouts, but he also was active in Community Theater, Civil Defense, the Farm Bureau, the Veterans Services Commission, and his Church.

I believe that his view on how he should spend his life was, "Provide for, teach, and love your family and then serve others."

EARLY LIFE

MY MOTHER

My mother was an amazing person! She didn't have the opportunity to further her high school education by attending college but, she did help raise two active children and worked part time. Despite the demands that placed on her life, she served her community and her country in spectacular fashion! My father, who stormed the beaches of Normandy on Day One of the invasion, was proud of his wife for all of it!

Her teenage years were not always easy for her. When she was eight, the United States entered the Great Depression which impacted her, her four brothers, and three sisters significantly. Two years later, her father died. She and her brothers and sisters could have "dropped out" of life, but they were determined to become successful.

She graduated from high school and two years later at the age of twenty, was married to my dad. Over the next five years she would give birth to a boy (me) and a girl (my sister). After she met and married my father, life again threw her a curve ball when the United States Army decided that they needed to borrow Dad for a couple of years.

It was during that period of time that she was forced to assume both parental roles. With the help of my grandparents, she carried on while she anxiously awaited the return of her husband. She was in her early twenties, yet every day she faced the real possibility of being notified that she was now a widow.

Given that background, she accomplished a great deal in her life. Although she completed high school with good grades, she was unable to afford to go to college. Despite that, she had intelligence and a drive to accomplish many things. She went from poverty, to meeting and sharing a stage with a President of the United States.

So, the question is, what kind of a mother was she? Mom was not a devoted cook. She was great at casseroles and, during harvest time, would organize the whole family to prepare and freeze corn, green beans, peas, red beets, carrots, and many other vegetables taken from Dad's garden. We would put many boxes of vegetables and fruits into a large freezer for use throughout the year.

Just like Dad, she had a calling for community service. She was a Girl Scout leader for more than 30 years, positively impacting the lives of many young women. When Mom was in her 80's she would get phone calls and visits from her former scouts.

As a district representative, she would take on the Girl Scout cookie sales on a grand scale. I remember a semi-tractor trailer truck backing into our driveway and unloading countless cartons of cookies.

These cookies were then stacked in our dining room area. At times, they were 6 to 7 feet high and would fill most of the room.

She would then call the leaders for all of the units in town and schedule them to come pick up their troop's cookies. When they came, Mom had organized their orders and would hand out cartons or boxes through

EARLY LIFE

our dining room window. Somehow, everything seemed to work out due to her attention to details.

While she was primarily a stay-at-home mom, she would often be asked to work as a secretary or as a part-time bookkeeper at local schools. She took this time to further her education by taking post high school graduate courses.

Her skills and attention to details were reflected in the meticulous ledgers where she kept track of the family income and expenses. Every penny of income and every penny spent was listed. She would even record the purchase of an ice cream cone!

When she was not busy at home or working part time, she had many interests. I have already mentioned the Girl Scouts, but another deep interest in her life was working with the local community theater.

Over the course of many years, she had leading roles in plays such as A Streetcar Named Desire, Arsenic and Old Lace, and The Cemetery Club. She also directed plays including seven musicals. She directed her last musical when she was 80 years old!

When she wasn't acting or directing, she would sell tickets, work with costumes, act as the stage manager, or do basically anything else that needed to be done. As she neared the end of her involvement with Carnation City Players, she was selected by the state to be enshrined in the Ohio Community Theater Hall of Fame. She also was made an honorary life member of the local community theater. In 2022, the local community theater did extensive renovations on the box office and placed a plaque on the wall which stated that this was the Mary Beth Schulze Community Theater Box Office.

Despite her active involvement in Girl Scouts and community theater, her greatest contribution in service to others was in the DAV. When my dad got back from the war, he joined the Disabled American Veterans (DAV). Mom joined the DAV auxiliary. Both were active in this organization for many years.

DISABLED AMERICAN VETERAN'S AUXILIARY
(Laying a Wreath at Arlington Cemetery & My Mother Assisting President Ford)

As I have told you, my father served in the United States Army during World War Two and was a part of the invasion force at Normandy. He was wounded and received a Bronze Star and a Purple Heart for his service during the invasion.

When he came back to the United States, he became active in the Disabled American Veterans. This non-profit organization was formed to ensure that combat veterans from all branches of the military could lead a full and productive life despite suffering debilitating wounds while defending our country. For a number of years, Dad served in various offices of the DAV, including as commander of the post in Alliance.

My mother was active in the Disabled American Veterans Auxiliary. She served as commander of the local post and then became active in various positions in the State of Ohio DAV. After almost 30 years of loyalty to this important cause, she was asked to run for Commander of the Ohio DAV. Despite quality opposition, she ran for and was successful in attaining the top position in the state of Ohio.

After serving as the commander of the Ohio Disabled American Veterans Auxiliary, my mom became active on the national level. She served in several positions and, in 1975, she was selected to become the national commander of this vibrant organization of more than 54,000 women from across the United States.

My mother, who came from a small town in Ohio and who had never flown in an airplane, was about to board a jet to fly to Hawaii and be sworn in as the leader of the United States Disabled American Veterans Auxiliary! She and my dad were about to embark on a yearlong

EARLY LIFE

adventure. My mother became the first national commander of the Disabled American Veterans from Ohio.

During her tenure in 1976, she would visit almost every state to talk to local DAV members and to local, state, and federal officials. On one of her first official visits, she was given a small handheld bell as a memento. She was thrilled and told everyone how much she appreciated the gift. Soon after, she was presented with a bell every time she would make a visit to a local chapter. By the time she left the office, her collection numbered well over one hundred bells!

She was invited by the United States Army to tour the White Sands Missile Range where she was given a tour of the facility accompanied by the Base Commander who was a Major General. This is the same base where, seven years earlier, I was trained to fire ground to air missiles when I was a Private First Class on active duty.

As commander of the DAV Auxiliary, she was asked to present the Molly Pitcher Award to Archbishop Fulton J. Sheen for his contributions to national security. My mother was privileged to meet him and talk to him on a trip to New York City. He was the highest ranked Catholic clergyman in the United States at that time.

She also sat on the Valley Forge National Awards Panel to help choose the Freedom Foundation Award winner. There, she was joined by state and federal officials from across the country.

She met with Happy Rockefeller, the wife of Vice President, Nelson Rockefeller. She also hosted the wife of the United States Secretary of Defense, Donald Rumsfeld at a dinner in Washington, DC.

As commander, she presided at the Women's Forum on National Security which was held in the nation's capital. This important gathering was attended by leaders of the Disabled American Veterans Auxiliary, the American Legion Auxiliary, the Women Marine's Association the Marine Corps League Auxiliary, the Navy Club of USA, Auxiliary of the Gold Star Mothers, AMVETS Auxiliary, the Catholic War Veterans of the USA, the Daughters of the Union Veterans of the Civil War, Goldstar Wives of America, Ladies Auxiliary of the Military Order of Purple Heart, and the Navy Mothers' Club of America.

In her capacity as commander Mom opened, moderated, and closed the proceedings which were attended by many other dignitaries, including members of Congress and representatives from the White House.

Since this was the year of the United States Bicentennial Celebration, she was invited to participate in a number of other events. She was asked to help dedicate a new National Service Headquarters for the Veterans Administration. She was asked to escort President Gerald Ford to the dais for his dedication speech, after which she briefly addressed the audience. She then escorted President Ford back to his waiting vehicle. She received a nice personal letter from both Gerald and Betty Ford thanking Mom for her service to our country.

My Mother with President Gerald Ford

EARLY LIFE

The other major events which she was asked to attend made the greatest impression on her. She was invited to place a wreath on the grave of the Unknown from the Revolutionary War and another wreath on the Tomb of the Unknown Soldier in Arlington cemetery.

FEBRUARY 26, 1976
ARLINGTON NATIONAL CEMETERY
WASH. D.C. MARY BETH SCHULZE,
PLACING WREATH AT THE TOMB
OF THE UNKNOWN SOLDIER.

Sometimes we shape the path of our life and sometimes we just follow it. My dad did not want to go into the Army and try to kill people. My mother was unsure that she was worthy enough to participate in a most profound military ceremony. They were just plain people . . . good people . . . real people. They were not super heroes, but they were there to represent all the people who love this country, despite its flaws.

THE WHITE HOUSE
WASHINGTON

March 18, 1976

Dear Mary Beth:

It was indeed a genuine pleasure for me to participate in the Dedication of the Disabled American Veterans National Service Headquarters on March 3. I was happy to be greeted and escorted by you and Lyle Pearson at this event.

I want you to know of my deep appreciation for your personal efforts in making arrangements for the Dedication. You helped to ensure success on this memorable occasion.

With warm personal regards,

Gerald R. Ford

Mrs. Mary Beth Schulze
National Commander
DAV Auxiliary
9606 McCallum
Alliance, Ohio 44601

THE WHITE HOUSE

Mrs. Mary Beth Schulze
National Commander

EARLY LIFE

THE WHITE HOUSE

April 2, 1976

Dear Mrs. Schulze:

President Ford and I are grateful for the opportunity to join your many friends in expressing congratulations on your becoming the first woman from Ohio to serve as the National Auxiliary Commander of the Disabled American Veterans Auxiliary.

Certainly this is an outstanding achievement which is recognition of your dedicated involvement and leadership qualities.

We regret that we were unable to join you at your testimonial dinner but wanted you to know we were thinking of you and wished to send our very warm wishes.

Sincerely,

Betty Ford

Mrs. Mary Beth Schulze
Alliance, Ohio

REFLECTIONS

My mother was a fan of the Today Show on television and was particularly fascinated with the 100th birthday celebration on the Smucker's jelly jars. On more than one occasion she expressed her desire to have her picture and name on the jars and to have Willard Scott or Al Roker acknowledge her living to be 100 years old.

Now, to qualify she needed to live at least until January 29th, 2021. Three weeks prior to that milestone, she passed away, falling a bit short of her goal. Knowing how much she wanted to gain that recognition; I contacted the people at Smucker's and asked them if they minded me completing her dream by having her 100th birthday label attached to eight jars of Smucker's jelly. That way, I could give a jar to each of her children and grandchildren at her memorial service.

The Smucker's people couldn't have been nicer. They referred me to their website for a prototype label and Mom's dream came true!

EARLY LIFE

MY SISTER

My sister Pamela (Pam) was born in Alliance, Ohio in March of 1947. At that time our family lived on Glenwood Drive and Dad had built an additional bedroom to accommodate a family of four.

She has proven to be a remarkable person who has a heart of gold and is blessed with many talents. She has two children and two grandchildren, all of whom turned out great! Both of her children have positions of leadership in local industries.

In selecting her husband Fred, she made one of the wisest decisions in her life. He has proven to be not only a good provider in material ways but also in many other support aspects.

During our early years, I was a proud big brother and now 70 plus years later, I still am. Considering how stubborn I really am, it is amazing that Pam has been able to put up with me and still be my friend as well as my sister.

When she was young, Pam enjoyed all of the family outdoor activities. She loved her rabbits and her puppy dog. She was active in Girl Scouts and traveled to Idaho to attend a national Girl Scout activity.

When she graduated from high school, she chose not to go to college. She was certainly smart enough to succeed, but due to financial and medical considerations she never got a college degree. As she was about to graduate from high school, she began to search for a job which would allow her to work with and help people.

Being the talented person that she was, she initially received training in cosmetology. This was interesting to her but did not satisfy her need to assist people in crisis.

She then received training and certification as an Emergency Medical Services person. She was quite well suited for this important job however, after a period of time responding to serious medical emergencies, she had seen too many children seriously hurt or killed, and she decided to acquire a new skill. She became a respiratory therapist. This important position satisfied her for years and she excelled at it.

In addition to holding these service positions, she decided to look at a job that would satisfy her life interests instead of concentrating on how much the job paid. She decided that she wanted to be an actress!

During school and for many years thereafter she starred in Community Theater productions. She was not only an actress, but also directed plays. She was known for her superb acting and was eventually hired to do commercials for a local grocery store chain.

Later, she received the honor of being asked by a nearby medical school to portray herself as a patient to their student doctors. These "would be" doctors were tested on their interaction and observation skills. After each pretend visit to these student doctors, Pam and a faculty member would evaluate and comment on the students' performance.

Pam lived on a 55-acre farm near Alliance with her husband, Fred. The farm was once owned by my grandma and grandpa. It was then purchased by my mother and father. We felt that it was important to keep this hideaway in the family.

Pam and Fred moved to the farm and built a new house with an extra bedroom, bath and sitting room so that our mom could live with them. She took care of Mom for over 14 years until Mom moved into an assisted living facility. I will always be grateful to Pam for looking after our mother.

I recently sat down with my sister and asked a lot of questions such as, "What is the first memory you have about your childhood?" She thought about it for 10 to 15 seconds and then said, "Do you remember that year we had a huge snowstorm which left two-to-four-foot snowdrifts?" (1950)

You were about seven and I was about three and we wanted to go outside and play. Dad looked outside and said that we could, but he wanted us to wear something special on our feet. He went to the basement and came back with two pairs of homemade snowshoes.

EARLY LIFE

He had attached straps to two pieces of plastic and attached buckles to the straps. We got our coats on and ran outside. Dad put the snowshoes on us and lifted us to the top of the nearest drift."

At this point in her remembrance, Pam started to laugh and then continued with her story. "You were walking ahead of me and I was trying to keep up. Suddenly, your snowshoe dipped into the snow and you went face first into a drift. I laughed so hard and I will never forget what happened."

When she wasn't laughing at me, Pam liked to visit Grandma Stanley's house and play hide and go seek and kick the can. She was often joined by some of our many cousins. Even though Grandma had eight children and almost 30 grandchildren, she always seemed to spend some time with each of us grandchildren individually.

Over the years, Pam had many pets at home including a dog and a cat and some rabbits. One of her favorite pets was her cat. When the cat adopted us, we named her Katze which is German for cat.

She was a loyal pet with a couple of unique traits. She was a hunter. She would leave the house only to come back to display her conquest. We would be inside and hear a loud and prolonged "MEOWWWWWWWW." We would go to the back door and find Katze hanging onto the screen. Behind her we would find her conquest. Sometimes it was a mouse or a mole and sometimes it was larger animals such as a rabbit or squirrel. We would praise her and then tell her to get it off the steps. The other thing I remember her doing was waiting for a neighbor's dachshund to pass our house, at which time, she would chase the terrified dog down the street.

Pam went to the same elementary school, middle school, and high school that I did. I asked her for other memories and she skipped ahead to high school days. Apparently, I was in college and she was in high school when she asked me to drive her and her friends somewhere. I had a Dodge Dart convertible which an uncle had sold to me at a very reasonable price.

On this particular day, I put the top down and Pam and her friends loaded in. I drove down a main street in town and began to cross a major railroad crossing. I had almost passed by the first crossing gate when the cars in front of me stopped. I looked in my rearview mirror and saw that the cars behind me had moved close to my car. Just then the crossing bells began to ring, the lights started flashing, and the closing gate began to descend onto my car.

Although the cars in front of me were clearing the tracks I couldn't back up because the crossing bar was lower than my windshield. I was reluctant to pull forward because I would have to cross the active tracks and I could hear the train bearing down at the crossing.

The front of my vehicle was not across the active tracks and, as we sat there, with screaming coming from the back seat, the train, blowing its horn, rumbled past us to everyone's relief.

My sister was a strong person. Although she faced many adversities, she would meet them head on and make the best of her situation. The most important thing I will remember about Pam was, whenever we were about to hang up the phone, she would say very sincerely, "I love you!"

I love you too, Pam!

My sister passed away while this was being written. I promised her a copy so I had better get busy and finish the copy I will bring her when we meet again.

MY CHILDHOOD
1943 TO 1949

I don't have vivid memories of my preschool years. What I do remember centers around times of crisis. I know that on one occasion, I was trying to climb up on the roof of our house and I fell and broke my arm.

EARLY LIFE

I was also riding in a car with my mom when a milk truck ran a stop sign and crashed into our car. The impact spun our car around. These were the days before child car seats or even seat belts. Despite the lack of safety equipment, neither Mom nor I were injured.

By the way, for you younger folks, when I say we were hit by a milk truck, it was an actual truck that would drive around the residential neighborhoods leaving bottles of milk on the front porch according to previous orders received from the homeowners. There were also bread trucks which delivered bread to the homes. With the new emphasis on grocery store and restaurant deliveries, we seem to be returning to the past!

The last memory I have from that time, was an incident where my dad was driving our car with Mom and me in it. He stopped the car and pointed at a dog that was walking slowly beside the street. He said, "Look at the foam around the dog's mouth. That dog has rabies. We need to call the police!"

Since this was long before cell phones, we turned around and raced back to our house which was only a couple of blocks away. Dad rushed into the house, called the police, and returned to the car.

We then went back to the street where we had last seen the dog. We realized that an older woman was walking on the other side of the street from the dog, going the opposite direction. We called out to her but she either couldn't hear us or chose to ignore us.

My father immediately pulled the car in between the dog and the woman. At this point in time, a police car pulled up and a policeman got out of his car. Dad moved away from the dog and the policeman drew his gun and shot the dog. We all felt bad for the dog but, at least no one got hurt.

As the fifties approached and I began school there were many things happening which I do remember.

THE 1950'S

The decade of the 1950's is often referred to as the "Happy Days." At this time, there was an era of economic growth, prosperity, and upward mobility for many who were willing to work hard and persevere.

In the 45 years before the mid-50s there had been three major wars, a horrible genocide called the Holocaust, and the detonation of two atomic bombs on the mainland of Japan. The Holocaust was responsible for six million deaths, and the atomic bombs took 185,000 lives. There was also a worldwide epidemic and a deep and protracted economic depression.

Despite the almost complete absence of war and major natural disasters in the mid to late 50's, the world was not free from turmoil. Certain political leaders in the United States spread suspicion and fear that the communist bloc was sending spies to the United States with the intent of overthrowing our democracy. This was known as the Red Scare.

A United States Senator from Wisconsin said he wanted to "save" our country by ferreting out and prosecuting every hidden communist supporter. The Red Scare included bomb drills carried out in every school. This was when children were taught how to hide under their desks in case Russia or China decided to drop bombs on our homes and schools. These drills may have been more damaging to our psyche than mandatory face masks!

The communist ideology contrasted with the majority conservative values of our country. A former Army General, Dwight Eisenhower was elected to the presidency in 1952 and again in 1956 but the Cold War did not fade away.

The Russians were the first in space as they sent a satellite into orbit and they would soon send astronauts into space. Just about 100 miles from our southern border, Fidel Castro successfully led a revolution in Cuba and established a socialist/communist government.

EARLY LIFE

The civil rights movement was beginning to heat up as minorities realized that, often due to prejudice and segregation, their happy days had not yet arrived. Activists like Dr. Martin Luther King Junior, Malcolm X, and Rosa Parks were demanding equality and, as the protests grew louder, the next decade would experience the beginning of some important social reforms.

To get some idea of the tensions which existed in this decade you should go to the internet and pull up the song, "We Didn't Start the Fire" by Billy Joel. In 1989, Mr. Joel was talking to a 21-year-old acquaintance who was lamenting how hard it was to grow up in the 80s compared to the 50s. Joel's song's response, while not self-explanatory, points out that life can be difficult, even during Happy Days.

My elementary school years were very family oriented. I had parents who loved each other and who taught my sister and me about life. They encouraged us to explore whatever interested us.

I took lessons on the saxophone and got involved in Little League baseball and Scouting. I was not very good on the saxophone, a little better in baseball (I made the traveling team) and I dove enthusiastically into Cub Scouts and then Boy Scouts.

My dad started a Cub Scout pack and built it up to a large group of involved boys and their families. When I got to Boy Scout age, he became scoutmaster of the troop and provided a way for each scout to learn about a variety of life skills and earn merit badges to recognize their accomplishments.

As I was beginning to become a young man, he began an Explorer Post where we looked at and worked on areas of interest in the adult world. His enthusiasm never waned and his accomplishments resulted in recognition of his exemplary service by the Boy Scouts. The greatest result of his caring was not recognition, but the number of his former Scouts who were successful in their profession and personal lives. I attained the rank of Life Scout and proudly wore my fifth year Pipestone award.

I believe that those early years of learning, which my dad made possible, helped me to feel confident in my abilities and gave me guidance on how to conduct my life. My father taught us Scouts that the Scout oath and Scout laws are to be lived, and not just memorized. 60 years later, I still remember them and try to live by them.

Below are the Scout Oath and Scout Laws that my father taught us to live by.

SCOUT OATH

On my honor I will do my best to do my duty to God and my country and to obey the Scout Law; to help other people at all times; to keep myself physically strong, mentally awake, and morally straight.

SCOUT LAW

The Scout Law has 12 points. Each is a goal for every Scout. A Scout tries to live up to the Law every day. It is not always easy to do, but a Scout always tries.

A SCOUT IS:

TRUSTWORTHY. Tell the truth and keep promises. People can depend on you.

LOYAL. Show that you care about your family, friends, Scout leaders, school, and country.

HELPFUL. Volunteer to help others without expecting a reward.

FRIENDLY. Be a friend to everyone, even people who are very different from you.

COURTEOUS. Be polite to everyone and always use good manners.

KIND. Treat others as you want to be treated. Never harm or kill any living thing without good reason.

OBEDIENT. Follow the rules of your family, school, and pack. Obey the laws of your community and country.

CHEERFUL. Look for the bright side of life. Cheerfully do tasks that come your way. Try to help others be happy.

THRIFTY. Work to pay your own way. Try not to be wasteful. Use time, food, supplies, and natural resources wisely.

BRAVE. Face difficult situations even when you feel afraid. Do what you think is right despite what others might be doing or saying.

CLEAN. Keep your body and mind fit. Help keep your home and community clean.

REVERENT. Be reverent toward God. Be faithful in your religious duties. Respect the beliefs of others.

While there are many similarities between elementary school then and now, in other ways my experience was a bit different than today's children experience. Today, kids can research any issue they want to simply by getting out their iPad or phone. My parents saved up money to buy a set of encyclopedias that were informative, but were bulky and outdated before they even went on the shelf. My sister and I got a lot of use out of those expensive books but they couldn't match today's electronic research.

Speaking of electronics, cell phones today serve as cameras, calculators, calendars, weather forecasters, a post office, a news source, a meeting place, a radio, a television, a library, a bank and much more! As I was growing up, our phone just allowed you to call someone – most of the time.

These were the days when a telephone call had its own unique style. First, pick up the phone receiver (that's the thing you hold up to your mouth and ear). It was stuck on the end of a cord which limited your ability to move around. Then you'd listen to be sure that your neighbor was not on the line (yes, we did have a party-line phone). Next dial the five-digit number on a rotary dial or, if you were making a long-distance call, dial 0 and talk to the operator to get the help you need. Of course, there were charges for most long-distance calls.

No, the 50s were not before the invention of television. Even prior to World War Two, there were inventors working on a commercially feasible TV.

After World War Two, television began to become more common. The average television viewer had a small-screen black and white set which carried maybe three stations and relied on an antenna to bring in the signal. The antenna was an array of aluminum tubes which did not receive a signal from a satellite (there was only one in space at that time and it wasn't ours.)

Color TV was on its way but it took a lot of fiddling with the knobs to get a good picture. My Grandma Stanley had one of the first in the area and all the grandchildren enjoyed watching The Wizard of Oz turn from black and white to color when Dorothy steps out of the house and into colorful Oz!

The contents of the television shows were not as technically sound as today and they certainly did not have the adult language or visuals of today's shows. Some of the shows were live and you never knew for sure how the audiences would act out.

In my elementary school days, I was part of the "Peanut Gallery" who liked to watch a marionette named Howdy Doody with his buddy, Claribel Clown. I was so into this program that my parents bought me a "Howdy Doody" marionette of my own. I don't remember when "Howdy" was thrown out but, if I had him today, I could probably get a lot of money for him.

As I acquired a taste for screen entertainment I began to watch Captain Video, I Love Lucy, Kids Say the Darndest Things, Twilight Zone, and Maverick among other shows. My parents were careful to limit my screen use and to create lots of opportunities for outdoor exercise.

EARLY LIFE

As I entered junior high school (middle school), my interests turned to sports and girls. I will talk about my sports activities and girls in later sections of this book, but all I will relate here is my deep interest in the three S's during these formative years. Those three S's were: school, sports, and social activities.

Unfortunately, I did not have an inner drive to excel in school. I did what I needed to do to get into college, but I did not become the valedictorian. I also did not make the National Honor Society when the teacher "blackballed" me because I would not sign up for her A.P. class.

Sports, especially football, consumed my time and I have maintained a deep interest in it to this day. Girls interested me then, but also baffled me and continue to do so to this day.

For someone who witnessed violence firsthand, my father was a pacifist. If a conflict arose between me and anyone (including my sister), he would tell us to talk it out. He expected me to probe the depths of why the other person was acting in an improper way and he expected a peaceful resolution to take place.

However, it didn't always work out that way! When I was in my early teens, I loved to play baseball. If I could find a group of friends, we would go to a field, choose teams, and play.

If I could only find one or two friends, we would grab a ball and our gloves and play "catch." There were times when I couldn't find anyone to catch, so I would get my glove and ball, and go into my backyard. I would throw the ball as hard as I could, straight up into the air, settle under the falling ball, and catch it.

One day, as I was playing catch by myself, a boy who lived behind us on the next street came into our yard and stood watching. I asked him if he would like to play catch and offered him a glove. He said he didn't want to, so I began to throw the ball straight up again.

As I closely watched the ball descend, this boy moved closer to me. I threw the ball again and he ran to where I was standing and hit me in the stomach. I was shocked! The ball fell to the ground and I hollered, "Why did you do that?!" He just laughed and ran back towards his home.

A few days later, I was again in my backyard playing catch by myself, when that same neighbor boy appeared. I told him that I was mad at him for hitting me. He said he would not do it again. So, I threw the ball in the air, but sure enough, he ran up and hit me again. He then ran back home.

At this point, I sought out the advice of my father. He said we need to talk it out. He instructed me to follow him and we made our way to the boy's house. A discussion then ensued with the boy and his father. His father refused to believe that his son had done anything wrong. So, we left them and went home.

A little more than a week later, the boy was back. I put down my glove and ball and asked him why he was hitting me. He replied, "I just wanted to see you drop the ball."

I told him he would have to go home until he stopped hitting me. He swore he wouldn't do it anymore.

I threw the ball, he ran toward me, and I stepped to the side and hit him in the stomach. He ran home crying and he never came back. The lesson I learned was that you should always avoid violence if you can, but you need to be prepared to defend yourself!

In my junior high school days, I became addicted to a TV show about Perry Mason, a polished and accomplished attorney who created an interest in me that would eventually inspire me to go to law school. At about 14 years of age, I locked into law as my future. This was quite a goal considering that no one in my extended family (including aunts, uncles, and cousins) had ever graduated from college, let alone law school.

The other major hurdle to a legal career was the cost of a doctorate level education. My father never made more than $12,000 a year as a newspaper printer. Despite the leap of faith which was necessary to make my dreams become real, my parents never tried to change my vision to something more realistic.

EARLY LIFE

Throughout my teenage years I had a love for music. Early on I found a record case which my parents had filled with 78 RPM records. This music was popular in the 1930's and 1940's.

I would take our record player down in the basement and play their classics over and over again. I believe that this visit to the past gave me an insight into what my parents went through during the Depression and World War II.

As I entered high school, my taste for music changed from swing to rock and roll. Elvis, Chubby Checker, and Little Richard, blended into The Beatles, The Rolling Stones, and many others.

Most of these singers sold their music on 45 RPM records. I still have some of my favorite recordings on 45's! Of course, now I could get my phone and call up SPOTIFY to play these rock and roll hits.

Meanwhile, as I mentioned, I was a typical teenager who loved sports, music, and girls, not necessarily in that order. The late fifties and the sixties were the birth of rock and roll. Elvis was an icon who lived life in the fast lane, yet he agreed to be drafted into the army.

The British group called the Beatles was about to invade the United States, and I learned to dance slow dances.

When I would go to the Hanger, which was a place in our high school to hang out and dance, I would watch and appreciate the skills of the girls and boys who learned to "jitterbug" while watching American Bandstand on TV.

As soon as a slow song came on, I was on my way to ask one of my favorite girls to dance. It wasn't until "The Twist" came out that I felt comfortable fast dancing.

When I wasn't playing or watching sports, dancing at the Hangar, or studying for my Latin class, I liked to read books. I had a wide range of favorites but my interest in mysteries led me to the Hardy Boys series. I still have over 20 Hardy Boys books on my bookshelf which I will occasionally pull out and read.

STATE SERVICE AND SUPPLY

While my father would have told you that I was not handy with anything involving construction or repair, I worked in an industrial supply store for several years while I was in college.

Getting the job was not too hard, since my grandma's second husband owned the business. I guess he figured since Grandma was going to give me money ($500) toward my college tuition, he could at least get some work out of me. Since this book is about what helped shape my life, I need to briefly address my employment at State Service and Supply.

When I went to work there, I didn't know a hex head cap screw from a lock washer. I soon learned the difference between those as well the difference between coarse thread and fine thread. I also learned what a V-belt was, and I got an inside glimpse at how difficult running a small business can be.

I learned that the people you are serving will offer no sense of loyalty if they can save a penny. I learned that my advice was not valued as much as I thought it should be.

For instance, a semi-truck pulled into our loading dock and the driver said, "I've only got a little box. I don't need your help." I looked at the box and realized it was a keg of flat washers. I knew it was much heavier than it looked and I said, "I'll get the hydraulic cart."

"No need," said "Mister Smart" and he pulled it to the edge of the truck. He then took a breath and promptly lost control of the 240-pound box of flat washers. That box hit the floor, broke open, and sent ¾" flat washers throughout the back of the store. I spent many hours picking up flat washers!

I also learned that a salesman has to have a lot of self-confidence. We had one named Ron, who came to work just as I discovered a Garter snake nestled in the drill bins that were hanging on the wall.

EARLY LIFE

I told Ron what was happening and that I was getting a stick to coax the little fellow out. Ron's reply was, "Step aside. That's just a Garter snake!" With that, he reached into the bin, let out a screech, and withdrew a finger with a little spot of blood on it.

The snake dropped to the floor where I secured his head with the stick and then released him in the field next door.

During the time that I worked at SS&S, it seemed to me that my grandpa had a problem with alpha males working there. However, it wasn't just salesman and truck drivers who presented him with problems.

Before I came to work there, someone broke a window and entered the building after hours. They rifled through desk drawers and file cabinets. It did not appear that they stole any merchandise and, in fact, they left a note saying, "Next time, leave more money." It was obvious that they were most likely misguided kids.

Within six months after that break-in, a second one occurred. This time, however, they stole tools, including carbide tipped drills. This was the last straw.

My grandpa confronted the Sheriff and told him that his deputies took over two hours to arrive for the call. Grandpa also explained that he lived next door to the store and owned a rifle. "If I see anyone breaking in again, I am going to shoot them," Grandpa declared.

The sheriff warned my grandpa that he was only allowed to shoot them if they were actually inside the building, to which my grandpa replied, "By the time you get here, they will be inside."

Sometime later that year the Alliance City Police conducted a search of a house and found the drills stolen from my grandpa's store. They arrested two men and charged them with breaking and entering, grand theft, and later filed murder charges for a death that occurred at an unrelated burglary!

LET ME TELL YOU MY STORY

THE 1960'S

As I entered high school and then college, the dynamic 1960s kept life interesting. I believe this decade was accurately portrayed by Professor Greg Travalio in a prologue to my prior book, "Welcome to the Army." Here is what he said:

There is a reason that the 1960s are still viewed as an iconic period of our history; it was a time of uncommon domestic turbulence and international peril, and at the same time, an era of extraordinary promise.

In 1960, the torch truly passed to a new generation of Americans. The first Catholic president of our country promised that we would bear any burden to ensure the survival of freedom – a promise that would be sorely tested in the coming years. His promise would arguably lead us into the most divisive international war in American history and bring us to the brink of global annihilation-and then we would step back.

The sixties brought us art and ideas that still reverberate in our society and throughout the world: rock and roll, civil rights, feminism, the sexual revolution, and drugs. It was the decade in which we continued – with increasing commitment – to make good on our promise of equality for all. It was during this period that both the Civil Rights Act and the Voting Rights Act were enacted by Congress. But this commitment was not shared by all, nor was it without tremendous upheaval. In a horrifyingly short period of time, we lost to assassination a president, a presidential candidate, and the leader of the civil rights movement. I remember being in college in Pittsburgh on the night of the killing of Dr. Martin Luther King Junior, and watching the eerie orange glow from the fires in the nearby Hill District. I was frightened to the core and wondered aloud what would become of my country.

This was also a time of rapidly increasing economic and technological change. During this decade, the Beatles released their first single, Wal-Mart opened its first store, the first Super Bowl took place, the Peace

EARLY LIFE

Corps was formed, Woodstock happened, and ARPANET (the beginning of the Internet) was developed. This was the era of the space race with the Soviets and the U.S. in a desperate race for space supremacy. Russia was first to send a satellite (SPUTNIK) and to have an astronaut in space. They also had the first unmanned rocket on the Moon, but the U.S. put two men on the moon.

These changes brought material wonders to most of us that we could not have dreamed of even a decade before, but they also brought dislocation, confusion, and disorientation to many. It was in the sixties, to a great degree because of the economic and technological boom, that we began to experience the growing inequality gap that plagues us today.

During this period, the Berlin wall was constructed to emphasize the might of the Soviet Union in Europe. This got dicey close to home when the U.S. sponsored an unsuccessful invasion of the small island of Cuba by rebels, less than 100 miles off our shores. Not long thereafter, the world held its breath during the tense days of the Cuban missile crisis. It was only later that we became aware how close we had come to nuclear war. Even so, as a young teenager I remember vividly thinking about the possibility that I might never grow up.

It was in the early sixties that President Kennedy sent the first contingent of 3500 troops to a small Southeast Asian nation called Vietnam to train and advise the sitting government. Kennedy's successor, Lyndon B. Johnson, began to expand the U.S. presence in the Republic of Vietnam. By 1969, there were more than one half million U.S. servicemen in the Vietnam theater. In order to sustain this pace of warfare, the military was forced to draft many young men—a decision that profoundly divided the country. Many of those drafted were genuinely opposed to the war. Some demonstrated this opposition by leaving the country or going to jail. At some point, the need for manpower became so severe that it encompassed some who were, at best, only marginally fit to serve.

The North Vietnamese and the Viet Cong began the Tet Offensive, and antiwar protests exploded at home. The Democratic National Convention in Chicago was disrupted by demonstrations, and in 1970, college students were killed at Kent State in Ohio by National Guard soldiers.

This was the setting that my friend Dennis Schulze found himself in. He had spent the last seven years in college and at law school and was studying for the Ohio Bar Exam. He was almost 25 years old and was married to his college sweetheart. His focus was on starting a family and a profession, but he was walking into a real world. Over the next five years, he would face not only decisions, but events that would happen regardless of the decisions he made.

This is his story.

>   COL Gregory Travalio, USA (ret.);
>   and Lawrence D. Stanley, Professor of Law Emeritus,
>   The Ohio State University College of Law

MY GRANDMA

My grandmother on my mother's side was named Mary although we always called her Grandma. She lived to the age of 91 and was one of the toughest human beings I ever met. I never heard her complain about her hardships; she just met them head on. Grandma was born in Pennsylvania in 1890. At the age of 21 she married Glen Akins, a businessman.

Nine children were born of this marriage. One died at birth and the remaining eight consisted of four boys and four girls. One of those girls was my mother.

EARLY LIFE

In this photo, Grandma is on the porch and all eight of her children are pictured too. One of the men in the car is my grandfather.

The family moved to Ohio where Glen was a good provider. Unfortunately, he died in his forties from a gallbladder problem. At his death, the youngest child was 15 months old. At this time, the country was headed into the worst economic depression it had ever experienced. Mary and her children lived the next ten years in poverty and the four years after that with World War II in progress.

In order to survive, Mary began a roadside restaurant and sold corn to passing motorists. The money coming in was so meager that, at Christmas time, the children were thrilled to receive an apple or an orange as their gift. Mary was well liked in her community and others would try to help her out when they could.

LUCKY SEVENS

One day, two sheriff's deputies, who often ate at my grandma's restaurant, were talking to her about the difficult times that the country was facing. They asked about her eight children and how her restaurant was doing. As usual, grandma didn't complain, but she admitted that times were tough.

The next day, the deputies approached her and asked if she could do them a favor. They said that they needed someone to store a piece of evidence that had been used in a trial.

She told them that she would love to help them, but she didn't have much room in either her house or at the tiny restaurant. They assured her that what they wanted her to store would fit on her counter next to the cash register.

She agreed to help them out and, on their next visit to the restaurant, they walked in with a confiscated slot machine. They set it in plain sight and told her to be sure to keep it cleaned out because they didn't want too many coins in it.

Truckers, who stopped at the restaurant, enjoyed the attraction and the deputies continued to frequent the restaurant.

GRANDMA'S HOUSE

By the time I was six years old, Grandma had married again and had raised my mom, my aunts, and my uncles to be productive citizens. I have many happy memories of going to Grandma's house. There was a huge weeping willow tree in her side yard. It took two of my cousins and me to touch hands and reach around the trunk of the tree. If the limbs were not trimmed, they would touch the ground forming a hut that we could hide in.

EARLY LIFE

Since I had 28 first cousins on my mom's side of the family, there were always lots of playmates. There was also a small orchard nearby with several types of fruit trees including apple, cherry, and plum. During the summer and fall you would often find several children sitting in these trees eating the tasty treats or throwing them at each other.

When we were not sitting in trees, some of the cousins would get on a swing which hung from two ropes on a large branch of the willow tree. They would see who could swing the highest. Other, more adventuresome, cousins would play "spin the sitter." That was a game where someone would sit on the swing while others would turn the seat and the sitter until the ropes could no longer turn. When they let go of the swing it would propel the sitter faster and faster in a spinning motion.

Sometimes when the spin stopped, the sitter would get out of the swing and stumble around in a dizzy stupor. Sometimes the sitter had just had lunch and the results were more dramatic! Other pastimes for the cousins consisted of kick the can, hide and seek, and a baseball game called 21.

Meanwhile, the adults might be found inside playing a card game called 500 or, if they didn't have the proper number of players, they might play Hearts. Later, they often watched the new diversion called a color television. I will never forget watching the movie, Wizard of Oz, and the excitement when it changed from black and white to color. Of course, one of the adults would have to jump up every now and then to adjust the set since the picture was very unstable.

There were always animals at Grandma's. For a long time, she had two dogs named Kane (pronounced Connie) and Wahine. We were told that that meant boy and girl in Hawaiian. They were rat terriers and both lived about 20 years.

In addition to the dogs, there were always chickens. These creatures provided many eggs, which I often had to remove from under a hen, and they served as a popular meat dish. As a young teenager, I would help prepare the chickens from the egg layers to the fried chicken.

The process for preparing the birds for cooking was different than going to the store and picking out packages of chicken pieces. The adults, primarily uncles, would go to the henhouse and capture one or two of the chickens. They would then bring them to the chopping block. At this point, we children would climb into the willow tree or some other safe area and the chicken would face a guillotine type of demise.

When the chickens stopped moving, the children would climb down from the tree and help with the preparation of the chickens to be fried. Each of us would be assigned a task. Some would grab the dead chickens by the feet and dip them into very hot water. Some would pluck the wet feathers off the chickens and some would singe the pin feathers off over an open flame. The adults then finished the preparation process and took them to Grandma to cook.

The chickens lived in a fenced area which had a metal building where they nested. One of the worst jobs I ever had was cleaning out the chicken coop. I would start by wearing as few clothes as modesty would allow and put a face mask on. Unlike the facemasks of the pandemic, my mask was more like a handkerchief. When I finished the cleaning, every inch of me would be covered in dust and who knows what else!

Chickens were not the only birds which Grandma raised. She also had peacocks. They were beautiful birds which would strut around with the males spreading and shaking their colorful tail feathers. These birds would issue a plaintive cry which sounded like "helllllp." At night, or even in the day, visitors who had not been there before would ask, "Is that someone calling for help?"

In my first year of college, I wrote a paper about a strange noise that was coming from the darkened mist surrounding Grandma's house. I told the true story of a hole in the fence and the cry in the distance of "helllllp!" I never identified what was making the cry as I recounted the search, capture, and the return to the enclosure. I received an A+ but the professor

EARLY LIFE

admonished me that the A+ would revert to an F unless I told her what it was that escaped in the night.

The last animal I will talk about was not owned by Grandma but by her neighbor. Grandma and I were in the kitchen when we heard strange sounds outside. Looking out of the window we could see a large hog rooting up Grandma's yard. Grandma shouted at me to get him out of my yard! I ran outside and was confronted by a large pig that weighed at least 300 pounds! I said in a very quiet voice, "Get out of here" while waving my arms. He didn't move and I didn't move any closer. Just then, Grandma came swiftly out of the door with a broom in her hands and moved aggressively toward the animal and smacked him on the nose with the broom! He squealed and turned and ran home.

Despite all the action outside, I will probably most remember the wonderful foods that Grandma made. She always had a lot of family there and, on special occasions, she would put two large turkeys in two roasters and have eight or nine pies cooling on the porch. After these big feasts, there were a lot of dirty dishes and pots and pans. My uncle Bill would always volunteer to wash the dishes and would then volunteer me to dry them.

As time passed, many of my cousins grew up, moved away, or found new interests. I was still a frequent visitor at Grandma's house. I remember going there one time when I was in high school and Grandma asked me if I would like to earn some money. Since I was planning to attend college, I quickly replied "Sure, but what do you want me to do?" (After all, it couldn't be worse than cleaning out the chicken house, could it?) She took me out to the side yard and pointed at the once majestic willow tree. Time had been hard on her. She had broken limbs and an insect infestation of the leaves. Grandma said, "I have been told that I should remove this before it becomes a hazard."

She then asked me if I could cut the giant willow tree down, chop up the wood and have it hauled away. I looked at this beautiful work of nature that I had spent so many hours with. I remembered climbing, swinging, and hiding under it. I knew it was just a matter of time before it would be felled. I looked at the enormous trunk and its limbs reaching to the sky. I told grandma that such a task would be difficult. Suddenly, she said, "I will pay you $100." I immediately said, "Of course I will do it."

One hundred dollars seemed like a fortune. It would be a great start to my college fund which, although I was working, was meager at best. After the deal was done, I studied the task before me. I couldn't just chop it down. The trunk was enormous, and I didn't even have a chainsaw. I decided that the major limbs would need to be removed first. That would entail climbing up the tree and sawing the limbs off. I also needed the limbs to fall in a certain direction and that would mean pulling a rope up the tree, tying the rope around the limb being cut, and having someone cut the limb while someone else pulled the rope. I soon realized that meant that I needed a partner in this job.

I sought out a good friend and showed him the tree and the plan to accomplish the job. I told him he could earn $50 to just help me out a little bit. I soon realized that $50 did not sound as tempting as the $100 that I thought was going to be all mine.

My friend Bill was a smart person. I knew I couldn't fool him into the belief that this was a minor endeavor (he ended up being the valedictorian of our high school senior class) so I appealed to our friendship. He agreed to help, and I assigned him to the tree while I had held the rope on the ground. (I was not going to let the valedictorian dictate terms.) We (Bill) removed a number of branches until each remaining limb and the trunk were too big to cut with a handsaw. Seeing our struggles Grandma then hired a professional to finish the job. By the way, she did pay us and gave us $100.00 each!

Despite the influx of funds, by my third year of college, I was getting low on tuition money and was planning on working fulltime for a semester or two. Without my asking, Grandma gave me $500 to cover my school bills. In my senior year she repeated this generosity. I am not certain that I would have completed college if it were not for my grandma!

I was very close to my Grandma Stanley and it was not just the money that she gave me. Although she had little formal education, she had a way of imparting certain life skills. Many times, her advice rang true, but not always. More than once, she told me that, "If your nose itches, you are going to kiss a fool!"

When I was a teenager, another thing I learned from Grandma was, "The best way to fight off a cold is to mix honey and whisky in a cup and swallow fast!" I never got to see if this remedy was effective because my parents never had whiskey in the house.

Grandma's house (The tree on the left is the one that Bill and I chopped down!)

BILL AND HIS FAMILY
(A Tornado, Two Fires, and a Flood)

My Uncle Bill was one of my favorite people. He was the youngest of the Akins clan and we shared many fun times. These included fishing trips to Canada with his wife, Bev, and their children.

Karen and I also had a wonderful trip through Germany with them. We stopped at bed and breakfasts and we visited so many castles that, as we approached one of these giants, Bev said, "Bill, could you go back to the car? We forgot the camera."

Bill's reply was a classic. He said, "Don't worry. We have so many pictures of castles that we can borrow one of them and say that it is this castle."

Bill was the best man at our wedding and when he and Bev would come back to Ohio for work, or just to visit, they would be sure to come see Karen and me.

As nice as Bev and Bill were, they had a lot of bad luck, especially when it came to their houses. When they lived in Ohio, Bill, who was a commercial contractor, built a beautiful house out in the country. Eventually, they moved to Indiana and asked me to watch over their house until it was sold.

One day, I pulled into their driveway and saw the back door standing wide open. I cautiously approached until I could see that it had been forcefully opened with a hammer or some other blunt object. I went to a neighbor's house and called the sheriff's department. They said that they only had two cars out in the entire county but they would get right on it.

An hour and one half later, the deputy arrived and he entered the house. He found it empty, but someone had apparently had a party. The dining room and kitchen had cake and ice cream all over the place!

Meanwhile, back in Indiana, months passed and Bev and Bill lived in another nice house in an upscale subdivision. It was Palm Sunday and Bev and Bill had invited another family over for dinner. The skies clouded up and the wind got gusty and stronger. Someone looked out of the window and saw the dog house being propelled out of the yard and they heard an ominous rumbling. They did not have a basement, so Bill shouted for all of them to lay in a huddle on the kitchen floor.

All of a sudden, the doors and windows blew in and the roof lifted off and sat on an angle against the back of the house. The tornado began sending debris sailing into the air! Outside, the friend's van had lifted in the driveway and flipped top down onto my uncle's car. Inside, the adults were frantically checking the children for injuries. Amazingly, other than the emotional impact, there were only minor cuts and bruises.

As they went outside, they could see the path that the tornado had taken. A row of houses in the subdivision were leveled. Those which didn't have basements were almost wiped clean and those with basements were gaping holes in the ground! My uncle's house had been more fortunate as it appeared the tornado veered left at the last moment.

Bev was a nurse and she and Bill ran outside to check on the neighbors. One lady, two doors down, had just stepped out of the shower. She was picked up, towel in hand, by the wind and carried about ½ mile into a cornfield. Another neighbor was not home at the time but lost most of his possessions, including two gold medals which he had won at the Olympics.

Bev found survivors, and although the street was blocked by downed cables, she managed to get them to a place where the emergency squad could retrieve them. After the emergency squad arrived, she and Bill headed back to their house. On the way they passed a large metal utility tower. It had been twisted like a pretzel.

My Uncle Dale and I went out to Indiana the next day to help Bev and Bill. The devastation was unreal! Their house was a total wreck and much of their personal property was damaged or missing.

Weeks later, they received an envelope from someone who lived in Ohio. When they opened it, they found mail with their names on it and a note saying that the mail had been found after tornados went through Yellow Springs, Ohio.

Back in Indiana, Dale and I searched through rubble in the yards surrounding the house. We were looking for anything of value, including the two gold medals that the neighbor had won at the Olympics. Unfortunately, we never found them.

When it was determined that it was relatively safe to enter the house, we slowly moved through the debris to find what we could save. As we entered what was left of the master bedroom, we were astonished to see a nightstand sitting upright with a vase on it with the flower still in it! The steel utility pole was twisted like a pretzel by the wind but the flower remained safe!

My Uncle Bill and his family had survived a traumatic experience and moved on. As they rebuilt and refurnished, they stored much of their new furniture in my Uncle Bob's barn until they finished building a new house. Unfortunately, the barn caught on fire and they lost everything!

The family remained strong and, as Thanksgiving approached, they had moved into their new house. The neighbors invited them over for Thanksgiving dinner and their hearts were grateful that none of them had been hurt in the tornado or the fire.

After enjoying the food and the company, they got in their car and headed for home. As they did, they saw a black cloud of smoke and heard the sounds of emergency vehicles. Their house was on fire! Even though no one was hurt, the spirt of Thanksgiving was gone.

A few years later, my uncle's work took the family to New Mexico. There were no tornados or fires. But, here, near the desert, a flash flood entered their house and destroyed some of their possessions! To my amazement, they accepted their fate and moved on.

EARLY LIFE

Uncle Bill and his wife, Bev

LOOKING BACK

I hope that this glance back at the first twenty-one years of my life has shown you how fortunate I was to have a family that provided me the support and the love that I needed during my most formative years.

During the next two chapters, we will see how my friends and my education also gave me a foundation to build on.

Then, as I begin my journey as an adult, we will examine other major factors in my development.

Dennis and a close friend

Chapter 2

FRIENDS

YOUR FAMILY can have a profound effect on who you turn out to be. A loving, caring, supporting, faith-based family can provide the opportunity to develop your skills and help you position yourself for success throughout your lifetime.

A dysfunctional family can create barriers to success. A family lacking in morals or one which does not value the effort needed to succeed can make it difficult for you.

However, your family is not the only factor that will influence how you develop during your formative years. Friends can be a powerful influence on who you become. The friend who is "cool" because he is in a gang or he sells drugs can be a negative influence on how you evolve. Other friends can instill in you the traits of kindness and achievement.

At every stage of life, or at least part of it, you will have the opportunity to make friends who will share life with you and add or detract from your progression to the person you want to be. I was fortunate. My friends almost always were supportive, moral, and provided me with good examples of how to live my life.

My first recollection of friends happened to be in my own family. My cousins, who lived in the duplex I shared until I was five, were the ones I looked to for fun times. We were young and innocent, but we did not always follow the rules. I remember climbing up on the roof and falling off and breaking my arm. I had to accept responsibility. This was my decision, not my cousins'!

ELEMENTARY SCHOOL

We moved to Glenwood Drive when I was about to enter school. My first school was named Parkway Elementary. This environment provided lessons in life as well as in reading, writing, and arithmetic.

Much of my interaction with the other students was on the playground. Kickball was a favorite pastime as were footraces. I was not very fast as a runner, but a good friend of mine whose name was Johnny won every race! Usually, a red-haired girl named Valerie was right behind him much to the chagrin of all the boys who did not like losing to a girl.

I think Valerie wanted to be my friend, but I was a bit intimidated by her aggressive demeanor and her success at sports. It wasn't until junior high that I came to appreciate being around self-confident girls. I have since learned that some of my best friends have those traits.

In the classroom, there were opportunities to meet many children who were different than me. One was a child at a desk near mine who would dip his fingers in a paste jar then lick the paste until his fingers were clean. He even began to drink the ink provided in art class until the teacher put a stop to that.

During my elementary and middle school days, another source of friends was the Boy Scouts. My dad, along with my mother, organized and promoted the formation of a Cub pack with boys ages 5 to 10 years old. This group was then divided into dens of five to 15 boys per den. Cub Scouting was my introduction to new friends who came from different backgrounds and who had an infectious enthusiasm to learn new activities and grow confident in themselves.

My Boy Scout Troop

JUNIOR HIGH

As I moved on to junior high school, my world of friends opened a little wider, as I moved from Parkway School and its protective nurturing environment. The diversity of my fellow students in junior high created new opportunities to develop friendships with boys and girls whose first decades of living and learning included more hardships than I had experienced.

In order to understand this dynamic a little better, I should explain about my hometown of Alliance, Ohio. Alliance was and is a small town of approximately 20,000 people that was economically based on industry which peaked during World War II and shortly thereafter. These companies produced items for the war, including traveling overhead cranes (the world's largest), guidance systems for submarine torpedoes, garage door openers, rubber bands, military vehicle parts, and a variety of other products.

This industry helped create a cadre of millionaires, numbering in the mid-30s. They provided a positive work environment for skilled workers and managers, and they presented opportunities for advancement of the lesser skilled workers. Many of these workers had moved out of the southern United States seeking a better economic life.

When the war was over and the country settled into the doldrums of the 50s, new jobs were harder to come by. Soon, the owners of many of the industries moved South to rebuild their factories in areas which offered tax incentives and cheaper labor. The millionaires moved South and the skilled workers began to look for other opportunities, which turned out to be harder to find.

In the 1950s and 1960s, racial equality was very much an elusive dream. One of the results of this was the settlement of various groups into several separate areas of the city. Each area was classified or identified as acceptable or affordable to each particular group of people. I lived in a lower middle-class neighborhood. Most families were white, as was my family, and my dad was skilled in a trade as a newspaper printer. He never made a lot of money, but it was a steady income.

Many factors contributed to the polarization of the city. We had people who were economically disadvantaged. They settled on the other side of the railroad tracks. Many black families and poor white families would attend school at Stanton Junior High, while the more middle class, mostly whites, would go to State Street Junior High. The wealthier families would often send their children to private or parochial schools.

FRIENDS

My opportunity to have a broad base of friends was progressive: Parkway, almost all white, middle class; State Street, a broader base of backgrounds, but still somewhat racially imbalanced; and Alliance High School, a rich mixture of diversity, with the minor exception of rich kids who still went their own way.

One example of emergent diversity at State Street, was the students who lived at the children's home. This was an orphanage, which often continued to care for children into their teens, since the foster parent program was not as large or well-funded as it is today.

One vivid memory I have retained involved an incident on the playground when two teenage boys from the "home" got into a fistfight. Unlike some fights, these young men were physically punishing each other. Blood was flying and teeth were loosened. I'm not sure what would have happened if the teachers hadn't gotten involved.

The next day I saw these same two boys chatting on the basketball court with each other while they shot baskets. It seemed that they had been hardened to fight for their rights, but it was understood that, in reality, they were brothers joined by their circumstances.

When I was in Junior High, I was average in many ways. I was shorter than 5'8", I weighed less than 120 pounds, and I was not a star athlete.

I did have one outstanding physical trait though. I was double jointed in my knees! I could reach down, grab my foot, lift it, and then secure the leg by hooking my foot in front of me on my hip. This procedure gave the appearance of a leg amputation if I was wearing shorts.

One day, my friends and I were on the playground at State Street when they told me that they wanted to play a trick on the playground monitor, Mr. Vogely.

They hid me behind a storage shed and with one friend on each side, they pulled my shorts up to cover my right leg which had been tucked at my waist.

They then drug me over to where Mr. Vogely was while they shouted, "Mr. Vogely! Mr. Vogely! His leg is gone!"

The poor teacher shouted, "Oh my God!" and ran to meet us.

He quickly noticed no blood and the fact that we were laughing. At this point he ordered us to take me behind the shed and fix my leg!

As he joined us by the shed, he began laughing and told us that what we did was wrong. He never did turn us in to the vice principal, but I heard that the story made its way to the teachers' lounge.

As I completed my three years of middle school, I made some new friends who broadened my perspective of the world that I lived in. I was no longer in the protective cocoon of my elementary school.

FRIDAY NIGHT FIGHTS
(Attempted Armed Robbery)

When I was in middle school one of my favorite pastimes was going to the home games of the high school football team. They usually played on Friday nights in a local college's 10,000 seat stadium.

One Friday night, my friend Ralph and I were walking from our homes to the stadium. We were talking about "guy things" and we were not paying much attention to what was going on around us. The stadium was about ½ a mile from our neighborhood and it was just turning dark. All of a sudden, two men jumped out from behind some bushes and grabbed me around the neck!

Ralph started to run, so they concentrated on me. The one who was holding me by the neck held a broken glass bottle in front of my eyes and told me not to resist or he would cut me! I believed him and I did not struggle. What I did do was start talking. The thugs made it clear that they wanted my money and, as I quickly complied with their demands, I told them that I would gladly give them more, but I only had ten dollars on me.

The one with the beer bottle then said he might as well cut me. I am not sure what I said then, I just kept on talking. They finally got tired of my excuses and ran off. I never felt afraid as I walked about town, but incidents like this shaped how I observed my environment.

Later, Ralph said he could see why I wanted to be a lawyer because I talked them out of cutting me.

HIGH SCHOOL

In high school, friendships often took on a predictable pattern. Sports were an important part of school life. If you were on a team (football, basketball, track, and baseball) you had a ready-made group of friends. This did not mean that you would spend much time with your teammates during non-sports activities, but the coaches of these teams worked very hard to develop a closeness among all members of their teams.

FRIENDS – BILL

One of my closest friends in high school was Bill Sutton. Bill ran track and his time in the mile was not bad, but he was not going to win a lot of races.

So, Bill came to me and asked me to help him get better. He needed someone to time his practice miles and to call out each lap time. I agreed to help and we looked for a track to practice on. Alliance had a college which had a stadium with a quarter mile track. The problem was they locked the gate when the college track team was not using it.

Bill was determined to get better and he was also determined that we could climb over the wall surrounding the stadium. So, for two entire track seasons, we climbed over the wall and Bill got better and better. He will never be remembered as a premier miler, but his determination to succeed will live forever in my mind.

Training for track was not the only sport Bill and I shared. When we were at Scout camp, we got interested in archery. We both bought a bow and together would walk for miles out in the country, shooting arrows at targets like corn stalks. We never did get involved in bow hunting.

FRIENDS – CHARLIE

Football was the main attraction when I was in high school. Every Friday night home game saw about 10,000 fans gathered into the Mount Union College stadium to watch the local heroes win another game.

There were many victories in the late 50's and early 60's. When I was a sophomore, Alliance won the Ohio state championship in the level one competition. In my junior year we were 14th and in my senior year we were third. We were so good that three of my classmates went on to play in the NFL. Our high school team traveled all over the state to play top teams. Twice we flew in a chartered plane to the southern part of Ohio.

One of the primary reasons why we were so successful was my friend Charlie King. He was named the outstanding football player in the state of Ohio. He later was a star player at Purdue and then went on to play in the National Football League with Cincinnati and Buffalo.

In my senior English class, I sat right behind Charlie and he would often turn around so we could talk football. Charlie told me that he was going to play pro-football and since I was planning to go to law school, he would hire me as his agent. The plan sounded great to me; however, when Charlie turned pro, I was just beginning law school so he had to hire a "real" agent.

I learned a lot from Charlie by watching him prepare his body and mind at practice. He always gave the maximum effort. For instance, during the fumble drill, he would attack the ball carrier and then, when it was his turn to carry the ball, he would holler at the defenders who were trying to get him to fumble. He would mock them by calling them names and saying they were not real players. By the time the game rolled around, the other team didn't seem nearly as tough as his own teammates. As Charlie put it, "You can talk a good game, but to win you need to prove it on the field."

We went our separate ways after high school, but 35 years later, I called him up to see if he would come talk to the high school football team that my son was on. He immediately said "yes." It was a great reunion and he delivered a wonderful speech for the team. My son's team reached the state semi-finals that year.

FRIENDS - KURT

Kurt was a good friend of mine throughout junior high and high school. He was in my group of friends in the Boy Scout Troop and also in many of my school classes.

One day our troop competed in a swim meet against another Boy Scout troop in town. It just so happened that Kurt had been swimming competitively since he was in elementary school. He even had, and regularly used, a swim simulator in his basement. At times he held the record on a national level for his age group.

At the meet, as the competition got underway, we realized that we would have to give the other troops some advantages or there would not be any real chance for them to win.

One event was a four-lap relay featuring freestyle, backstroke, butterfly, and breaststroke. We let the other troop choose their four best swimmers, and we had Kurt swim all four laps. It was no contest. Kurt finished almost a full lap ahead of the other team!

The other troops suggested an underwater contest to see who could go the furthest without breaking the surface. The other troops had two swimmers who made one length plus about 10 feet. I counseled Kurt not to overdo it because there were further swim competitions to come, but he jumped in the pool for the underwater race and swam 2 full lengths of the pool.

When we were in high school, there was no official swim team at Alliance High School. Kurt went to the administration and talked them into forming a swim team. The team not only had a good season of matches with other schools, but Kurt qualified for two events at the state swim meet. He ended up winning the butterfly and the individual medley relay. He even set a state record in the butterfly event.

As we finished our senior year, Indiana University offered Kurt a full scholarship to compete on their swim team. Ironically, the Indiana team had two swimmers who held world records in Kurt's two best events (butterfly and backstroke). It wasn't until his senior year that he got to be the top dog. Then he really shone!

One of life's lessons which I learned from Kurt was that, to excel in any of life's challenges, you must truly want to succeed and you must be ready to dedicate your efforts to that end.

THE MOVIE PSYCHO

In 1960, Alfred Hitchcock directed the movie Psycho. Anthony Perkins starred as a psychologically troubled man who ran a motel in a remote area of the U.S. He lived in a dark two-story house behind the motel.

Janet Leigh played the part of a young woman who made the mistake of staying at the Bates Motel. In 1961, this classic horror film was in our local theater and my friend Kurt and I decided to go watch it. Kurt drove us since, after the movie, I was supposed to meet my parents who were fishing at my grandparents' farm.

The movie was chillingly graphic and the evil emanating from the Bates house made a lasting impression on both of us. Remember, this was 60 years ago and direct violence was not prevalent in movies or on television.

After the movie, Kurt drove me to my grandparents' farm which was fifty-five acres and was in a rural area with no houses nearby. We turned into the 1/4-mile drive and soon approached the dark and empty two-story farmhouse. Kurt looked at me and said, "Oh, my God. That looks like the house in the movie!"

Kurt then asked me if I really wanted to get out. I looked toward the farm house and then several hundred yards down to the stream to where my parents were supposed to be fishing. I saw the glow of a lantern and I said, "Yes. No problem, drop me off here." As I hopped out of the car, Kurt rapidly did a U-turn and raced down the lane past the farmhouse. I looked around and saw no signs of life. It was now too late to say no.

I was now in a totally dark environment next to the imposing and deserted house. I began to walk rapidly toward the stream, then I broke into a slow run. As I neared the light, I suddenly thought, what if that's not my parents. This was before cell phones so I couldn't call my parents. I stopped and tried to make out who was out there. I couldn't go back but I wasn't sure that I wanted to go forward.

Finally, I gathered my courage and called out to them. The response from my father calmed my fears. When I got to the stream, my parents asked how the movie was. I replied, "Oh, not too bad. It wasn't that scary."

This movie has remained one of my favorites.

CLUBS

If you weren't involved in sports, there were many activities and clubs available to help you meet people. Some got involved in plays and musical groups. I had "flunked out" of playing a saxophone in middle school, so that was not an option for me.

I did decide to get involved in the American Field Services Club though. This was the second largest club in the school (behind the athletic booster club) and its purpose was to promote the exchange of students with other countries.

I believe that the beauty of the Danish student we hosted in my junior year, and the fact that so many girls belonged to the club, may have sparked my interest. In my senior year, I was elected president of the AFS Club and I had some great experiences and made a number of friends.

Some of the students at AHS made friends through the power structure outside of the official school systems. They joined gangs. These friendships were often strong bonds to the point of encouraging the exclusion of anyone that was not an official member of their gang. I knew and got along with many gang members because I knew how not to challenge them. (You can read more about the gangs in the Education section of this book.)

We also had social friendships arising out of such activities as the "Hanger." This was a school sponsored dance club where we could take what we learned on "American Bandstand" and jitterbug, slow dance, twist, and do all of the other 50's and 60's rock and roll dances. One caveat to this was meeting girls. We learned quickly to not get too friendly with the girls who were dating athletes or gang members.

I believe that I had a significant and diverse group of friends in high school. Not all of them lived by the same commandments that my parents instilled in me. However, despite the temptations flowing through the

FRIENDS

school and the town, I never felt pressured to do something against my value system. I know that there was support amongst these friends, and when needed, the closest friends were there to help.

COLLEGE

The friends I made in college were a mix of old and new. I chose to go to Mount Union College which was located in my hometown of Alliance, Ohio, and a number of my high school friends also chose to attend locally.

The balance of the students provided a rich variety of backgrounds, even though there were less than 2,000 students. They came from different areas of the United States and even from foreign countries.

There were also opportunities to meet other students at dances, concerts, and athletic events. Some of the performers who appeared on campus in the 1960's included Dionne Warwick, Neil Diamond, and The Four Seasons.

The biggest impediments for me to make new friends were that I lived at home instead of in a dorm and I had to work to pay tuition so I didn't have time to join a fraternity. I did have some time to socialize, however, and I was steady dating by my senior year. My college social experiences were complete and fulfilling.

THE WARRIORS
(Vietnam, 9/11, and the Pentagon)

I graduated from high school in 1961. As I prepared to go to college, the world was in turmoil. On the other side of the globe a civil war between North and South Vietnam had intensified. The United States, in the mid-1950s, had agreed to support South Vietnam with money and our Army troops.

By 1963 a small group of Special Forces advisers had been increased to 16,000 troops. As I graduated from college and began law school, President Johnson was in the midst of significantly increasing troop strength. When I graduated from law school, the number of US soldiers in Vietnam had increased to more than 500,000!

Two of my good friends who also graduated from Alliance High School were Ralph Hunt and Bill Ruth. They both had been in the Boy Scout troop which I had been in and I had known them throughout elementary, middle, and high school.

In 1965, after we had graduated from college, Ralph and I drove to North Carolina to meet with the admissions people at Duke University. Ralph had decided to enter the ministry and had been accepted by Duke in their school of theology.

I wanted to evaluate whether I should apply to Duke or continue with my plan to go to The Ohio State University College of Law. I decided to go to OSU and Ralph enrolled at Duke and began his studies to become a pastor.

I later learned that Ralph had changed his mind about his career path. After one year, he withdrew from the Duke University and, in May of 1966, he joined the United States Marine Corps to be trained as a helicopter pilot.

Ralph completed training and was sent to the Republic of Vietnam. In June of 1968, he was killed when his helicopter was shot down by a missile. I did not learn about Ralph's death until a couple of years later. It struck home hard because Ralph was confident in his decision to serve the Lord and was then suddenly headed in a different direction.

Thirty-three years later, my friend Bill Ruth was serving in the military at the Pentagon. He had joined the Marine Corps and been trained as a helicopter pilot. He served in Vietnam and then left active duty. He was later recalled to serve in the Persian Gulf War. His service eventually brought him to the serve at the Pentagon in Washington D.C.

FRIENDS

On September 11, 2001, members of Al Qaida hijacked four commercial airplanes in the United States and used them to perpetrate the most devastating terrorist attack in U.S. history. Two of the airplanes crashed into the twin towers of the World Trade Center in New York, killing almost 3,000 innocent people. Another 25,000 were injured in this attack.

The remaining two airplanes headed toward Washington, DC. United Airlines flight 93 became a battleground in the air as the passengers fought with the hijackers. The struggle resulted in the airplane crashing into a field in rural Pennsylvania.

The last plane, American Airlines flight 77, was flown to Washington D.C. and deliberately crashed into the Pentagon. As a result of this terror attack 184 people were killed.

The youngest victim was three years old and the oldest was 71. My friend Bill was in his office on that day and died serving his country. A Pentagon memorial has been constructed and, in that tree-lined lawn area, there are 184 benches. One of them has Bill's name on it.

I realize that life is filled with risks. Sometimes we are faced with increased risks because of the decisions we make. Being in the military can be dangerous, but it is because we have brave brothers and sisters that we are still a democracy and one of the best countries in the world to live in.

I salute my fallen brothers for their sacrifice.

LAW SCHOOL

When I was twenty-two, I graduated from college and moved to Columbus, Ohio to attend law school at The Ohio State University. I was leaving my hometown and found myself without the close support of the friends I left behind.

At OSU, I was joining 200 first-year law school students in my class, and while I would spend a lot of time with them and make new friends, I didn't know any of them previously. My best friend became my roommate. There was a separate part of a dormitory, located near the law school, which was set aside for law school students. I soon found a whole new group of friends.

We fell into a pattern of study and play. During the day we would attend class or study intently. As we entered the new (to us) world of law, there were many deep discussions of its meaning.

Soon I realized that I needed an activity to relieve some of the stressors of law school. I decided I would try to work in some pickup games of basketball on a nearby outdoor court.

At night, five to ten of us might visit a pizza parlor or a dilapidated restaurant bar called "The Last Roundup." These moments of comradery gave us a chance to relax and break the tension of the demands of law school.

This routine was fun, but the best was yet to come. I had been in Columbus for a little over a month when life was about to take a different direction. However, you will not get to know what happened on October 15th, 1965 until my section on dating!

FRIENDS - DUNCAN

Before and during my third year of law school, I was hired by the Columbus City Attorney's office and assigned to the Prosecution Division. While there, I met many people who were firmly established in the legal profession and made many friends.

Part of my duties included evaluating complaints of citizens and deciding whether a crime had been committed. If I determined that the conduct complained of was a crime, I would issue an arrest warrant.

FRIENDS

If the facts of the case sounded interesting, I would often go to Municipal Court and sit in on part of the hearings. There was one municipal judge who I always enjoyed watching in action. Judge Robert Duncan brought a certain energy to the job, and you could tell that he had a deep concern for the alleged victims and the alleged perpetrator. After court we used to talk about his work and his philosophy about life. These times together would later prove very valuable to me and the direction my life would take.

ARMY FRIENDS

When I graduated from law school, I spent approximately three months with no time to worry about enjoying my friends. I needed to pass the Ohio State Bar Exam. To assist with accomplishing this daunting task, I and most of the other law students immediately began a review course designed to prepare us for this three-day test.

At night I would study for the bar exam and during the day I would work at the Columbus City Prosecutor's office. I had now married and we had no cash savings, so I had to work both day and night.

Then, before I could take the exam, in August of 1968, I began a completely new chapter of my life. I was drafted into the United States Army. Within three months, I was separated from my best friend, my wife Karen. I was put on a bus headed to Fort Dix, New Jersey and soon I met 199 new friends in Company A, 4th Battalion, 1st Advanced Infantry Training Brigade.

This diverse group of men were expected to bond together in eight to ten weeks to the point that, someday, they would be willing to risk their lives to protect their fellow soldiers.

In reality, the members of my basic training company, the members of my advanced infantry training, and the members of my missile training unit often did not meet the definition of friends. The training we were receiving was too intense to allow many social interactions.

If I got to really know one or two of my fellow trainees, it would be with the knowledge that we had little time for friendship to form and that within eight to ten weeks a training cycle would end and I would probably not see any of my fellow trainees again. Once my training ended, I was assigned to a duty station where there were many more opportunities to make friends.

While I was stationed at Fort Benning in a replacement company, I was given a direct commission into the Judge Advocate General's Corp (JAG - Army Lawyers). I was then assigned to Fort Devens, Massachusetts. Since this was not a training assignment, or in a war zone, Karen was able to join me and we were assigned on-base housing. Incredibly, I stayed in this assignment for four years.

In this setting, Karen and I made many friends. The legal support for the base and all of New England came from the office of the Staff Judge Advocate which is where I worked.

Most of our friends during this time (1969 – 1973) were other army lawyers and their spouses. Most of them had been assigned outside of the United States and they were at Fort Devens to finish out their time until they were discharged from active duty. Occasionally a new JAG would be assigned there, but within a year or so, they were usually transferred to the RVN (Republic of Vietnam).

Karen and I were very fortunate to be able to socialize with my fellow lawyers and their spouses. They told us about living in foreign environments and I gained an insight into the legal advice that they were called upon to give to the commanders.

The Army Lawyers and their spouses had experienced life in the fullest. Most had been separated for at least one year while they completed their hardship tour (usually to the Republic of Vietnam). In addition to Vietnam, some had been stationed in Europe, Korea, or South America.

I also learned how inventive they could be. For instance, all of us in the law office would socialize with each other. On some occasions, we would eat at nice restaurants which required reservations during peak hours.

We were having difficulty eating at these restaurants until one of the captains, Paul G. said, "Leave the reservations up to me!" Sure enough, we started having much better luck and we asked him how he did it.

Captain G then told us that he would make the reservations as "Doctor Paul G." When we pointed out that we weren't doctors, he pointed out that we had Doctor of Jurisprudence degrees. We could see that he was technically correct.

I'M A CIVILIAN

In February of 1973, our family moved to Marysville, Ohio as I prepared to enter the active practice of law in the civilian community. The previous years had been a series of unknown circumstances which propelled us into a world of friendships which would have to be special or they would melt into memories.

Now we were settling down into an environment which promised more stability and more of an opportunity to form lasting friendships. We have now lived in our hometown for more than 50 years and we have met and become friends with hundreds of people.

Many new friends were introduced to us through school activities as our children entered school and participated in sponsored activities. Both Karen and I became friends with people we met in our professions, and some, we just had opportunities to interact with and enjoyed their company.

It is interesting to me that, it seems, our circle of friends has grown and become much more important to us as the years go by. As I gained new friends who had traveled the world, I gained an appreciation for how limited my experiences had been. I learned about new foods and even began to use chopsticks when I had Asian food. To this day, I use them and enjoy the challenge of picking up rice with my sticks.

As Karen and I grew older, we sadly saw a number of friends move from the area for various reasons. Others remained friends but on a casual basis.

A surprising group of friends remain "good" friends to this day. We share entertainment and celebrate special days. One group took on a special status. That is our "Supper Club."

BREAKING BREAD
(A Supper Club More Than 45 Years Old)

Friendship can be defined in various ways. I like the definition which says that it is a relationship between people who like each other and enjoy each other's company.

FRIENDS

Soon after Karen and I moved to Marysville, we met and became friends with four other couples who were approximately our age and who seemed to have similar values and interests. The interesting thing about these couples was not their similarities but in fact their differences. Two of the couples tended to be in the liberal political camp and two of the couples would classify themselves as conservatives. The fifth couple (Karen and I) were rather independent and could not be categorized as liberals or conservatives.

Despite their political differences, these five couples were so compatible that we began to have all 10 of us to each couple's house for dinner. We soon began to arrange our calendars to meet every 4 to 6 weeks while alternating between hosting a dinner at someone's house and eating out at a restaurant.

We would ask the host couple to choose where we would go when we ate out, and we tried not to repeat any restaurants. Fortunately, we lived near Columbus, Ohio and had our choice of many different eateries. At times, when we met at someone's house, we would choose a theme (for example we've done a murder mystery theme) and always, when we were eating at someone's house, we would have each couple bring a food item as requested by the host couple.

Scheduling these dinners was no easy task. All the individuals were either in a demanding job such as judge, attorney, teacher, businessman, psychologist, engineer, etc. or was active in the community.

Another time factor was the family situations. We started to have children and with that came responsibilities. Despite these challenges, all five couples remained faithful to our group. It was not unusual to have everyone at our gatherings.

The time began to pass. Children started elementary school. Children graduated from high school and headed off to college. Our sons and daughters began their own lives with new jobs, marriages and eventually, they provided us with grandchildren.

There were many reasons to drift apart. In fact, other than strong friendship there were not many reasons to continue our dinner club at such a high level. The same five couples continued our friendships and we continued our dinner club. On average, we would meet every six to eight weeks. No one moved away. No one got divorced. So far, no one has died. And no one got tired of each other's company.

It has now been more than 45 years that this group of friends has been sharing stories about their families, helping each other when help was needed, maintaining a deep affection for each other, and of course, breaking bread together.

HOW I BECAME AN ACTOR

Since the early sixties, my mother and sister were active in community theater. Both enjoyed this activity and were accomplished as actors and, later as directors. Both received accolades from Community Theater organizations as well as the general public. My mother was inducted into the Ohio Community Theater Hall of Fame. She was still directing plays at the age of 80!

My sister appeared in numerous productions, including regional competitions. She was asked to be in advertisements shown on local TV stations and, a nearby medical school asked her to participate in student instruction by playing the part of a patient interacting with the would-be doctors.

My father got involved in designing and building set decorations and props. For the play Pajama Game, he built a sewing machine which would safely explode and catch fire.

He also designed and built a prop that gave the illusion of a knife thrower throwing knives around the body of a young lady. The lady was standing before the board with an apple on her head and the conclusion portrays the apple being split and falling to either side of her head.

FRIENDS

You might have noticed that I have not mentioned my shining accomplishments in theater. That is because I didn't have any, unless you count me setting up folding chairs to accommodate the overflow for "Oklahoma."

Let's fast forward ten to twelve years after my family began their stage debuts. I had graduated from college and law school and had served on active duty in the Army. I was now a civilian living in Marysville Ohio and practicing law.

Marysville had a community theater group, and Karen and I had enjoyed attending their performances. One day a friend of mine asked me to go with him to the tryouts for a play. I told him that I had no desire to try out but I would accompany him if he wanted me to. He said that would be great.

We arrived at the auditorium where the auditions were going to be held. The director sat on the stage and would invite several actors up at a time to read a part. My friend went to the front of the auditorium to await his call and I sat in the back row and watched.

After about 45 to 60 minutes, the director called for a break. She still had ten to twelve people who hadn't yet read for a part.

As I sat there, my friend came back to where I was sitting and asked for my evaluation of his performance. I was saying that I thought he did great when, the Director approached us and asked to speak to me. She then asked when I was going to audition. I told her that I was just keeping my friend company and I did not intend to read for a part. She then asked me for a favor. She needed another male to read the script to properly complete the auditions. At her urging, I agreed to help.

After the readings, the director spoke with about 8 to 10 people and then came to talk to me. She said that she had the perfect part for me and would like me to consider accepting it. I must admit that I was sort of surprised and proud that she thought I was good enough to get a part. I asked what the part was.

The Director said the play was a melodrama and that I would be the narrator. I wasn't sure what that meant but I figured I would give it a try. It turned out that I had more lines than any of the other actors in the play.

At times, I would be interacting with the characters in the play and, at other times, I would speak directly to the audience. It was an enjoyable experience and over the next few years I participated in other plays until my busy law practice and being in the Army Reserve took up most of my time.

I never became a great actor but I believe that my community theater experience helped hone my skills before juries in the courtroom, where I had some good results.

HOW I BECAME A SINGING STAR

When you live in a small Midwestern town, you often have an interest in community organizations such as the local hospital or the YMCA. In Marysville they had an annual hospital fundraiser which featured people from the community performing a variety show consisting of songs, dances, and comedy skits. It was called "Fall Frolics" or "High Fever Follies" and it took place in the school auditorium.

A professional director was brought in to choose the acts and assign who would do them. Over several years, I had participated in comedy skits and, since I had no singing or dancing ability, as the tryouts for the show drew near, I decided I would once again do a comedy skit. The director advised everyone who wanted to be in the show that they needed to have a song to sing at try-outs even if you were a dancer or an actor. There were songs, dances, and skits already chosen for the show by the director and it was just a choice of who did which one.

I went to a local music store to ask for help. I told the clerk that I needed to sing a song and it needed to be an easy one to sing. He suggested that I choose a country tune, and directed my attention to one

FRIENDS

called "It's Hard to be Humble When You're Perfect in Every Way" by Mac Davis. Later it was performed by Willie Nelson.

I took the song home and tried to sing it with no one around me. It was an easy song to sing and I felt as comfortable as I could since the audition would just be in front of several people including the director. The day came and I tried to remember that it didn't matter what the song sounded like. I was going to be in a comedy skit where I was confident. The director seemed nice and when she told me to begin, I relaxed and sang the song a cappella.

I finished. She thanked me and told me when the skits, songs, and dances would be announced and who would perform them. When decision day came, I was shocked to learn that I was chosen as a singer and that I would be performing the very song which I had chosen for my audition. As soon as I could, I got ahold of the director and protested the assignment. She just smiled and said, "I know you will do fine."

On opening night, we had 500 to 600 people in the audience and as I peeked out at them from behind the curtain, my mouth went dry and my breathing irregular. I was having a major panic attack!

The director pulled me aside and told me that she had been doing this for a long time and she had confidence in me. On my queue, I went out on stage and sang every word without fainting! I repeated the performance the next two nights to similar audiences.

I was shocked that I was able to do something that seemed so difficult and was even more shocked later, when I was asked to perform the same song at the local air show and balloon rally with thousands of people in attendance. The positive words of the director and the support of my fellow cast members helped me face the challenge and win.

To this day, I have remembered the words to that song and, if encouraged, I will get up in front of a group of people at a karaoke and sing my song. However, I will only do that if the prior singers weren't that good, and the audience has been enjoying a few adult beverages.

LET ME TELL YOU MY STORY

LYRICS TO "HARD TO BE HUMBLE" BY MAC DAVIS
(Later performed by Willie Nelson)

Oh Lord it's hard to be humble
When you're perfect in every way
I can't wait to look in the mirror
Cause I get better looking each day
To know me is to love me
I must be a hell of a man
Oh Lord It's hard to be humble,
But I'm doing the best that I can

I used to have a girlfriend,
But I guess she just couldn't compete,
With all of these love-starved women,
Who keep cowering at my feet

Oh, I probably could find me another,
But I guess they're all in awe of me
Who cares? I never get lonesome
Cause I treasure my own company

Oh Lord it's hard to be humble
When you're perfect in every way
I can't wait to look in the mirror
Cause I get better looking each day
To know me is to love me
I must be a hell of a man
Oh Lord It's hard to be humble,
We're doing the best that we can

FRIENDS

I guess you could say I'm a loner
A cowboy outlaw, tough, and proud
I could have lots of friends if I wanted
But then I wouldn't stand out from the crowd

Some folks say that I'm egotistical
Hell I don't even know what that means
I guess it has something to do
With the way that I fill out my skin tight blue jeans

Oh Lord it's hard to be humble
When you're perfect in every way
I can't wait to look in the mirror
'Cause I get better looking each day
To know me is to love me
I must be a hell of a man
Oh Lord It's hard to be humble,

We're doing the best that we can
We're doing the best that we can

    All our friends have influenced our lives in one way or another, but this group of friends has made a profound positive impact on our lives!
    I hope that you can tell that I have learned a lot from the friends I have made. The next chapter will delve into my education. It will touch on both the formal education and the life experiences where, by interacting with others, I have learned a great deal and my life has been enriched.

Chapter 3

EDUCATION

EDUCATION IS AN IMPORTANT component in everyone's life. If you do not experience quality learning, your life will be shallow and your opportunity to improve will be greatly diminished. An important point is that everyone learns, not only from formal education, but also from life experiences. The question is, are we learning the right information?

We begin to learn early. If I was a month old and I cried, my parents would probably come to see what was wrong. The odds are good that I would be given a bottle of formula or would be changed out of my wet diaper. Either way, I would have learned a lesson that would prove to be useful throughout my life. If you need help, you have to call out.

As we grow older, our learning broadens into knowledge which extends beyond our limited childhood world. Books might be read to us; we might watch computers or television. These feed us information which may prove useful if true.

When you think about it, that is partly what this book is about. It is about sources of learning that will hopefully improve your life. Family members are an early and very important part of that learning experience. Sometimes the family members need help, perhaps a grandparent or even a sibling might accept that role. Sometimes the parents may be assisted by professionals such as Head Start teachers and other preschool instructors.

Early in life, friends provide a source of knowledge. Hopefully these friends are learned and selective in what they're teaching you. While learning is a wonderful thing to acquire, many people have been taught incorrect, hurtful, or even hateful information which has scarred their lives and often ruined many others. Race supremacy is a primary example of hurtful learning.

As you leave the shelter of your family unit, the source of learning can shift to your spouse and eventually your children. There is certainly a continuing learning environment. Has your significant "other" learned that force, intimidation, and deception are ways to get what they want? Do your children whine until they get what they want? It is extremely important to determine what every important person in your life has accepted as preferred acceptable behavior. It is also important that you realize what lessons you are being taught and determine whether these standards are going to help you live a happy and productive life.

This chapter, which I have entitled Education, primarily explores the formal education which I've received throughout my life. The balance of this book delves into informal education.

My school experiences were rather traditional. I attended public schools in elementary, junior, and senior high schools. I then attended a small private liberal arts college which was located in my hometown, and I followed that up with law school at a large state-run university. Subsequent to law school, I received instruction in the United States Army and over the years I've participated in many continuing education sessions as required by the Ohio Supreme Court. All together I have received formal education in 75 of my 80 years.

A significant informal source of my early education was from my parents. My father, in particular, would quietly give me and my sister many insights into knowledge needed for life. He excelled in explaining how things worked and what we needed to do to ensure that they would continue to work.

Dad and Mom provided us with books and encouraged us to read and understand them. My father also built bookshelves in my bedroom, which were big enough to hold hundreds of books.

Even though neither of my parents had attended college. I was certain that they were hoping I would do so. They did not do this by putting pressure on me. But they had an ability to instill a desire in me to complete postgraduate classes.

EDUCATION

ELEMENTARY SCHOOL

In 1948, I was enrolled in kindergarten in Parkway Elementary School. This school building was almost 20 years old, but it was in good repair. At this point in time, the school serviced kindergarten through 6th grade. It was located on a winding street in a residential neighborhood. My family's house was just 1/2 a block from the school building. I walked to and from school with no fear of danger. Violence against children was rare and we were allowed to roam our neighborhood at an early age.

Behind the school was a large playground where, for the next six years, I would spend many hours running, playing dodgeball, and interacting with my fellow students.

I don't remember how many students were in the school. But I do remember that the student population at Parkway was not very racially diverse. The city of Alliance had a minority population of around 10%. But the housing patterns were such that I do not remember any children of color attending Parkway.

In addition to attending classes and playing on the playground, my strongest memory was being part of the school patrol. Since all of the students had to cross an active street to get into the school, there were concerns for the safety of the young children. Rather than hire an adult to be a crossing guard, the Superintendent formed and trained upper-class 5th and 6th grade students to control traffic.

We were formed into two teams. One for the front of the school and one for behind the school. We were issued long wooden poles with a flag on the end saying stop. We also were issued a belt which went over our shoulder and around our waist and displayed a metal badge indicating our rank.

At any one time there would be two students with poles and flags and they would be wearing badges bearing the title "patrolman." They would move the flags into the traffic lane at the direction of the student

99

standing beside them, who was wearing the badge of a sergeant. The two students in charge of the entire operation were the Captain and the Lieutenant who would watch over the actions of the others and give assistance and advice.

In fifth grade, I was the Lieutenant, and surprisingly, for the times, the Captain was a girl. The school patrol was fun to be in because you got to feel important. And at the end of the school year, patrol members from all over the state were given a bus trip to Washington DC to visit the monuments and museums. My mom even went as a chaperone.

As I was about to enter the 6th grade, I was looking forward to going back to school. I was going to be in the senior grade, and I was going to be promoted to Captain of the school patrol.

Then came the announcement. There were too many children in the district, so a decision had been made to transfer the Parkway incoming 6th grade students to a nearby elementary school. There went my feelings of security. There went my unchallenged seniority, and there went my command of the school patrol.

BUS BOYCOTT

When I was about to enter the sixth grade at Parkway school, the growing population of Alliance created an overcrowded condition in the schools. This led the school board to transfer our entire sixth grade class from Parkway School to Lincoln Elementary School. Lincoln was about 1½ miles from Parkway and the procedure was that we would gather at the Parkway playground and a school bus would take us to Lincoln and then bring us back to Parkway in the afternoon.

We began the school year and the bus picked us up and went directly to Lincoln. We missed some of our friends who were in other grades but it seemed as though that was the only drawback. This was my

EDUCATION

first experience riding a school bus since I lived less than a block from Parkway School.

It wasn't long before we, the sixth-grade students, realized that the bus driver was not an easy person to get along with. He was always grouchy and he demanded strict adherence to his commands, regardless of how arbitrary they might be. He was not interested in our concerns.

A group of my friends and I decided that we did not have to put up with this. Other than our parents, we did not know who to complain to. We decided to talk to the principal at Lincoln School but that did not get us anywhere and the principal told us to do what we were told.

My friends and I talked about our options, and all of us agreed that we would rather walk the 1½ miles than ride the bus. We began to boycott the bus ride and walk to school instead. What started off as a small protest grew until there were only three or four students riding the bus.

In an effort to remedy this situation, the driver would stop at Dairy Queen and buy ice cream cones for those students who continued to ride with him. Some of our group decided to try riding the bus again but they quit riding for a second time and told us that the driver had gotten worse rather than better.

Eventually, the school officials became aware of the situation and called in the bus driver, who said it was a small group of instigators. Some of the students were called in and we explained our concerns. The bus driver was reassigned, and we began to ride the bus again. A small but important lesson about addressing wrongs.

Looking back at what we did, I am not certain what I would think if I found that my children were walking that distance to school. Times change and so do the challenges parents face. I do know that I gained some degree of satisfaction that the system eventually worked, and we were listened to, instead of being treated as mindless children.

JUNIOR HIGH

As I entered the 7th grade, I attended a different school for the third year in a row. Parkway was my first and at that time my most meaningful school experience. The thing is, I was inching toward adulthood, and I was receiving lessons in life. Usually, life is not static. We begin to experience new environments, and with those changes, our knowledge is broadened. At times, we are sheltered from a world that can be challenging and at times cruel.

State Street Junior High School was a dramatic change of environment. Boys and girls from different parts of the city were called together to learn more about life and to share their experiences. The style of teaching was different. Instead of having a primary teacher who would be with our class most of the day, we had classes in different rooms. Our schedule took us from one class to another where a teacher who specialized in a single topic would be located.

Most of the friends that I made at Parkway traveled with me over to this new environment, but they did not necessarily end up in the same classrooms.

We were transitioning from a protective homeroom teacher to experts who had different expectations and different personalities. I soon discovered that a great deal of my learning would be how to relate to these teachers and utilize the information they provided to be successful in school and in life.

The school building itself was certainly in need of attention. One day, as I was sitting at my desk, I heard a noise that sounded like window blinds being released and suddenly flying upward, flopping all the way. This was followed by a cloud of dust and debris.

I heard students right next to me cry out. It's then that I realized a section of the ceiling had come loose and fallen on three of my classmates! Fortunately, no one was seriously injured.

EDUCATION

I dusted myself off and the next day, we were back in the same classroom. I don't remember if the class was able to concentrate on what the teacher was saying, but I know that no one fell asleep in that classroom for a long time!

School levies were not popular during the 1950s, and the need for a new building would not be successfully completed until I was well out of high school.

State Street had a playground area, just as Parkway did. However, the activities which took place there were markedly different. I soon learned life lessons were not confined to the classroom. The foot races and dodgeball turned to turf wars and dares. On several occasions a fight would break out and a teacher would be needed to stop the hostilities. Sometimes there was just a push or a threat of violence without any follow through. At other times, there were real punches thrown and blood would start to flow.

State Street Junior High, where the ceiling collapse occurred

ALLIANCE HIGH SCHOOL, THE AVIATORS

In the 1950's there was only one high school in Alliance, OH and the student body consisted of about 1400 students. My graduating class had 468 students in it. The student body was very diverse and we had students from upper class families, middle class families, and those that lived in poverty. There were groups such as jocks, geeks, and gang members.

When I look back at my high school experience, I realize that while it was not the education that professional educators would strive to create for students, it did provide me with a significant base of knowledge.

Alliance High School was built in 1911 to 1914, at the same time that my grandparents were watching World War One envelop the world. The school was eventually demolished in 1974. When I attended this school, the building was in a major state of disrepair. When there was significant rain, water would cascade through the roof and pour down two of the back staircases from the second to the first floor. Since the classrooms were almost 40 years old, they were cold in the winter and hot in the summer.

ALLIANCE HIGH SCHOOL ACADEMICS

As I began my high school studies, I had several important academic decisions to make. I had known in junior high that I wanted to go to law school and that meant declaring for College Prep.

Other choices would have been Practical Arts (Home Economics/Industrial Arts), Language Arts (English/French/Spanish /Latin), and Fine Arts (Music/Sculpture/Etc.).

Since I knew little about the real legal world, I felt compelled to take Latin (2 Yrs). It wasn't until I entered law school that I discovered the need-to-know Latin was largely imaginary. I could have taken French or Spanish and been equipped with a second language I could actually speak!

EDUCATION

Another mistake I made was applying for and receiving entry into Advance Placement English. Ordinarily this would have been a good college prep course, but I did not get along with the teacher. I suffered through this course in my junior year, but I was looking forward to a different teacher in my senior year A.P. English class. Guess what. As I entered my senior year, I discovered that my problem teacher was being given the senior course! I immediately tried to withdraw from A.P. and sign up for regular English, but they wouldn't let me. It was against the "rules."

The only way I could get out of this class was to have one of my parents come to school and talk to the counselor. I talked to my mother and she reluctantly agreed to withdraw me. The counselor tried to talk her out of the request, but we stood firm.

I completed the regular course, was accepted into college, and got an "A" in my first English course in college.

Not to be outdone, my nemesis A.P. teacher blackballed me when I was nominated for National Honor Society. If you visit my house, you will not see a framed certificate admitting me to the National Honor Society. Big deal!

I had a couple other course selection problems in high school. I asked to have a typing class but I was told that typing was for secretaries and, since I was going to college, I didn't need or qualify for the class. I still can't type, but I guess that is my fault at this point in time.

I experienced another course dispute when I signed up for home economics. I was told the boys take industrial arts and the girls tale home economics. I asked why and was told that the "rules" said so. After several discussions we reached a compromise. If I would take industrial arts, they would let me take home economics. I agreed.

In industrial arts, I sort of made a magazine rack. I did better in home ec., although I can only remember baking some cookies.

GANGS & GANG FIGHTS

It was not a scary thing to be in school, but it had its moments. There were significant gangs roaming the halls that might have been compared to those in West Side Story except they couldn't sing or dance! Every once in a while, they would mix it up and blood would be spilled on the streets. The Cleveland television stations would immediately proclaim these as race riots, even though they were really gang fights. For the average student, there was not too much to fear from the gangs unless you tried to date or disrespected their women.

Occasionally someone would encounter a gang member who probably had been drinking or was high on pot, and a felony or at least a misdemeanor might result. For instance, one day I was walking down a hall in the lower area of the school building and another student approached me. He blocked my path and said, "You want to see my knife? I'll let you see my knife if you give me a quarter." With that, he pulled out a switchblade knife and flipped it open.

I'm not sure if I had any money on me, but I knew I shouldn't encourage him to treat me like an ATM machine. "Gee Tuck, I'd love to see it, but I ain't got no money," I said. Just then, another student walked into the hall and he pocketed his knife and walked away.

Knives were the most common weapons of choice. One day we had a surprise locker check carried out by the local police and items seized included 53 knives and three guns. Another time, the industrial arts teacher discovered a student making a single shot pistol in shop class!

I even had friends who were members of the gangs. (Pharos, Deacons, etc.) I didn't necessarily "hang out" with these friends, but we knew each other and I enjoyed talking to them.

One night, I was walking home from the Hanger, (described later in the Clubs section) when two teenagers stepped out in front of me. I stopped and heard a noise behind me. I turned and saw that there were two more. It didn't look good!

Then, I recognized one of them as a gang leader who I would talk to every once in a while. I said, "Hey Sammy. How are you doing?" Sammy looked at me and then nodded his head to his friends. Just as fast as they had appeared, they were gone.

GIRL GANGS

The girls were not exempt from acting disorderly at times. There was at least one recognized girl gang. One day, I was walking down the hall, two girls began to shout at each other. Then the swearing began. I was trying to ignore the altercation; however, fists started to fly and hair pulling began in earnest. I stopped to watch.

A male fine arts teacher ran to break it up. He was not real big however, and the girls, being off balance, fell into him and all three went down to the floor. Just then, a burly football coach arrived on the scene, bent down, and grabbed the two girls by their hair. He stood them up and marched them off to the vice principal's office.

Meanwhile, the fine arts teacher was trying to find his glasses. I spotted them and gave him the badly twisted spectacles. Everyone then went on their way to classes, but I learned some new words that day!

EXTRACURRICULAR CLUBS AND ACTIVITIES

I don't want you to think that school was just chaos. The academics were adequate to instill a basic education in those students who desired one. We also had many extracurricular clubs and activities.

The Booster Club was the largest group in school followed closely by the American Field Service. This was a club who communicated with students from foreign countries and who sponsored an exchange program. In my senior year, I was the President of this club. I was genuinely interested in the foreign exchange, but it was also a great way to meet girls since 90% of the club was female!

MOUNT UNION COLLEGE

Upon graduating from high school, I applied for admission to Mount Union College. (Now known as The University of Mount Union.) It was the only college or university that I applied to. There was no running to get the mail; I applied and was accepted.

For the next four years, my experiences with higher education differed somewhat from that of the majority of other students. I didn't have money for the dormitory or dining package, so I became a commuter student since I could live for free at my family's home.

In order to pay for the fees related to tuition and books, I needed to work. These factors made it difficult to fully integrate into extra-curricular activities and the college social life.

I was asked to pledge to a fraternity (Sigma Nu), but the time commitments required to be a good pledge brother led me to decline.

I did have a social life, however. I attended sporting events and I dated, but nothing serious. All in all, MUC did prepare me for law school and gave me a strong educational foundation for life.

EDUCATION

LAW SCHOOL

When I was 22 years old, I graduated from college with a joint degree in history and political science. I had gotten decent grades at Mount Union College, but I had applied to attend law school at The Ohio State University and their standards for admission were rather high.

In the 1960s, The Ohio State University College of Law would admit around 200 students each year. In the first year, approximately 70 of those students would drop out or be asked to drop out. I felt I was ready, but I had some major hurdles to overcome.

As required, I took the law school admission test (LSAT) and scored in the 99th percentile. That sealed the deal. I was on my way to Columbus to accomplish my lifelong dream!

As I prepared for my first day of law school, I really had no idea of what it would be like. I knew the work would be intense and it would include subjects which were totally foreign to me such as torts, constitutional law, foreign trade and investments, civil procedure, etc.

Many of my classmates had one or more relatives who were already practicing lawyers or judges, and some had worked summers throughout college at law firms as clerks. They knew what case precedent meant, or the difference between legislative law, common law, and constitutional law. I, on the other hand, was entering a new world. In a way I was fortunate to not know these things. I was not wise enough to recognize my deficiencies and worry excessively about them.

I knew that the school's objective was to educate and qualify young men and women to practice law. They hired brilliant professors to impart the information necessary to accomplish these tasks. The question was, would I be able to relate to these scholars?

As I mentioned, the first-year class of law students numbered 200 students. Our class was divided into two sections. My section consisted of 97 men and 3 women! (In today's classes at OSU there are more women than men.) As I sat in the classroom and looked around at the expectant faces of my classmates, I was sure that all of us wanted the same thing—to be reassured that we would be successful. For many, this hope was dashed on the first day.

One of the first professors to address us began by telling us that our success or failure was primarily dependent on our own efforts. He went on to say that we would be exposed to more work, more thinking, and more stress than we had ever experienced in our lives.

He then told us to look at the person on our left then look at the person on our right. This was significant he said, because by the end of that school year one of the three of us would be gone. He went on to say that the individuals who didn't make it through the first year would have either dropped out on their own or they would have flunked out. At that early point in my experience as a law student, I wondered what it would be like to skip law school and be a teacher.

I knew that I needed to study more than I ever had before. I began on the right path and was pleased to learn that the law was not as much of a mystery as I had imagined it to be. (Except possibly constitutional law.)

I began the year with the best of intentions. I stayed up late. I read the assigned lessons and extra readings. What I found was that no matter how much I applied myself, there were many others who were driven to extremes. They lived in the law library, they studied until two or three in the morning, and they had no life other than law school.

I decided to adopt a more balanced approach. I would study, but I would enjoy life as well. I very much wanted to become a lawyer, but I did not believe that the fanatical approach was the way to go.

For example, I needed exercise, so I would go to the local basketball courts in the afternoon to get involved in a pick-up game. There I got my blood circulating. (Sometimes dripping on the court.)

One day, I was chosen for a team and when we matched up, I found I was playing man on man against a fit young man who was about 6'1" and weighed 230-250 pounds. We began to play and my opponent would get the ball and drive to the basket. It didn't seem to matter whether I was in his way or not. He did this time after time and I was feeling the effects of the pounding I was taking.

Now, you have got to realize that there were no referees and the unwritten rule was "no blood – no foul." After the game ended with a victory for them, and they left the court, I asked one of my team members, "Who was that guy?" My friend replied, "Oh, he is the starting fullback for the Ohio State Football team!"

Another escape I had from studying was an almost nightly visit to either a local pizza place or a nearby bar. This usually would occur at about 11pm and my friends and I, after satisfying our hunger and thirst, would hurry back to our apartments of the dorm designated for law students. There, some would resume studying until 1,2, or 3 in the morning. I went to bed.

The third distraction I allowed turned out to be the most important event in my life. I met and courted Karen, who two years later, I married. I have a section in this book regarding that relationship. However, I want to point out here that, whatever study time I lost dating was more than made up for when Karen would insist that we study in the law library. To my dismay this happened often. It may also have helped get me through law school.

A MAD PROFESSOR

One of the biggest differences between college and law school were the professors. At Mount Union the faculty all seemed nice, although some of them were more difficult than others. For instance, I had a Spanish professor who started his class with 34 students and, by the time of the final exam, we were down to 12. Apparently, there were 22 students who were smarter than I and dropped the class. After the final exam, eight of us passed his class and I got my only D in college! We were allowed to retake one class for credit and, on my second try, I received a B which really upset my professor!

I don't know if you have ever seen the 1973 movie "Paper Chase." In that film, a tyrannical law professor terrorizes first year law students with the specter of flunking out. His teaching method seems designed to suggest that "If you are not "Elite," what are you doing here?"

My first and second year of law school at OSU had one such professor and I ended up having his class for constitutional law (first year) and an international business law course (second year).

He had a seating chart and, when he was going to ask a question, he would say "Mister . . ." (again, there were only 3 women out of 100 classmates) and as his finger stopped, the section of the class that he was about to choose would all look down and sink into their seats. He would call on a random student and demand that this poor soul defend a position on a legal issue. No matter which side the student took, the professor would humiliate him or her by arguing against his position and backing up his rebuttal with case citations and statutory or common law precedent.

The style of this professor was so intense that he was known and feared throughout the school.

There were at least two examples of his fervor that I remember. One time, the fire alarm went off during class. Students began to rise out of their seats to leave the building. The professor shouted, "SIT DOWN! SIT DOWN!" He then asked what was going on and a student told him that it was a fire alarm. The alarm was steady and seemed to be growing louder. The professor then said "Oh, it's probably just a test; now where was I?"

It wasn't until a fireman in full regalia opened the door and ordered us out, shouting, "Everyone out!" that there was a scramble to the exits.

EDUCATION

My last view, as I left the room, was the professor throwing a marker at the screen behind him. It turned out that it actually was a test and the professor never left the room despite threats of discipline against him.

The second incident, in another class of his, happened on a Saturday. Now, I don't know how a class got scheduled for 11:30 AM on Saturdays but it did.

One Saturday, at about 10:30 AM, I was studying in the law library when a classmate of mine approached and asked me if I had heard about the building repairs. I told him that I hadn't and he said that they were going to turn off the electricity in the entire law school building at noon. He then asked me if I thought that the professor would cancel his 11:30 to 12:30 class. I told him that I doubted it but at least we would only have half of it.

At 11:30 everyone gathered for class and I was anxious to see if anyone would ask the professor if we were going to have the class. No one was dumb enough to approach him though, and class began. At noon the lights went out. The room was suddenly pitched into total darkness. The room had no windows except for two small panels on the doors. The doors opened onto an interior hallway which had some light coming from adjoining rooms. As he did with the fire alarm, the professor showed a complete lack of awareness when he shouted, "What's going on? Who shut off the lights?"

One of the students, emboldened by the darkness told him that they were working on the building and that the electricity would be off for all afternoon.

Students started to get up and head for the doors. Suddenly, the professor shouted, "Everyone back in your seats!"

He then instructed the students in the back of the room to prop open the doors. This resulted in two dim shafts of light protruding about 4 to 6 feet into the room. He then resumed his lecture which lasted until almost 1:00 PM.

I did not get a D in either class that I took from this professor. In fact, I got an "A" in both classes. I truly believe he scared me into achieving those grades!

When working on this book, I wondered whatever happened to the good professor. If he was still alive, he would be about eighty or eighty-one years old. On the off chance that I could track him down, I Googled him. I was impressed and humbled to find out that he had not wasted his professional life since I was a law student in his class. He was a professor emeritus at a top Ivy League law school. His curriculum vitae was 14 pages long. He was an author of numerous books and articles. He was also in the top 50 in the entire world for legal citations.

I couldn't believe it. I found this professor who had given me two A's . . . and he was world renowned! There was a phone number on the site, and I decided to call it and reconnect with the man I feared most in law school.

I got a recording saying that "This is the office of Professor . . . and he is not in now. Leave your number and he will call you back." I did leave my name, number, and a statement that I was his student at The Ohio State University College of Law. I did not expect him to call me back and I was surprised when my phone rang about an hour later. It was him!

Before I could begin to ask questions, the caller verified that he was indeed "Professor X," but he never taught at OSU and he thought he knew who I was looking for. He went on to say that a person of the same name, who had also been a professor of law, had practiced law in NYC after teaching at OSU.

I apologized for bothering him and asked him how he knew his namesake, my former professor. He replied, "When I graduated from law school, I was hired as an associate at a New York City law firm. When I reported my first day, I approached a group of receptionists and asked where I needed to go." They said, "What is your name?" After I replied, one turned to the others and said, "My God! We have got another one!"

My former professor and the eminent scholar I was speaking on the phone with had been members of the same firm!

THE ARMY EDUCATION

After completing high school, college, and law school, I believed that my days of formal education were over. Then the U.S. Army offered me an "invitation" to learn new skills in the setting known as Basic Training, Advanced Individual Training, and Missile Training.

I was sent to Fort Dix, New Jersey for approximately five months of intense classes explaining how to kill our enemies and not get killed in the process. I then was sent to White Sands Missile Range where I learned to shoot down airplanes.

These educational classes, for the most part, were conducted in the woods and in the desert. There was a sense of urgency driven by the realization that a failure to learn these lessons did not get graded by A's or F's, but ultimately by whether you lived or died!

My formal education as an enlisted Army recruit continued with learning which airplanes were U.S. planes as opposed to Russian or Chinese. We were encouraged to shoot down enemy planes, but not our own planes.

My formal education in the JAG school continued as a student and an instructor over the next 30 years.

In my civilian practice, I kept up with continuing legal education (CLE) until I retired in 2022. The Supreme Court of Ohio required this to be accomplished by all practicing attorneys.

The JAG School in Charlottesville, Virginia

WHAT I LEARNED AS AN ARMY LAWYER

After my enlisted training in the U.S. Army (which you can read more about in the military section of this book), I returned to a more traditional school at the Army Judge Advocate General's School in Charlottesville, Virginia. There, I spent eight weeks learning about the profession of being an Army lawyer.

My primary assignment for the first year and a half of active duty was to defend soldiers who were accused of breaking the rules. There were a lot of rules and a lot of errant soldiers. In that year and a half, I was appointed to represent 168 defendants.

During the last two and a half years of my active duty in the JAG Corp, I was a Legal Assistance Officer. I had four attorneys in my office and several law clerks. We would provide advice to our clients regarding estate planning, real estate, contracts, personal injury, and may other legal matters.

EDUCATION

Our clients consisted of active-duty soldiers, sailors, airmen, and marines. Since Fort Devens was the largest military base in New England, we were kept busy providing advice and I learned a great deal about the practice of law.

In addition to court-martials, I was sent all over New England to teach our troops about the Uniform Code of Military Justice, aka "The Rules."

I was also asked to teach certain courses at the JAG school in Virginia. These opportunities to serve as an instructor meant a great deal to me since I was only a Captain. The usual practice was for them to only ask Lieutenant Colonels or Colonels. The students were attorneys from all over the United States.

Chapter 4

DATING & MARRIAGE

THE RELATIONSHIP between two people is often the most important component of your life. It can be a powerful force providing comfort, love, support, and companionship. Or, it may be a cause for concern, confusion, anger, and disappointment.

At times, bonding with a parent, a sibling, or a child is the focus. Often, it is your spouse who becomes the center of your universe. I loved and revered my parents and my sister. I love my children and grandchildren as much as can be imagined. But the love between my wife and me has made my life the blessing it has been.

My history of dating would not make Casanova envious. When I began dating in the eighth or ninth grade, these were primarily parent approved (sometimes parent arranged) gatherings where I would go to a party and spend time with a girl after which, her parents and mine would pick us up and take us home.

LET ME TELL YOU MY STORY

As I moved into high school there were more activities and more independence. While this provided me more opportunities to ask girls out, I discovered that many of the girls I was interested in dating were going steady with someone else.

I was a friend to many of the coolest girls in the school, but our conversations were often about their athlete boyfriends. They felt comfortable sharing their feelings with me and asking for advice. I could dance with them at the "Hanger" or share fries with them at Heggy's, but a formal date – did I really want to tick off that 230-pound defensive end?

High school was a culture where relationships were formed based on expectations. The captain of the cheerleaders would date one of the captains of the football team and so on. As a non-athlete student, I could interact with any of the most desirable girls in school if I was not perceived as a threat by their boyfriend.

When I began college, it was a different dynamic. My relationship with girls seemed more based on an assessment of what kind of wife she would be, and would she be a fun friend until we both decided that it was time to get serious or to move on. I still had casual friendships with girls, but my expectations were to find a life mate.

I enjoyed dating Sherry, although she lived a distance away. I had a more serious relationship with Maria; however, we eventually mutually agreed to move on.

I will not dwell on my dating prowess, as incredible as it may have been, but, on October 15, 1965, when I first met Karen, my future was set and my mission was clear. I was to love her with all my heart and to hope that somehow that love would be returned.

You may wonder how Karen and I first met. That was a life incident that I will NEVER forget.

DATING & MARRIAGE

HOW I MET YOUR MOTHER
(A Bet Which Changed My World)

It was a cool fall night in Columbus, Ohio, in October of 1965. Less than two months earlier, I had packed almost all of my possessions, gotten into my car, and left my family home.

I had graduated from Mount Union College and been accepted into law school at The Ohio State University. I would soon begin a rigorous post-graduate program that was demanding on my time and attention.

I won't say that in the first two months I spent all my time in the classroom and studying in the law library. My fellow first year students and I would often take some time out late at night to hit the hot spots on High Street for pizza and beer.

The problem was, I was having more stress than fun. At OSU, I had entered an exciting environment filled with interesting people and some really attractive women. Yet, I was spending the few free hours that I had, washing down pizza with beer accompanied by the same guys I saw in class every day.

You should know that my class had 97 men and three women in it. I needed to get back on the social agenda which I had been building at college.

That night in October, a friend of mine from Louisiana and I decided to find some real girls to talk to (and of course impress). It just so happened that an undergraduate freshmen mixer was in progress in a nearby building. We talked about skipping the pizza and beer and instead crashing the dance (after all, since we were in our first year of law school, we technically were freshmen).

My friend was a little bit concerned that due to the tender age of these undergraduates (18 or 19), we sophisticated men of the world might get bored and wish that we had gone for the pizza.

To keep things exciting, we came up with a plan. If we were successful in gaining admittance to the dance, we would separate and have a bet on which of us could dance with the girl whose home was farthest away from Columbus, Ohio. A six pack of beer was riding on this bet.

We approached the dance with anticipation and apprehension. Would we lie if they asked us if we were freshmen? Would there be consequences If we were caught lying? You should know that, at this time in history, institutions of higher learning were very protective of the young ladies entrusted to their care. There were no dorms with men and women on alternating floors. There certainly were no dorms with a mix of men and women on the same floor.

Even though we men could leave our rooms at night and roam the streets all night if we wished to, women had a curfew and had to sign out before leaving the dorm at night. They even needed to indicate where they were going and who they were with!

My friend and I had no trouble getting into the mixer (I guess we didn't look like men of the world) and we began our bet by separating and walking onto the dance floor to identify and dance with a girl who didn't look like or talk like a Midwesterner.

As I walked by a number of very nice-looking young women, I saw one who was just plain beautiful. I determined in my mind that I would dance with her no matter where she was from.

As I walked up to the group of girls, I heard her speak and she had the strongest New York accent that I had ever heard! There may have been some girls there from Australia or Singapore, but I was willing to settle for the East Coast of the United States.

I asked the young lady to dance and she said yes. At this moment in time, my life changed forever. As we danced, I didn't expect her to just melt in my arms (and there was that pesky bet I had made) so I began talking to her. She told me that her name was Karen and that she was from Valley Stream, New York (very important information). She asked me where I was from and I replied that she probably had never heard of my hometown but I was from Alliance, Ohio.

She responded, "Oh, really?" She then told me that she had just gotten a letter from her brother who was in graduate school in Michigan. He told her that he had a job interview in Alliance, Ohio, with a major industry there.

After getting over our amazement about her brother going to my hometown, we found out that she had one sibling, her brother, who was my age, and I had one sibling, who was a sister, who was her age.

We also discovered that one of her roommates was from Port Clinton, Ohio, which was where my roommate was from! I'm not sure how we discussed this, but it turned out that we were both Lutherans. This was interesting because in college I had been dating a Catholic girl while she had been dating a Jewish boy in high school.

I don't remember if I danced with anyone else that night, but I do know that I asked Karen (my dance partner) for her phone number and hoped to talk more with her soon. She gave it to me and my big concern was that she had made up a number since I didn't even know her last name.

When my law school friend and I got together to compare notes, he claimed that he had danced with someone from Long Island, New York also. We ended up declaring a draw. We then invited some friends in and got some pizza and beer to celebrate a great evening.

A week or so after the mixer, I finely got up the courage to call her and was thrilled when I heard her voice on the phone! I asked her if she would like to go to a movie, and she said that would be nice.

Our first official date was the movie "Those Magnificent Men in Their Flying Machines." I was thrilled to get to know her better and I discovered that her 19th birthday was happening in December.

Karen in high school

KAHIKI

So, I wracked my brain trying to think of something to do for her birthday that would impress her. I hadn't known her long enough to buy her an expensive gift. My roommate suggested that I just take her out to dinner. He told me that any girl would appreciate a break from dorm food.

I wasn't thrilled with the suggestion as I envisioned stopping in at a local White Castle for some sliders. Then it hit me! Take her out to dinner but not to the restaurants I might happen to frequent. After all, she was a girl from New York City where they had fancy restaurants with many kinds of food.

DATING & MARRIAGE

I asked around to my classmates and was told that I should take her to an upscale Polynesian restaurant called the "Kahiki." So, I made a reservation and took her there! This grand structure seated 500 people and was listed on the National Register of Historic Places. It featured gigantic fish tanks with many different tropical fish. There were gas-ignited fireplaces and palm trees.

The food service was exotic and extensive and it was served by men and women in native dress of the South Pacific Islands. While we were eating, entertainers sang, danced, and played Polynesian musical instruments. The prices on the menu did not compare favorably to what I was used to paying at a restaurant, but we had a great time.

As we both headed home for Christmas break, I wondered if I would ever see her again. The reality was that there were reasons to believe we might be too different to end up in a long-term relationship, let alone a marriage. For example:

1. She was young and wanting to experience life.
2. Her family lived in New York and mine in Ohio.
3. She was sophisticated. At least she had experienced a wider range of life. Compared to her range of life experience I was a hick.

On the other hand (as my favorite Broadway character Tevye would say):

1. At that stage of my life, I looked "not bad." (5'11", 160 lbs.)
2. I was in law school.
3. I drove a convertible.
4. Her roommates thought I was hot.
5. We had kismet relationships which brought us together.

We continued to date until the summer break. When we returned for the fall semester, I was not sure how firm our relationship was.

I came back to school ready to express my love. (No—wait. I can't use that word yet. It's too early.) I did bring back a gift which I gave her before she had a chance to break my heart.

Karen had trouble sleeping. She had five roommates, a difficult academic schedule, and probably angst regarding our relationship.

I bought her a clock radio!

As I explained to her, she could turn on a station with soothing music and set a time when it would automatically turn off.

She seemed touched and she never told me about wanting to date around until we were happily married.

OUR FIRST YEAR OF DATING

There might have been another reason why Karen was willing to continue dating me. She hated to study alone and all of her roommates seemed busy with other interests. I was always there to spend study time with her. She couldn't really help me too much in my studies (Constitutional Law, Torts, Civil Procedure, etc.), but I had some experience with her basic subjects until it came to chemistry.

With five roommates she didn't even try to study in her dorm, but she was thrilled when she found out that I could take her as a guest to the law library. The rooms were quiet and the librarians were trained to keep it that way.

When I got bored with studying, I would slip out into the hall next to the water fountain and she would eventually find me there, shooting the breeze with classmates. I would estimate that I spent twice as much time in the law library then I would have if I wasn't dating Karen.

After meeting Karen and starting to know her better, my primary focus shifted from completing law school to winning her heart.

DATING & MARRIAGE

Over the first eleven months of 1966, we spent most of our time together going to concerts, movies, and dances. When we wanted to be alone, we would get a picnic basket of food and a blanket and hop in my car to go to a nearby park.

We also attended athletic events together and I treated Karen to a seat at a basketball game in Saint John's Arena. We were in the very last row. The court was so far away that the six foot five players looked about two feet tall and, during the Star-Spangled Banner, the flag was below us! When football season began, we were closer to the players, but we were in the end zone.

We continued to go to movies, concerts, and dances. When the weather cooperated, we would often go on picnics. We enjoyed each other's company while sitting on benches in the OSU Oval. We always enjoyed the show the squirrels put on. (Karen is not a big squirrel fan now, since they get into her flowers and destroy them.)

This nearly one year period of learning about and learning to love each other became the basis for over 58 years of as perfect a marriage as a couple could hope for!

WILL SHE SAY YES?

Another time we got to spend quality time together was when I offered to drive her home to New York for the holidays. When Karen was at Ohio State, she did not have the use of a car. So, my offer to drive her home relieved her parents of a long drive to Ohio and back to New York only to repeat the trip to get her back to school.

It worked out well for me also. I got to spend 11-12 hours alone with her and I got to spend a week with her in New York. This was the first time that I got to meet her parents and try to impress them with the company their daughter was keeping.

By December of 1966, I was ready to "pop the question" and ask Karen to marry me. We had discussed the subject of marriage, but neither of us had committed to this most important decision.

I was 23 years old and had completed the first of two years of law school. I was ready to commit to spending the rest of my life with Karen. However, I knew that, at age 20, Karen may have wanted to enjoy her single status a bit longer even though we had spent much of the last 14 months together and each of us had expressed our love for each other.

I decided that I was certain in my love for her and that I was going to ask her to marry me. If she said no, or asked to postpone, I would honor her decision, but I would continue to love her with all my heart.

With my mind made up and Christmas fast approaching, I enlisted the help of my parents and we began to look at engagement rings. While in college and law school I had worked, fulltime in the summer and part time during the school year. However, it was only with the help of my Grandma Stanley and my parents that I was able to pay the expenses of the education I was receiving. I was surprised at the high prices of engagement rings! They did have some in the price range I could afford, but if I wanted a real diamond the stone would not be very big.

I finally selected a ring and it is *not* true that you needed a magnifying glass to see the stone. Let's just say that it was not ostentatious!

Now I started thinking about when, where, and how I should give her the ring and ask the most important question I would ever ask.

I decided that I would wrap the ring as a Christmas present and give it to her at her parents' house on Christmas Eve. I knew that her parents would be there and that was alright whether she said yes or no. I didn't expect any of her friends to be there.

I bought a cardboard cylinder and placed the wrapped ring in the bottom of it. On top of the ring, I placed 4-5 other small wrapped gifts to keep her from suspecting a ring gift before she opened the last present.

Christmas Eve was a happy holiday with Karen, me, and her mom and dad snacking on cookies and getting ready to open gifts. Then, the doorbell rang and Karen's best friend paid a surprise visit to say Merry Christmas! Of course, Karen invited her to stay while we opened presents. By that time, I was beginning to panic because I was about to ask Karen to marry me and I didn't know what her answer would be!

It was now too late to remove the ring from the cylinder and I couldn't think of a reason not to give Karen her present until the next day. So, I asked to go last and everyone began to give and receive presents. I could see the joy everyone was experiencing and I didn't know what to do except give Karen her gift.

As she reached into the cylinder, she pulled out a small gift which she received enthusiastically. Four or five small gifts later she reached in and pulled out a small box which she opened, and I said the only thing that I could (and the only thing I wanted to say) with a little bit of a stutter.

"WILL YOU MARRY ME?"

She looked very surprised and then said "YES!" We all cried.

It seemed like a good time to celebrate. The optimist in me had decided to bring Champagne and glasses. Soon the crying turned to laughter.

Despite the initial uncertainty, more than 58 years later we are still celebrating that question and her answer.

WE ARE ENGAGED

1967 started off on a high note with Karen wearing a small diamond ring on her finger. We decided to set the date of the wedding for September 9th, 1967.

The next eight months were filled with preparations. Karen's mom took on many of these while her dad arranged the plans for the reception.

For the last four months, Karen was immersed in her major of Family and Human Development. Yet, she was in constant contact with her mom regarding the dozens of wedding preparations.

When she returned to New York in May, things got even more hectic.

Karen told me who she wanted as her maid of honor (a friend since 3rd grade) and as her bridesmaids. There were three bridesmaids plus the maid of honor, so I needed to come up with four groomsmen to balance the wedding party. With the blessing of my dad, my Uncle Bill agreed to be my best man.

Karen's family lived comfortably, but were not rich. They had paid for her tuition at OSU by establishing a bank account and depositing a savings bond each month while she was going to middle and high school. Because of the cost of a wedding, Karen asked if I would mind a nice, but not fancy ceremony and reception.

I was from a small town in Ohio where the reception often consisted of going to the church basement for cake and punch or some other soft drink. The "fancy" reception parties came after the main group left the church and close friends and family came back to someone's house where real food and drink was consumed.

With that history in mind, I expected similar happenings for our reception. After I talk about the ceremony, I will tell you the "rest of the story."

Prior to the ceremony, Karen and I met with the Pastor of the Lutheran Church of which Karen and her family were members. The Pastor was very likeable and supportive. He didn't require any pre-ceremony counseling, but he did offer us an opportunity to talk about the commitment we were making.

We sent out invitations and, although I didn't expect a large turnout from any relatives and friends because of the significant travel time, we started receiving a nice number of acceptances from out of state family and friends.

THE NIGHT BEFORE

While the ceremony went wonderfully, I should probably tell you how I almost ended up in jail the night before our wedding!

No, I was not at a wild bachelor party! In fact, a couple of my cousins, my sister, and I decided to take a walk in the city park which was located right next door to Karen's parents' house.

It was a beautiful evening and the park seemed well suited to give us a quiet place to talk. There was enough of a moon to see the road into the park and we had just stopped to talk seriously about married life when all the sudden a car entered the road behind us and another car emerged in the park ahead of us. Five men jumped out of the cars and shouted, "We are the police! Stay where you are!"

We were shocked and I was wondering if they really were the police since they were not in uniforms. They quickly demanded to know who we were and what we were doing in the park at 10 pm at night. They advised us that the park was under curfew from dusk to dawn and we were therefore guilty of trespassing.

One of my cousins then pointed at me and exclaimed, "He is a lawyer!" This in fact, was not true since I still had to complete my third year of law school and I had not taken or passed the bar exam yet.

I was suddenly the center of attention and, knowing that many police officers are not big fans of lawyers, I asked how we were supposed to know about the curfew. One of the officers (they had shown us their credentials) walked me back to where we entered the park and pointed to a sign attached to a post which clearly stated the closure time and the law which would be broken if a violation occurred.

I agreed with the officer that a clear warning had been given and told him that I should have seen the sign, but my mind was filled with thoughts about my wedding which was happening tomorrow.

The mood of the police changed dramatically when they heard I was about to be married. They suddenly started to congratulate me and even patted me on the back.

The police gave us a warning and then sent us back to my soon-to-be in-laws'!

Karen on our wedding day

THE CEREMONY

The date was set and on September 9th, 1967, Dennis & Karen Schulze would become husband and wife! The time flew by. Karen had a bridal shower hosted by her best friend, Donna. Out of all the gifts she received, I believe that the nicest one was a bride and groom wall hanging made by Donna on which the soon to be groom (me) and the lovely bride (Karen) stood hand in hand.

Soon it was the day of our wedding at Abiding Savior Lutheran Church in Valley Stream on Long Island. The ceremony joining us together for life is somewhat of a blur, but I do know that every major part went right.

I didn't see the bride on that special day until she walked down the aisle escorted by her father. (She looked absolutely gorgeous!!) Both of us answered the Pastor's questions in the proper fashion, including the "I do!" Next was our grand exit when the rice (actually bird seed) was thrown on us.

Later in my life I was able to look at our wedding album and confirm that it was a joyous occasion and we both smiled a lot. Even later still, when I was an acting judge in Marysville Municipal Court, I had the good fortune to perform wedding ceremonies for more than 20 couples and, each time, I thought about my good fortune and hoped that each couple would be as lucky as I.

THE RECEPTION

Remember my description of an "Ohio wedding" from earlier? I was used to the wedding being in a church with a reception of finger foods, sandwiches, and cake in the church meeting room. After the main reception, close friends and family might come to the bride's or groom's house for more substantial fare and stronger libations.

Despite the plea for a budgeted reception, this was not an "Ohio" wedding. About 150 people accepted the invitation to a sit-down dinner of prime rib. I was also not expecting the differences in wedding gifts. There was a table for gifts and those people from Ohio who were able to attend, gave us a nice assortment of housewares to get us started as a married couple.

The New York guests, for the most part, did not place any wrapped gifts on the table. I didn't say anything to Karen however, and after we finished eating, I found out why. Karen took my hand and said, "Let's go meet the guests." We approached an aunt and uncle of hers. After greeting, shaking hands, and some chit chat they pulled an envelope from a pocket and gave it to Karen. She then passed the envelope to me.

I figured this was a congratulations card and so I started to open it. Karen said, "Let's wait until we greet everyone." After meeting and chatting with over 100 people, I understood that most of the people from New York gave us similar envelopes.

Karen took me into a room reserved for her and we opened one of the envelopes. In it was a one-hundred-dollar bill! Karen explained that while this was a major gift to us, not all the envelopes would yield the same bounty.

As the guests continued to party, Karen and I got in our car and headed for the Pocono Mountains in Pennsylvania. Yes, someone tied tin cans to the back of my car, but some kind soul removed them at my request.

Karen and I at our reception

LET ME TELL YOU MY STORY

OUR FIRST YEAR AS HUSBAND & WIFE

Back at OSU, we moved into an apartment about four miles from the campus. This was it! No roommates (except for each other) and our first real home to share.

Of course, there were a few negatives to deal with. For instance, we didn't have the money to afford a table to eat our meals on. We decided to use Karen's clothes trunk as a table and we sat on the floor to eat at it. (More than 55 years later, I probably would have trouble getting up off the floor.)

Also, we were not within walking distance to the law library. And we had to cook many of our meals since a restaurant would be too expensive. Thankfully, Karen was a good cook!

Despite these minor inconveniences, we were in heaven with a loving relationship and the promise of a lifetime of support and affection!

Our primary focus this first year was on me finishing my third, and last, year of law school and Karen finishing her third year of Family and Child Development.

During my first year of law school, I did not work until summer break, at which time I worked in a two-person law office specializing in criminal law, domestic relations, and worker's compensation. My income was minimal, but I learned a lot about the actual practice of law.

The attorney doing criminal law and domestic relations did not make a lot of money unless a wife walked in to file for divorce against her really rich husband. The worker's compensation lawyer would send me to an exclusive clothing store in his brand-new Cadillac to pick up a dress for his wife which cost $100! That was a lot of money to a law student.

Married life was even better than expected. I discovered that Karen was everything I could have hoped for. She had an amazing capacity for living life and she continually made it clear that she wanted to enjoy that life with me.

DATING & MARRIAGE

I can't remember any serious differences of opinion. I am sure that we didn't always agree, but more than 50 years later, I can't remember any time where either of us got upset and stayed upset. We were from two very different backgrounds; however, we joined into a relationship which allowed us to love each other and respect each other for who we were.

Both Karen and I completely believe we are a team. We have our individual beliefs, goals, and our own distinct personalities. Despite the differences, however, we now were part of each other's lives. We were so comfortable together that we did not have any doubts that God meant for us to be together for the rest of our lives. To this day, this is still our blessing.

WE'RE AN ARMY FAMILY NOW

As I was going into my third year of law school, I sought out some advice from an attorney I met who worked in the prosecutor's office. He said that I should apply for a job in the prosecutor's office. It didn't pay much, but I would meet a lot of people who could be helpful once I graduated.

I applied, interviewed, and was tentatively offered a job. Then came the unexpected question. "You are a registered Republican, aren't you?" I had never been that interested in politics and at 18 years old, I had registered as a Democrat, which was the party of choice for my parents.

My answer to questions was, "I will be a registered Republican by tomorrow." It actually took a little longer, but I became a proud member of the party and was hired to issue arrest warrants by the Columbus City Prosecutor's office.

It was while I was in the prosecutor's office that I met Robert Duncan, a Municipal Judge, who would later write a letter of recommendation to the Army in support of my being accepted into the JAG Corps.

LET ME TELL YOU MY STORY

In the spring of 1968, I celebrated my third graduation in eight years. I had become an alumnus of Alliance High School in 1961, of Mount Union College in 1965, and of The Ohio State University College of Law in 1968. With each of these there were challenges, twists, and turns which could have ended my formal education and sent me to work in a factory.

As I completed law school, I was very blessed for having the opportunity to further my education. Now that I was married to a beautiful, intelligent, and loving young lady, I was ready to seek out a job which would provide my family with years of security and the opportunity to engage in a profession which would provide me with additional learning and a sense of satisfaction.

Before I even began a job search, I was offered a job that would pay me a little over one hundred dollars per month, would separate me from my wife for at least a year, and would teach me how to kill people.

This was a job that I couldn't refuse. No, it wasn't the mob who came calling. It was the United States Army. Despite my law degree, the Army decided they had a greater need for warriors than for lawyers.

The second year of our marriage was not as kind to Karen and me as the first. In August, 1968 (after 2 extensions by the draft board) I was on a bus bound for Fort Dix, New Jersey to begin basic training two weeks before our first anniversary.

I suddenly went from the glow of love and companionship with Karen to facing the reality that we would be separated for six to eighteen months while I completed training and a very possible year of service in RVN (The Republic of Vietnam). We also faced a real possibility of my suffering a serious injury or even death.

A more immediate concern arose as our first anniversary drew closer. As a trainee, I was not allowed to spend time with anyone but my fellow trainees during the early training period.

That would not do! I told Karen to come down to Fort Dix on a Sunday to be with me on our very important first anniversary. We were

DATING & MARRIAGE

not training on that day and I snuck out of our company area to meet her. She brought a blanket and a picnic basket filled with goodies and I risked a court martial as we disappeared into a nearby woods. It was a wonderful day for us to reaffirm our love for each other.

After the anniversary picnic, Karen went back to school and I completed basic training, advanced individual training, and ground to air missile training.

With nearly six months of separation while I was trained to be a soldier, the time had come for me to find out whether I would: 1) continue to be an enlisted combat soldier and be sent to the RVN, 2) apply to OCS (Officer Candidate School), or 3) be accepted into the JAG Corps and serve as an army lawyer after being commissioned as a captain with a four-year active service obligation.

It turned out that I was selected for the JAG Corps and was sent to Charlottesville, VA to receive two months training in military law, again without Karen.

In May of 1969, I was ordered to report to Fort Devens, Massachusetts to begin my first duty assignment as an army lawyer. Karen soon joined me and, after nine months separation, we moved into base housing on a beautiful military facility. Devens had a commissary (grocery store), an exchange (department store), a golf course, swimming pool, tennis courts, a theater, a lake, hiking trails, and an officer's club (restaurant & bar).

Our house was a twin single ranch style with another couple living in the adjoining half. The JAG office was a close walk from our house and the units stationed at Devens included the Army Security Agency, the Tenth Special Forces Group, a combat engineering battalion, and the Base Command Staff.

The JAG office provided legal services to all of the units stationed at Devens as well as all family members and retired military members living in New England.

Karen enjoyed the amenities and played tennis, golf, and walked on the trails. However, she soon learned that the salary of a Captain with under two years of service was just over $560 per month. So, she applied for and got a job in a nearby nursery school.

Having spent a great deal of our marriage living apart, we soon found out that the demands by the Army on my time were great. I reported to the office on a Monday and was handed a file and told I would be trying my first case on that Thursday! In the next year and a half, I would try 168 court martials.

Despite the heavy workload in the JAG office, we were able to enjoy the beautiful post and we were introduced to the Army social life. We began to socialize with the couples who were associated with the JAG office. We learned about foods that other couples had been introduced to at duty stations all over the world. We also enjoyed the surrounding New England Communities. Boston was less than 40 miles from Fort Devens and we often took trips into this interesting city for a meal, a play, or a historical tour.

When I received my assignment to Fort Devens, I was advised that I should not get too settled in because I was likely to be reassigned to RVN or ROK (Republic of Korea).

After a year and a half, I was still at Fort Devens, while other JAG officers had come and gone to different places, including Vietnam. I, however, had heard nothing from the Department of the Army regarding my next assignment.

Karen and I discussed our shared desire to have children, but I didn't want to miss a year of our child's life while I was in a war zone. After a year and a half at Devens, we decided that we didn't want to wait any longer. So, when the calendar turned to 1970, we learned that Karen was pregnant.

DATING & MARRIAGE

THE ENERGIZER BUNNY

To this day, my wife Karen likes to keep busy. The previous sentence is like saying the Pope is Catholic. In our younger days she was in a bowling league and we often played tennis. She loved to hike and ride a bike. She even rode around the perimeter of Central Park in New York City on a rented bicycle.

Now, if it is not raining or over ninety degrees, she sometimes walks with friends. She has hiked up the steep trails at Watkins Glen, New York. She is in a golf league and golfs at least once a week.

She loves to cook and entertain friends at our house. She always cooks great meals for us. She loves to eat out, especially with our supper club friends. The supper club has consisted of the same five couples for over 45 years.

She will spend hours cleaning the house and working on the lawn or in her flower gardens. Often, when we return home, she will get out of the car and head for the plants that she has all around the house. It is only after she tends to them that she will come in the house.

Museums, movies, and plays are important to her. We often have season tickets to the Broadway series in Columbus, and we love to attend plays at nearby Otterbein College.

She loves to travel, whether it is a few hours away in the Amish country, Lake Erie, or to a state park. She also loves to travel to the other side of the globe. (See the Travel Section for further details).

We are not near an ocean (Lake Erie is 2 ½ hours away) but one of her favorite pastimes is walking on the beach at the ocean. I still get questions about why can't we see the sun set over the Atlantic Ocean. She is a saint when it comes to helping people. She was a home-based Head Start teacher for 27 years and her dedication and calm demeanor still draw praise from the now grandmas, parents, and former children.

She is now a Stephen Minister in the Lutheran Church and works with a senior citizen who needs a friend. In our county, she has a large circle of friends whom she assists and encourages when they are facing life's challenges.

She loves to shop and go to craft shows where she will often get gifts for friends. Birthdays are important to her, especially the birthday cake. When she provides a cake to a friend, they love it and since it's a gift they don't worry about the calories.

She likes to read books, sometimes as many as three at a time. She also enjoys book clubs even though she would rather meet in person then over a Zoom call. Her women's club calendar is full with several social or benevolent organizations at one time.

During her junior year of college, Karen took a painting class. She enjoyed it, but it wasn't until our older years that Karen began painting more and we got to see what a talented artist she is. We even have some of her artwork hanging in our house.

We have started to attend online classes at The Ohio State University. If you are 60 or older you can take the course for free. Both of us are Ohio State University football fans, although I believe that I might have more interest than her. Last year, she got a decorative sign which she set next to the TV. It said, "We interrupt this marriage for football!"

The most important activity in Karen's life is her family. For the last 4 to 5 years, she was frustrated by her inability to interact in person with our two children and our four grandchildren. Our daughter and her family lived in Minnesota until 2018 when they decided to move to Florida! Either place is a long drive.

Our son and his family were an even greater challenge, especially if you were driving. They lived in Singapore! (At the time of this writing, we found out that their next assignment is in London, England so we'll be traveling once again!)

Like any good mother or grandmother, Karen will dispense bits of wisdom to our children and grandchildren that she has accumulated over the years. She hopes that they are listening to her just like she listened to her mother . . . <u>most</u> of the time.

As you can see, my wife lives life to the fullest. In fact, on a pillow she has, there is a credo that reflects Karen's life. The pillow simply says "Live. Laugh. and Love."

It should come as no surprise that her friends have given her the nickname of the Energizer Bunny.

Karen playing donkey basketball for charity

1973 – 1993

In 1973, Karen and I moved our family home from Fort Devens, Massachusetts to Marysville, Ohio. The next 20 years of our marriage focused on raising our children. We had a precious daughter who was two years old going on twelve and a soon-to-be-born son who turned out to be just as intelligent and capable as his sister.

The times we spent with these two were happy and enriching for both Karen and me. Despite the many hours we spent teaching, protecting, and encouraging our children, both Karen and I found time for honing our skills in our chosen professions (lawyer and Head Start teacher). We also found time to enjoy many of the things which life offers. I believe that we had an excellent mix of family, spousal, and individual activities.

Karen at a restaurant while we are out exploring

THE EMPTY NEST

When our children left home to finish their schooling, meet and marry their precious spouses, and begin their own families, Karen and I felt an emptiness. It didn't last long because we discovered that there was still a wonderful world out there which provided us many opportunities to experience new good times.

We also got to watch our daughter and son do wonderful jobs of positively shaping each member of their families into fantastic people.

OUR 50TH ANNIVERSARY
(A Golden Anniversary)

Karen and I were married on September 9, 1967. We spent our first anniversary having a picnic while hiding in the woods near Fort Dix, New Jersey. I was in Army basic training, and I was not allowed to have contact with anyone other than members of my unit and the training staff. This was true even on that Sunday when no training was going on.

Such a disregard for rules could have resulted in disciplinary action against me. I believe that some 50 years later, the statute of limitations has run out, and I am free to admit that I risked discipline to spend a few hours with my wife on our special day.

Over the years, the celebration of our marriage on September 9th has held a special place in our hearts. When we moved to Marysville in 1973, we continued recognizing our anniversary by going out to eat or going somewhere special with friends. We asked a couple that we had met to join us and they asked when our anniversary was.

When we told them, they excitedly said, "We were married on September 9th! What year were you married?" It turned out that on September 9th, 1967, at 11:00 o'clock a.m., when Karen and I were getting married in New York, Bill and Joyce were getting married in Florida!

That began a tradition of celebrating a joint anniversary which has continued to this day. Over the years we have had many memorable times together. We have gone sailing on Lake Erie, visited Amish country in northeast Ohio, visited Las Vegas, and twice have gone to the island of Aruba.

As the significant golden anniversary approached, Karen must have thought that I had "lost that loving feeling." There was no special trip planned to a tropical island. We weren't even going to Vegas. We were going to eat out with Joyce and Bill. As much as we would enjoy being with them, this day was special since it marked 50 years together!

We began the drive to the restaurant, and I told everyone that I needed to stop at my law partner's house to sign a document. Karen asked, couldn't it wait until tomorrow? Bill and Joyce, (who were in on the surprise) said, "Oh, let's stop and say hello. We would love to see her house."

We entered the street where she lived, and a lot of cars were parked in her driveway and on the street. Karen immediately said, "She has a party going on. Let's not bother her now."

With the urging of Bill and Joyce, I ignored Karen's concerns, and we pulled up to the house. Again, over Karen's objections, we all got out of the car and walked to the back of the house where a pool was located and the sounds of music could be heard.

We walked into the pool area and saw many people who started clapping. As she began to recognize her friends, she realized that this was her party – our party and how much she was loved! She began to cry!

Over 60 of our friends were there including Karen's college roommate, friends who lived a distance away, and almost all our closest friends. Around the pool, people were enjoying live music, the poolside bar, the fire pit, and the festive atmosphere of a significant event.

One of Karen's favorite experiences is buying a cake for someone's birthday. That night, I made sure that we had a huge sheet cake with lots of frosting proclaiming 50 years of love. It was almost like we were getting married again!

For the next few hours, we shared remembrances with our friends of the wonderful life we have lived together. Who needs Aruba?

DATING & MARRIAGE

50 YEARS & GOING STRONG

Fifty years! It sounds like a long, long time and it is. But when you have been blessed by God with the opportunity to enjoy every phase of life—wise parents, caring friends, loving spouse, and children—you are willing and able to leave behind each major time in your life and look forward to the next adventure.

Even as we reach that "senior status" with its increasing ailments and the certain loss of those family members and friends who helped shape our lives, our base of faith helps us look forward as much as we look back.

Once armed with the comforting relationship of a marriage, I joined my partner to experience: the United States Army, the challenges of a professional career, the obligation of serving my community, the opportunity to travel to many destinations around the world, the thrill of participating in and cheering on sports, and growing in our faith to put it all in the proper perspective.

WHAT IF

Everyone has moments in their lives where they stop and wonder, "What if . . ." This is natural.

What if . . .
I was not accepted into college?
I didn't get a very high LSAT score to get into law school?
I didn't survive the first-year law school cuts?
I didn't pass the bar exam?
I didn't get into the JAG Corps?

I was the first of my family to graduate from college. If I had not been able to go to college, I probably would have gotten a job in Alliance, OH in retail service or in the factories that provided many of my family members with a living.

If I had gotten into college, but not been accepted into law school, I would have been looking to use my degrees in history and political science. There was not a huge job market for history majors.

If I did not get into law school or I didn't survive the first-year law school cuts and pass the bar, I probably would have become a teacher which is an important component of our society, but would have changed my life in many ways.

If I didn't get into or finish college, and if I didn't get accepted into law school at OSU, I would never have met Karen. I can't imagine what joys of life I would never have experienced.

In addition to never meeting the love of my life, I probably would have been drafted by the Army, trained as an infantryman, and been sent to RVN, where more than 58,000 American men and women were killed in a senseless war.

Chapter 5

CHILDREN & GRANDCHILDREN

THE PRIMARY PURPOSE of this book is to highlight the events in my life which have helped me develop and shaped who I am. Aside from my wife and my parents, there has been no greater impact on me than that of my children.

Karen and I have been blessed with two wonderful children. Both are intelligent, loving, and wonderful parents to our grandchildren.

Now that both our daughter and son have celebrated their 50th birthdays, it is interesting to look back and see how their lives were impacted by their early family, friends, their education, their choice of a spouse, their chosen professions, and their acceptance of the teachings of the Christian religion.

Since they have both evolved into wonderful people, it is tempting to claim some of the credit as their parents. However, after establishing their foundation, we must recognize that their decisions, as influenced by their adult lives, have provided them with the success they have achieved.

It does appear that both of our children are helping to build good foundations for their children, and that is wonderful for Karen and me since everyone knows that grandparents love to brag about their grandchildren!

CHRISTINA

I was on active duty with the Army when our daughter Christina was born. It was January 10th, 1971, and it was a cold, snowy night at Fort Devens, MA. Karen and I were watching the Tonight Show with Johnny Carson when Karen, who was nine months pregnant, began to have contractions. We called the doctor, who said that he would meet us at the hospital.

The base hospital was a modest structure which had been built around 30 to 35 years before. It consisted of a series of two-story wooden, barracks-style buildings connected in no apparent order. The doctor showed up in a sweatshirt and blue jeans. He was young, but he was an excellent doctor, who kept us at ease with his humor and his calm demeanor.

Christina was born around 6:00 in the morning, and our world was enriched and changed in a way we could not imagine. After a day's respite, Karen, Christina, and I went home to introduce our new daughter to our previous dependent, our dog, Daffodil (or as we called her, Daffy Dog). Christina and Daffy Dog would become close friends.

The next two years gave us an insight into the wonderful being that had been brought into our family. We could tell early on that Christina was intelligent, and we soon learned that she was fiercely independent.

She loved to explore the world around her. When her travels took her to our dog's vicinity, Daffy would show the patience of Job putting up with a tail grab or an ear pull. Christina was never truly aggressive, and Daffy never ran to us to complain. If it was naptime, Daffy would just find a bed to jump up on.

In 1973, when Christina had turned two, we left the army to move to Marysville, OH. It was there that I began an active practice of law and Karen was hired to start the Head Start program for the county. It was there where Christina learned to have her way with babysitters and anyone else she interacted with.

I recently sat down with our daughter, Christina, and our son, Greg, to ask them what they remembered about their childhood years. Christina remembered roaming through the woods near our home in Marysville. She enjoyed playing with Barbie dolls and her dogs.

When we moved to a new neighborhood, she would try to go visit the neighbors and Karen would have to keep an eye on her, so she didn't get lost or bother someone.

Christina loved the flowers in the neighbors' gardens and would occasionally get in trouble for picking them. In the summer, she loved Derby cars on the hill behind our home and sledding there in the winter. Christina enjoyed running through sprinklers and spending many hours at the nearby municipal pool. She also had a Big Wheel which she raced down the hill. She always liked the holidays, especially Easter with its bunny.

Not all the memories were pleasant, however, and when I asked her what she didn't like, she mentioned that Mom would occasionally fry liver and onions which Christina didn't like the smell of. She also reminded me that she once fell down our basement stairs.

She remembers being concerned about the paddling policy in her elementary school. I know she never got paddled, but a good friend of hers did. We eventually moved to a new house on Boerger Road, which was located just outside the city limits. It was next to a couple of cornfields, and she told me that her friends had a Cornfield Club where they would stomp out a path to the center of the field and would then stomp out a big square to have a meeting place. They used this area to hide from their parents.

She admitted riding her bike into town without telling us, and she also admitted getting into a fight with a friend where she bit her on the nose. On the side of good memories, she remembers going to the Dairy Queen for an Oreo cake milkshake.

Our new neighbors had a daughter that was Christina's age and Christina used to go next door to play in their treehouse and on their trampoline, both of which got a lot of use from all the neighbors' kids.

She remembers that soon after we moved out into the country, there was a huge snowstorm and the electricity went out for more than a few hours. So we all huddled in front of the fireplace, which was a very inefficient move to stay warm, but it was the only source of heat we had.

Christina attended our church-sponsored preschool. However, both she and Greg went to public school from kindergarten through high school.

As I mentioned earlier, Karen was instrumental in the beginning of the Head Start program in Union County. She would spend more than 25 years building the program through her dedication and inspiration. These efforts often called for her to involve me and both of our children in building the curriculum.

Christina remembers her mom was making a video on fire safety for the Head Start children, and she and Greg showed the proper way of crawling to safety in a smoke-filled room. In order to make the scene realistic, I bought a couple of cigars and puffed and puffed to fill our living room with smoke. They then crawled across the floor while being filmed at floor level.

My contribution to this effort was not limited to cigars, however. The fire safety video needed some flair to hold the attention of the students.

So, Karen filmed the sounds and action of the emergency vehicles leaving the station to respond to actual emergencies.

We also staged a ladder rescue where Greg was carried down a ladder from a two-story window by a fireman. Then, Karen wanted me to climb into the bucket of a hook and ladder which then extended 75 feet in the air. (I am afraid of heights).

I got in the bucket and grabbed onto the side of it so hard that my fingerprints are probably still there! Then, to my dismay, one of the firemen decided to climb into the bucket to join me. We bounced around and smiled for the camera. We then got out after the ladder descended and I practically kissed the ground.

Christina also remembers wading in a lake at a local golf course to retrieve golf balls, which she would then sell to the driving range.

In elementary school, she remembered movie nights and square dancing. In middle school, after the last class, she and her friends would go to an old-fashioned soda shop for candy and ice cream drinks.

This same establishment charged 5¢ for a cup of coffee. When the Honda manufacturing plant was being built in 1980, all of the major national television networks sent film crews to Marysville. I was in the drugstore/soda shop when an NBC camera crew came in and saw the sign saying "Coffee 5¢" and they laughed at the joke. It was only after they ordered four cups of coffee and were told that they owed $0.20 that they finally believed the price was real.

Christina began to reminisce about the jobs she worked at prior to college. She was a lifeguard at the Marysville pool, and she also taught swimming lessons. As a lifeguard, she once had to jump into the deep end of the pool to save a young boy who sank below the surface and was struggling to get to the top. We were very, very proud of her.

Karen and I believe that getting paid for work instilled some important life lessons in our kids. Christina also worked at a Dairy Queen, a

Burger King, and a Taco Bell. None of these were potential life vocations, but they paid for milkshakes and movies.

High school was a fun experience for Christina and she established a large group of friends. Karen and I enjoyed hosting some of their parties, complete with singing and dancing on our back deck. She was also a cheerleader, voted "best dressed," and was a member of the homecoming court. When her younger brother joined her at high school, she was a very protective big sister.

Christina's dating centered on a football star running back, and her longtime friend, Christian. They are still happily married and have given Karen and me two wonderful grandchildren. They live in Florida, near Saint Augustine.

When it came time to choose a college, Christina decided to stay in Ohio and enrolled at Miami of Ohio University. She majored in business and, just like in high school, she made good grades. She soon realized that business did not interest her and she switched her major to dietetics. It was then that she looked into nursing and completed her schooling in Columbus at Mount Carmel Hospital, where she graduated as a Registered Nurse (RN).

Upon graduation, she was hired by Mount Carmel to work in their orthopedics department. After a couple of years there, she applied and received a job in the Union County Memorial Hospital's ICU (Intensive Care Unit). She then worked in the ICU for over thirty years. Her decision to become a nurse was a perfect fit for her and she has helped countless people throughout her career.

As I mentioned, Christina and Christian are the parents of two children. At the time of this writing, one has graduated from college and is doing post-graduate work in nursing. The other is a junior in college and is studying construction management.

They are also proud parents of a Labrador Retriever named Daisy.

CHILDREN & GRANDCHILDREN

GREGORY

On May 8th, 1974, God blessed Karen, Christina, and me with the birth of a son and brother. We named him Gregory Jason Schulze. This epic event took place at Riverside Hospital in Columbus, Ohio and he was welcomed by each of us with love and anticipation. He was a big baby and the doctor who delivered him commented about his broad shoulders. He has also grown to be about 4" taller than I am.

Karen, who loves children, now had a daughter and a son to love, to protect, and to enjoy, as they developed strong identities which would serve them well.

During the first four years after his birth, we continued to live in a modest sized house (3 bedrooms, one bath, and a one-car garage). We began to look for a house to meet the family's needs and in 1978 we moved to a four-bedroom, two-and-a-half bath house with a two-car garage.

Greg was about to begin school. He, like his sister, attended preschool at Trinity, our church. As he began kindergarten, he moved to a public-school setting. He adapted quite well and learned about interpersonal relationships as well as substantive learning.

Much like his sister, he was an active adventurer. In fact, in three separate accidents he received a total of 32 stitches in his head.

Greg's interests included academics, athletics, and social opportunities with his friends. In the area of academics, he was on student council and he participated in debate and mock trials. He won science fairs and ran for Governor at Boy's State. He began a school newspaper and acted as its editor. In high school he also gained computer networking experience and he organized and conducted drug abuse seminars with the Ohio Attorney General and FBI agents as speakers.

Not only was he in the National Honor Society, but throughout junior high and high school he received all A's and was a co-valedictorian. He also was a National Merit Scholarship finalist.

Greg loved sports and early on played tennis and baseball. He then played basketball until he injured his arm diving into the bleachers while chasing the ball. Perhaps his favorite sport was football and his team made it to the state semi-finals.

When he wasn't studying or playing sports, he kept busy reading, playing the piano and trumpet, acting in community theater productions, and even sang a song in front of hundreds of people that I had sung years before. ("Oh Lord, It's Hard to Be Humble.")

When the opportunity presented itself, we took both of our children on vacations in such places as Hilton Head and Myrtle Beach, South Carolina, Charlottesville, Virginia, California, and Canada. We even were able to spend time in Hawaii while housesitting for my aunt and uncle.

After school, Greg liked to go to movies, do square dancing, fishing, ice skating, and sledding. He would even make movies with a video recorder.

While he was still in high school, Greg was offered a mentorship by the chief operating officer at Honda of American Manufacturing. Later he worked for, and learned from, senior management executives at a major construction company, the senior managers at Wendy's International, and Worthington Industries.

When it came time to choose a college, he applied and was accepted to six colleges including Duke, UVA, Cornell, and Northwestern.

Even though Karen and I thought that Duke would win out (he was visiting Duke when they won the national championship in basketball) he chose Northwestern. This allowed him to double major in engineering and business.

Upon graduation, Greg worked at Worthington Industries for a while and then went to North Carolina to get his MBA. This school offered him an opportunity to study in Chile for a semester, and Karen and I got to visit him down there.

After getting his post-graduate degree, he went to work for American Airlines. He moved to Dallas and was working on September 11th, 2001 when two American Airline planes were hijacked.

After almost 8 years at American, he went to work for Expedia Travel and he works there to this day. He now heads up Expedia's relationships with its partners (airlines, hotels, rental, etc.) and its media coverage.

He and his wife, Carrie, have two children. At the time of this writing, one has just graduated from college and one will graduate soon. They are also proud parents of a golden retriever named Kaya.

THEIR SPOUSES

Karen and I are very happy that our children have matured into responsible adults. One of the wise decisions they both have made is in their choice of a spouse.

Christina had known and occasionally dated a popular young man who excelled in academics and sports. (He was a football running back.) His name is Christian and he attended college to become a teacher and a coach. Although he was a good teacher, he eventually decided to become a financial planner. He has excelled in this profession.

Greg was attending Northwestern University when he met, fell in love with, and eventually married Carrie. She had attended college in the Chicago area and had been working as a social worker. She is an intelligent and personable young lady who has been the lynchpin for their family when Greg is traveling worldwide for his job with Expedia.

Both of our children's spouses have played a major role instilling both knowledge and morals in our four grandchildren. We are blessed that all four grandchildren possess intelligence, motivation, an appreciation for other people, and a faith in God.

GRANDCHILDREN

Karen and I have four grandchildren and like many other seniors, we think that our grandchildren are the best, the brightest, and the best-looking children ever born. Even if we take away the inevitable grandparent bias, we think ours are really awesome!

Each of our grandchildren has accomplished many different things in their young lives. However, one attribute which they all share is the way they treat people. They show that they truly care about others. Ego and envy are not part of their personalities.

MCKENNA

Mckenna was the first born. Since her mom and dad lived near us and were both working, Grandma and Grandpa got to spend a lot of time with her.

She had some of the traits of each of her parents. She was independent and determined to explore her world!

As she grew and attained knowledge, she set goals for herself. She has been successful in most of these, including graduation from college and deciding to follow in her mother's profession as a nurse. She is currently in an accelerated course at a Florida University and will soon begin her service of helping others who are in need.

McKenna has always been a hard worker who understands that she has a duty to add time and effort in succeeding in reaching her goals.

Grandma surprised McKenna with a graduation gift of a trip to Italy where both of them got to share time together again.

CHILDREN & GRANDCHILDREN

CAELAN

Our daughter's son is named Caelan. He is an athlete as well as a student. His father was a star football player in high school and he also ran track.

Caelan gave football and basketball a try, but then decided to concentrate on track. In his senior year of high school, he overcame surgery on his knee and placed eighth in the state of Florida in hurdles. This was quite an accomplishment!

Caelan is a huge fan of The Ohio State Buckeyes and is attending school at the University of Florida. In order to complete his dream season, in early 2025, his Buckeyes won the National Football Championship and his Gators won the NCAA National Basketball Championship!

When his family lived in Minnesota, Caelan loved to ride snowmobiles. Another sport he excels at is fishing. He has caught many big fish, both in fresh water and salt water.

Caelan is now finishing his studies of Construction Management.

TUCKER

Our son and daughter-in-law's children have also gotten a great deal out of life at an early age. Tucker and Kate lived in Singapore for five years and have traveled extensively throughout Europe and Asia.

In high school, Tucker's class took a trip to China. There they took a 9-hour train ride into the mountains where they hiked and did repelling down the mountainside.

Tucker also lived in the state of Washington, where he watched a mountain lion walk past his back door.

As a child, he was interested in automobiles and could identify just about every make and model. He also knew every state capital and the approximate population of each.

He enjoyed soccer and once played in a game where his team won 21 to 0!

He recently graduated from college and he has shown an interest in the environment. Will he do like his grandpa did and go to law school? No matter what he does, he will do great.

KATE

Kate is the youngest of our grandchildren by about one month. She, like her brother, had many unique experiences when she lived in Singapore.

One year while living there, her class trip took her to a rice farm where she walked into the rice patty behind a water buffalo.

Kate played softball and soccer and was elected Captain due to her skillful play and her sparkling personality.

In high school and college, she majored in Mandarin. This knowledge of a Chinese language should come in very handy if she follows her plan to make worldwide travel her profession.

She has continued to seek out adventures in world travel. Most recently she has lived in Australia while completing studies for Bates University.

While in that part of the world, she took up the challenge of bungee jumping off of a <u>very</u> tall bridge!

MCKENNA, CAELAN, TUCKER, & KATE

Even though all four of our grandchildren are still very young, they have shown the ability and the drive to contribute to the world around them.

My hope is that I am still around when they start their families. I would love to hold a great-grandchild in my arms.

CHILDREN & GRANDCHILDREN

Christina and her family

Greg and his family

Chapter 6

MILITARY SERVICE

WHEN I WAS JUST 25 years old, I reached a goal which I believed would be a major accomplishment of my professional life. I graduated from law school and prepared to take the Ohio bar exam to become licensed as an attorney.

Even though I knew that the Vietnam War was at its peak and there were 500,000 United States military personnel in Southeast Asia, I was so focused on my career goal that I did not appreciate the reality that I would likely be conscripted into the army. I never believed that I would be trained to be an infantryman and scheduled to be sent to a war that would claim over 58,000 U.S. lives. However, that is what happened!

If you believe in God, or at least the Ten Commandments, you should abhor war! People have engaged in warfare since the beginning of time and, as a result, millions of people have died, many more millions have been crippled, and countless millions have experienced the deep sorrow that comes with a loss of a loved one.

Having said that, our country cannot disband its military and destroy all our weapons. There are people in this world who continue to plan and carry out acts of terrorism. This type of aggressive behavior must be met and defeated by a well-trained and disciplined military force. Safeguards must be in place such as civilian control of the military and a recognition that we should not try to force a legitimate government to follow our directives for political reasons.

Today's armed forces are made up of men and women who make their own decision to serve. This is known as the "Volunteer Army." Throughout history, there have been times when people were conscripted to serve with little or no desire to participate. Some of those who did not volunteer fled to other countries to escape service and some have actually gone to jail for failing to fulfill their commitment to the country. Others have served by being drafted (chosen) by the military to serve for two years.

Since the military is needed, it is important that there is civilian control over the armed forces. However, history has shown us that civilian politicians are not always interested in doing what is best for the people. There must be a balance and controls over the President and Congress.

We cannot risk hiring thugs to do our fighting. We must have an intelligent well-trained force who know the rules and are committed to abide by them. Having spent 30 years in the Army, I am happy to say that, for the most part, we do have a military that understands its role and is willing to stay within those bounds.

This book does not provide an in-depth recounting of those 30 years of service. For a more complete story I would recommend that you go to Amazon or Barnes & Noble and buy my previous book entitled "Welcome to the Army."

THE UNITED STATES ARMY REQUESTS MY PRESENCE

It was spring of 1968 and my world was blossoming with accomplishments and hope for a wonderful future. During the last seven years I had attended and graduated from Mount Union College and then I was accepted at The Ohio State University College of Law and was able to survive the massive flunk out rate. Karen and I were married and would soon celebrate our first wedding anniversary.

Life was beautiful! What could go wrong? Ironically, what could go wrong was a job offer by the country's largest employer while I was still working for the Columbus, Ohio City Prosecutor's office and studying for the Ohio bar exam.

Passing this three-day exam was required to practice law in Ohio and, prior to taking the test, although all the applicants had spent three years in law school, just about everyone took a refresher course to stay out of the 20% who would fail the bar exam. I worked during the day in the Columbus Ohio City Prosecutor's Office, took the refresher course in the evening, and would then come home to spend time with Karen.

Even though I would be exhausted, I always tried to talk to her sometime during the day or at night when I was working or at the course. One evening, when I called her, she answered the phone by shouting, "You have been drafted!" It took me a moment to assimilate what she was saying and, although I had known this might happen, I was in shock and upset.

Yes, without even applying for a position, I was chosen to be the "best that I could be." The United States Army was asking, no *demanding*, that I give up my quest to begin my law practice and leave my wife two weeks before our first anniversary so they could teach me how to kill enemy troops and try not to get killed in the process.

When I got back to the apartment, I looked at the draft notice and realized that my reporting date was several weeks before I was supposed to take the bar exam! If I didn't take it in July as scheduled, it might be up to two years before I could take it.

The next day, I called my county draft board and explained that I had a very important test on July 30th, 31st, and August 1st. I explained that I was not trying to get out of reporting, but I needed to take the test now. I could not wait until my Army service was over and then take the test.

The clerk advised me that I should appeal in writing. I again pointed out that the bar exam was less than 60 days away and I needed to know now if I was going to be able to take it on time. She asked me for the dates of the test, and I told her July 30th, 31st and August 1st. She said that she would see what she could do but I really should apply in writing.

The next day, I talked to the city prosecutor about my dilemma, and he said that he would look into it. Three days later, I received a letter from the draft board saying that they were extending my reporting date to 5:00 AM on August 2nd. While I was glad to get an extension, the logistics for reporting one day after the test were impossible. That meant that I would have to prepare for and take the test, and plan my wife's living arrangements within a very short span of time.

I talked again to the prosecutor, and he said that he would call someone. He asked me how much time I would need, and I told him a month after the test would be great. He talked to the state draft board and they extended my time until August 27, 1968.

During the next two months, I talked to an Army Recruiter and ended up volunteering rather than coming in as a draftee. In this way, I was able to apply for Officer Candidate School. He also suggested that I apply for a direct commission into the Judge Advocate General Corps (JAG). He told me that it was a long shot since they were only taking one out of every 12 applicants into JAG but, if I waited and applied after I was on active duty, the odds dropped to one out of 7.

In addition to dealing with preparation to enter the Army and completing my studies for the bar exam, I helped Karen get ready for my departure. She decided to stay at Ohio State and complete her senior year.

We would not be able to live together for six to nine months while I attended training. As awful as that was, soon it was time to report to Fort Hayes induction center in Columbus Ohio.

A FEW GOOD MEN

As I walked into Fort Hayes, I was immediately checked in and told to stand with a number of other "volunteers' and "draftees." I soon found out that the Army way was a drill sergeant proclaiming loudly, "Everybody over here! I mean NOW! Hurry! Hurry!"

The group would then hurry and assemble there for a significant period of time until we were told to move again. I remember two other stops. I had a "physical" that took about three minutes and was performed by an enlisted soldier. The second stop was preceded by us being placed in a line and told to count off by fours. I was a "two" and was therefore told to report to a distant corner of the building.

There were about 15-20 of us in this corner where we waited. We were then approached by a Marine Corps Sergeant who greeted us by saying, "Welcome to the Corps, men. Our enlistees didn't meet the quota this month so you gentlemen have been volunteered! You should be proud to be in the best military in the world."

I immediately spoke up and said that I didn't volunteer for the Marines; I had volunteered for the Army. He looked at me and shouted in my direction, "Are you telling me you're not a draftee? You're a volunteer?"

I replied, "That's right, Sergeant. I signed a contract with the Army."

His very loud reply was, "Then get your . . . the . . . out of here and go find the Army!"

I have the greatest respect for the Marine Corps; I just don't think I was what they were looking for.

Later that evening we boarded a bus which took us to Fort Dix, New Jersey. Basic training is meant to form a cohesive unit, teach skills ranging from applying a tourniquet to firing a machine gun, and to instill the spirit to win as a team. A basic training company usually has about 200 soldiers. Each company has 4 platoons of 50 soldiers each, and each platoon has 4 squads of 12-15 soldiers.

My first full day in the Army I awoke in a wooden, two-story WWII vintage barracks. During the day did push-ups, pull-ups, sit ups, and ran. We also spent time in a classroom where we learned protocol and filled out paperwork.

With the paperwork done, we were escorted to a barber shop where, after a 10 second hair removal, I was chosen by the drill sergeant to be temporary platoon guide! I wish I could say that the sergeant recognized greatness, but the truth is that I was the second trainee out of the door and the sergeant thought the first trainee looked too stupid to be the platoon guide. I was platoon guide for 3 or 4 days, but then turned that job down and asked to be a squad leader instead.

There were two squads already assigned leaders and the two squads left consisted of a bunch of Midwest farm boys (Squad 1) and a bunch of New York City gang bangers who had been recycled after getting kicked out of a previous class (Squad 2).

I indicated that I would like to be the leader of Squad 1 since they were from the Midwest. The other squad leader said that he strongly wanted Squad 1 also. The sergeant pulled a deck of cards out of his pocket and said, "High card wins." I went first and drew . . . a 3!! The remaining squad leader with a smile on his face drew . . . a 2!

So here I am, living in a barracks with 49 strangers ranging from Mormons from Utah to gang members from New York City. We have all been given uniforms to wear which only differ by our name tag. Everyone has had his hair cut to the scalp and when we go anywhere, we march or run. We are not allowed to leave the company area unless we are with one of the NCO's.

The separation from the outside world even extended to banning visitors and phone calls except for an emergency call. Letters were allowed and just about everyone took advantage of that. I wrote Karen daily.

At the request of my fellow trainees, I began to write letters for them. When they found out that I was writing poetry to Karen, they asked for their wives/girlfriends to think they were poets.

I have included a couple of poems I wrote to Karen, but none of the ones that my fellow soldiers sent as their own.

A SMILE
A little smile
Sure helps my day
When it's smiled
That special way

MILITARY SERVICE

A special way
By that special girl
One sweet smile
And my head's awhirl
The sun grows bright
On the darkest day
The birds and the flowers
Seem to say
It's Spring outside
There's love in the air
Come join the lovers
Without a care
My knees grow weak
I can't breathe for a while
All because
Of that special smile

ONCE IN A LIFETIME A MAN MAY FIND
A woman who can bring him peace of mind
But it only happens to a lucky few
To find a woman as great as you.

When first we met my heart could feel
A throbbing love that was more than real
And as the years pass by, I see
The love for you will grow in me.

Every day as I dream of you
The flame of my love kindles anew
Knowing you has enriched my life
I'd like to say ---- Thank you, wife.

Ok, I am not a poet laureate, but we kind of had a lot of other stuff going on and this took our minds off of the situation we found ourselves in.

I should mention that a fellow trainee from Utah asked me to write a letter to his girlfriend asking her to marry him! I was reluctant to get involved in such a sensitive matter, but he convinced me to do it and I was happy when she said yes!

FURTHER TRAINING

The eight weeks of basic training were intense and filled with doubt and even fear. The objective of the Army was to mold the 200 trainees in our company into a cohesive unit. This was not an easy task. The diversity was significant. We came from many different areas of the country, from very different home and family experiences, with different education levels (some with no high school degree all the way up to doctorate level education), different ages (17-25), and levels of maturity.

Training demanded absolute obedience. You needed to work as a team (NO Rambos!) and to be serious about what you were being taught. Some trainees were National Guard or Army Reserve and would be going back home after the initial sixteen weeks. The rest of us would likely end up in Vietnam where our training might save our life. We were going to be introduced to rifles, bayonets, and various weapons. We were going to be put through a vigorous program of physical and psychological activities. In return, the Army was going to pay us $109.50 per month, plus food and lodging in a communal setting.

Following basic training, each trainee was assigned to 8 weeks of advanced individual training (AIT). There, the trainee would learn a skill such as cooking, truck driving, clerking, and many other civilian jobs. Others would be assigned to Infantry, Armor, or Artillery.

MILITARY SERVICE

The Army decided that I would make a fine light weapons infantryman! In that capacity I learned to fire a machine gun, throw hand grenades, and set up claymore mines and other weapons meant to kill people.

Some of the exercises we went through included live fire infiltration courses, prisoner of war camp, ambushes, defense of position, and, of course, the obstacle course.

While I was learning to kill the enemy, I applied for a direct commission in the Judge Advocate General Corps (JAGS). The Army lost my application papers . . . TWICE!

LOST APPLICATION

During the second week of AIT, we were in the field when I was approached by the company commander. The captain was aware of my request for a commission to the JAG Corps, and he asked if I had heard from my basic training company with a report on any progress on the application. I told him that I had not, and because of our training schedule, I was not able to call them.

He told me that the best way to follow through on this was for me to go to the basic training company and not leave until I had a satisfactory answer. He then went on to say that he was ordering me to go, and if anyone asked why I wasn't with my unit, I was to say that I was following orders.

I got a ride back to the main post and entered the basic training company headquarters. I didn't recognize anyone, so I started from the beginning. I explained why I was there and asked them to track down my application so I could check its progress.

The clerk seemed very helpful and he diligently searched the correspondence logs and the file drawers. After repeating his search several times, he suggested that I go back to my unit and he would let me know when he found the paperwork. Remembering my company commander's advice, I said no, I was going to stay until I had an answer.

At that point, the clerk went to get his first sergeant. Then his company commander came over. They searched the files. They searched the logs. They called their higher headquarters. And then they told me what I didn't want to hear. The application was lost!

I returned to my unit totally dejected. My captain could see that I was upset and he asked me for an update. Upon hearing the news, he immediately said, "No problem. You must have copies of the paperwork. We will just send it in through my company."

I thanked him for his concern. I did have copies of the application and its attachments. What I did not have were originals of the letters of recommendation. If I was facing seven-to-one odds against me, I at least needed originals of these important attachments.

He told me to get back in the jeep and have the driver take me to our company area. There, I was to call my wife and ask her to get new letters and send them to me as soon as possible.

I did as I was ordered, and Karen said she would go the next day and talk to the attorney, the municipal judge, and the city prosecutor. Two or three days later, we were in the company area when the CQ runner came and told me that I had a phone call from my wife. This was getting to be a pattern in my life.

I picked up the phone and said, "Don't tell me there was a problem getting the letters!"

She replied, "Well, there was a problem. Judge Duncan is no longer a judge with the municipal court." My heart sank. There went a strong recommendation, and from a judge no less.

Then Karen said, "I did track him down and he was willing to write a new letter."

Oh well, maybe his reputation is enough, I thought. Who needed a judge anyway? I then asked, "What is he doing now?"

Karen replied, "Governor Rhodes appointed him to the Ohio Supreme Court!"

The odds of acceptance just got a little closer to being in my favor!

THANK YOU FOR YOUR SERVICE

As I graduated from basic training and headed to Columbus, Ohio to be sworn in as an attorney in the Ohio bar, a couple examples of public sentiment gave me hope. Based on my experiences, some members of the general public were able to separate the actions of the brokers of war from the citizens who were caught up in the dynamics beyond their control.

I checked flight schedules, the prices of airline tickets, and the amount of money in my pocket and decided that I could fly "standby" from New Jersey to Pittsburgh and then from Pittsburgh to Columbus. At that time, a military person could fly for half price on a space-available basis. I went to the Newark airport and paid for a flight to Pittsburgh.

Upon arriving at Pittsburgh, I went to Allegheny Airlines ticket counter to get a ticket to Columbus, Ohio. Allegheny was one of just a few airlines that served this route on a regular basis. It was there that I found that the "standby fare" for Allegheny was three-quarters of the regular fare, not one half. I stood there, realizing that I did not have enough money to pay for the Columbus ticket. In fact, I probably did not have enough to pay for a ticket anywhere!

The ticket agent saw me standing there, in uniform, counting my meager funds, trying to figure out how I was going to solve this problem. He then asked me, "Soldier, how much money do you have?" I counted and then responded with the amount I had. He replied, "You weren't listening when I priced that ticket! That is the exact amount of the ticket." He then took my money and handed me back a dime, saying, "In case you need to make a call."

LET ME TELL YOU MY STORY

I arrived back in Columbus on Friday and had a joyous reunion with Karen. The swearing in was to take place at the beginning of the week, and there was a very important event happening on Saturday. As graduates of THE Ohio State University, Karen and I were (and still are), therefore, huge Buckeye football fans. When I realized that I would probably be in Columbus that Saturday, I looked at the football schedule and realized that the Buckeyes would be playing the Michigan State Spartans in a battle of top ten teams that very Saturday!

Before I left New Jersey, I had asked Karen to try to get tickets for the game since she and her roommates were eligible for student tickets. She didn't have a whole lot of luck, and was only able to get one ticket. This was a top national game. After talking it over with Karen, I decided we would go to the stadium and see if I could buy another ticket at a reasonable price. Given our financial condition, the price would have to be rather low. I told Karen to go in with the one ticket she had and I would hopefully meet her inside.

I was outside of the OSU stadium and was trying to find a ticket at a reasonable price, when an usher at one of the gates called out to me, "Hey, soldier! What are you doing?" I explained that I was on leave and I was trying to get a ticket. He called me over and said that he didn't understand why I needed a ticket since I was an employee. He then put an ID tag on my uniform and waved me inside the stadium. Karen and I witnessed an epic battle won by the Buckeyes, twenty-five to twenty.

For those of you who are not college football fans, I did spend time with Karen and I did go to the swearing-in ceremony. But if you ask me what my more memorable experience was . . . (OK, I am going to say the time I spent with Karen—we now have over fifty-five years of marriage together) but it was a damn good football game! You 'Bama fans know what I'm talking about. Roll Tide!

MILITARY SERVICE

SOLDIER OF THE CYCLE

My goal in AIT (Advanced Individual Training) was the same as it had been for Basic Training and that was to learn as much as possible in order to survive whatever lay ahead. This was 1968, and the Vietnam War was raging on. The United States armed forces suffered more than 58,000 deaths and many more soldiers and sailors were wounded.

After nine weeks of Basic Training, I was sent to AIT and the Military Occupational Specialty (MOS) which the Army chose for me was light weapons infantry (11B10). This was the world farthest from my previous world and was one of the most dangerous jobs in the Army.

There were 200 trainees in my company. We were Company A, Fourth Battalion, First Brigade, and we were going to be given eight weeks of advanced training. This time, we would be concentrating on the Army mission of finding the enemy and killing them.

Throughout this vigorous training, I did a decent job of preparing for combat (see my prior book, Welcome to the Army for greater detail). I was not the strongest trainee, nor was I the best shot (I did score "expert," however), nor did I come in number one in the physical training test (PT). I did everything asked of me and I felt that I was prepared to serve in whatever capacity they needed.

My fellow trainees were mostly younger, 17 to 22, (I was 24) and they were often more enthusiastic than I. I was not enjoying this experience, but I recognized the need to learn from it so that I could come home safely!

In the eighth week of training my First Sergeant told me to report to the captain's office. He went on to say that I was getting an award. I pondered the First Sergeant's words and wondered if he was joking. Then I remembered, First Sergeants never joke!

I reported to the company headquarters and was informed that, out of two hundred soldiers in our company, I had been chosen as "Soldier of the Cycle"! They gave me a bronze statue of an infantry soldier with my name on it and a designation as Soldier of the Cycle. I am not sure why I was selected but I treasure the recognition of my efforts. It certainly meant more to me than my participation ribbon from Little League Baseball.

The Soldier of the Cycle trophy I was awarded

At the end of AIT, I had still not been able to get my application to the JAG Corps for a decision. Instead, I was chosen for the Redeye Gunner School. This was a shoulder fired, ground to air missile that was designed to shoot down airplanes!

These three weeks of intensive training included classroom instruction on every aspect of the missile. It also included training to recognize

MILITARY SERVICE

whether a plane flying overhead was a Russian, Chinese, or American plane. This is very important information to have, especially for the pilot of the plane!

We also traveled over 50 miles into the desert where we would practice shooting at planes with a simulated missile launcher. The planes were real and were manned by the New Mexico Air National Guard.

After three weeks of training this way, we changed to a drone plane and real missiles!

I completed my missile school and was sent to Fort Benning, Georgia until the Army could decide where to assign me. The two likely options were to the Republic of Vietnam, where they needed a lot of infantrymen, or the JAG school if I was commissioned into the JAG Corps as an Army lawyer.

At Redeye Gunner School Missile Training

Posing with the Redeye Gunner School Insignia

THE JAG CORPS

Finally, my request for the JAG Corps was granted and I walked into a General's office at Fort Benning as a Private First Class and walked out as a Captain. I reported to the JAG school in Charlottesville, Virginia and spent the next eight weeks in intensive training on how to be an Army lawyer.

At JAG school, we learned about Army protocols, conflict of interest, court martials, as well as administrative hearings, government contracts, international law, status of forces agreements, claims by and against the Army, and so much more.

It had been around 9 months since Karen was able to be with me. During this time, she had graduated from OSU with a degree in Family and Child Development and I had received a training and certification as an infantryman, a missileman, and an Army lawyer.

We were going to be together again soon, unless I received orders to report to Korea or Vietnam. The JAG Corps asked me to list five duty stations where we would like to be assigned. They suggested that we might as well list Vietnam in order to get it out of the way, since most of us would be assigned there during the next four years anyway.

I decided that 9 months was long enough to be separated so I listed five bases on the East Coast. I knew that they could ignore my request and, since I was trained in infantry, I thought they might just assign me to RVN no matter what I put down.

To my surprise, they gave me my first choice, Fort Devens, Massachusetts! Karen and I would stay there the entire four years, even though other JAG officers came to Devens and were then sent to other places, including the RVN!

Fort Devens was a base located about 40 miles from Boston in the heart of American history (Lexington – Concord). In 1969, it was the home of the 10th Special Forces Group, a unit of the Army Security Agency, a combat engineering unit, and several other active Army units. The base provided a support staff of administrative, medical, legal, and security forces.

As a captain assigned to the base, we were provided with one half of a duplex to live in. The JAG office was about 3 blocks from our house. The base had a movie theater and a bowling alley, as well as a grocery store (commissary) and "department store" (base exchange). The base also had a beautiful lake and lots of trees. There was a golf course and an officers club.

My initial assignment was Defense Counsel. I would represent soldiers in criminal claims and discharge proceedings. I was handed my first case on the day I reported for duty and I was told that the trial would be in 3 days! Over the next year and a half, I represented 168 soldiers in court martials. The charges ranged from absent without leave, desertion, failure to obey a lawful order, disrespect to an officer to all the usual civilian crimes such as drugs, violence, theft, and serious vehicular incidents. (Again, for more details read "Welcome to the Army.)

After discussing the burnout factor with the SJA, I was reassigned to the Legal Assistance Office. There, we worked in estate planning, probate, torts, real estate, domestic relations, and civil litigation.

Our clients consisted of retired soldiers, active-duty military members, and their spouses. Our geographic area of responsibility included all of New England. I flew via helicopter to Intercontinental Ballistic Missile Sites (ICBM) within our area of responsibility to provide legal services. We also provided required training lectures to all of the Army assets including Recruiting Officers and ROTC instructors.

The authority to provide legal representation did not initially include the State Court system. This changed when the Department of the Army and three states (Colorado, Georgia, and Massachusetts) began a pilot program to allow JAG officers to represent soldiers in civilian courts even if they were not admitted to practice in that state. I was the first JAG attorney to appear in the state courts of Massachusetts.

When I wasn't trying court martials or providing legal advice, there were many special duty assignments which I was required to perform.

The JAG shop at Fort Devens was the only Army legal resource in New England. If a legal problem arose for any of the unit commanders or any other active duty or retired serviceman or their family members, our office needed to be available 24 hours a day, 7 days a week. That necessitated one of the dozen or so Army lawyers to take responsibility providing that assistance.

Each week the Staff Judge Advocate (SJA) would assign one of us captains to duty as a JAG on call. We needed to be available to anyone who was entitled to our services. This was before cell phones, so we were rather limited in where we could go and what we could do while "on call."

MILITARY SERVICE

One call I received stands out in my mind. It was late at night on a Friday or Saturday. My phone rang and the caller identified himself as the Provost Martial. This job was similar to a chief of police and I thought "Uh oh, what now?"

The Major told me that his M.P.'s had taken a civilian into custody. They took this action because, contrary to Army regulations, anyone seeking to enter a military base must be prepared to provide proof of who they are. This person refused to do this.

I asked the Major if he had talked to the civilian. He said, "Yes." I asked if the civilian had a valid reason for coming on the base. He said, "No, and I don't think she is for real."

The minute I heard that the person in custody was a woman, red flags went up. I asked the Major, "What do you mean she's not for real?" He said, "I think she is a guy. I may just reach down there and find out."

Although the Major out-ranked me, I immediately assumed the role of the Base Commander's legal representative. I firmly said, "Major, you are not to have any further contact with this person until I get there." Fifteen minutes later I walked into the military police compound and assessed the situation. There was an obviously agitated Provost Martial, several other M.P.'s standing around, and an attractive young lady seated in a retaining cell. She had long flowing hair and wore a slinky dress.

I asked the Major for a room where I could speak privately to the civilian and he ushered us into his office. As he began to sit down, I asked him to leave the room and, showing obvious anger, he left. I then turned to the young lady and told her that she did not have to talk to me, but if she didn't, we would have to consider her a trespasser on federal property. If that happened, we would turn her over to the federal marshals and they would process her at a federal corrections facility. I suggested that it would be better for her to disclose who she was and why she was on this Army base.

She then smiled at me and said, "Since you asked nicely, I will tell you." With that she/he reached up and pulled off his wig. He then gave me his name and address. I thanked him and told him that he would be given a letter barring him from entering Fort Devens again. If he violated that letter, he would be charged with trespass!

Just another night as a JAG Officer.

THE PROTESTORS DISCOVER DEVENS

The mood of the people of the US was divided regarding the Vietnam War. Some staunchly defended the need to stop the domino effect of Communist aggression, while others believed that there were political agendas by both major parties that fueled the war.

Those defending the war were finding it more and more difficult to justify the continued drafting of so many boys. The official military reports pronounced large numbers of enemy casualties and relatively few for our troops. Yet the number of deaths continued to grow.

There were many anti-establishment groups emerging and their rallying cry was "Stop the war." In Boston, with its large number of young adults and its liberal leanings, the outcry was loud.

Soon the protestors turned their attention from the small army activities near the harbor to the larger target thirty-some miles to the west. Fort Devens was a relatively open post. There were some fences and gates at the road entrances and the military police restricted the access at these points to individuals with legitimate business on post.

The post commander started getting reports of planned demonstrations at Fort Devens. A task force was formed to address this threat and I was appointed as one of the JAG representatives.

It seemed that Army Intelligence units (the branch I had considered) had infiltrated certain anti-war groups in Boston and become aware of

MILITARY SERVICE

two or three busloads of demonstrators who would soon be on their way to Devens. In fact, they gave us the exact number of demonstrators and the exact time of their arrival.

It was decided by the task force to allow the buses to park outside of the gates and to allow any peaceful demonstrations in the large lawn area outside of the base itself. No demonstrators would be allowed on the base, and if they came on base after being denied access, they would be captured, taken to the movie theater, photographed, fingerprinted, and then escorted off base. If they returned to the base itself, they would be arrested and turned over to US Marshals for prosecution in federal court.

The question then became, Who would capture the violators and safely transport them to the theater? It was decided that squads from the 10th Special Forces Group (Green Berets) would perform this duty under the supervision of the JAG representative. (ME!)

I met with the "snatch" squads and we had a very in-depth discussion regarding the purpose of their assignment and the rules they would abide by. I stressed the need to ensure that no demonstrators be harmed, even if they were resisting arrest.

One of the snatch team interrupted me to ask, "What if he is trying to hurt me, sir?"

I replied, "Are you afraid of those big bad hippies, sergeant?"

His retort was, "Hell no! No way they're hurting me!"

"That's our answer then. You secure them without hurting them, and bring them to the theater."

The buses showed up with the exact number of demonstrators we expected. They demonstrated for the TV cameras, but fewer than a dozen tried to come on the post. They were snatched (safely), brought to the theater, processed, and released.

ICBMS

Part of our country's defense system includes intercontinental ballistic missiles (ICBMs). These missiles may be armed with various types of warheads, including nuclear. They are stored in silos and dispersed throughout areas away from large population centers.

The JAG office at Fort Devens was responsible for supporting the legal needs of the troops assigned to this system. The legal assistance section of the office was tasked with this duty.

Because of the distances involved to get from the sites to Devens, it was decided that we would go to them. A schedule was set up and a helicopter was made available.

I began my "house" visits and soon found that there were factors involved that I hadn't expected. Although the population of New England is not congested, the air space can become so.

The pilot advised me that we needed to be aware of any commercial airliners taking off or landing because they created a jet wash that could be very detrimental to our craft, including interfering with the rotor blade. Also, small aircraft, which would likely occupy the same air space as us, did not always maintain a safe distance. This was demonstrated one day as we were descending into a missile site. A small airplane approached from behind and suddenly appeared just below us. The pilot pulled up and muttered something about wishing our craft had missiles.

Another thing I was warned about was the landing zone. We were not flying into airports. If we set down in a grassy area, we needed to be aware of small stones or other debris being sucked into the rotor blade.

After a number of flights, I realized that there was risk in everything, and the pilot was just giving advisories that his lawyer would recommend.

MILITARY SERVICE

NAIT

One of the additional duties that I picked up was serving on the Nuclear Accident Incident Team (NAIT). Because the Army had missiles with explosive warheads placed around New England, the possibility existed that there could be an accident or other incident involving these missiles.

In the event that something went wrong, the army established a team of experts to deal with any situation. The Fort Devens Nuclear Accident Team was made up of personnel from public relations, military police, medical staff, engineers, JAG, and other units.

I was the JAG representative. We were issued a duffel bag full of gear and told that we might be contacted at any hour, day or night. We would be expected to report within thirty minutes to a pre-designated spot, where we would be placed in a vehicle to be transported to the scene of the incident.

During my service on this team, we did not have any actual incidents to deal with, but we had several training alerts where we reported and were taken to a site where they had actors playing the parts of those who might have been involved.

On one occasion, we arrived at a site where a flatbed semi was sitting in a ditch. We were told that a missile was being transported when the truck went off the road. We were told that there was no warhead on the missile.

As I stood there with the command representative and the public relations representative, two military police approached us with a gentleman in between them. I greeted them and was told that the civilian claimed he was a reporter for the Boston Globe. At this point the civilian demanded to know what was going on. I asked him for identification and he handed me a card, complete with picture, which identified him as a reporter for the Boston Globe.

I was impressed with the role-playing and began to suspect that he might actually be who he said he was. I asked for a driver's license and he complied. I had a real-life reporter on my hands.

I then began to explain the nature of the incident and why it was being done. He was very interested and asked if he could do a story about this. I involved the public relations officer and we agreed that something could be worked out. The story was very complimentary to the Army.

AFTER ACTIVE DUTY

After leaving active duty, I initially decided not to stay in the active reserve. If I had stayed active, I would have been required to attend drills in Columbus and participate in two weeks of annual training at an active-duty Army base.

However, I soon realized that I missed the Army. As an Army lawyer, I had been involved in finding legal solutions when they involved international law and the laws of war. I had advised generals and individual enlisted men and women.

So, I changed my status from inactive to active reserves. I was assigned to a small unit of lawyers specializing in government contracts. From this modest beginning, over the next 25 years, I advised two-star generals regarding legal matters and I was a commander of a unit of more than fifty legal specialists.

ANNUAL TRAINING

When you serve in the Army Reserve, each year, in addition to regular drills, you are expected to complete a two-week annual training period

MILITARY SERVICE

(AT). Often, that training is with an active-duty unit that your unit would be assigned to if you were called to active duty.

There are times when the magnitude of your unit's regular assignment is such that the commander may say, "Stay here and get our unit's job done." Or sometimes, a unique opportunity comes along to provide an exceptional training experience that will benefit the unit.

I have already told you about my opportunity to teach at the JAG school in Charlottesville, Virginia. One year when I was attending a seminar at the JAG school, my son's best friend Steve was in his first year at the United States Naval Academy. Annapolis was about a three-hour drive from Charlottesville and I decided to call Steve to see if he would be available to go to dinner.

I would get to tell him what was going on in Marysville and he could show me the campus at the academy. He said he would love to see me and that he would get permission to go off campus to eat with me.

I decided to wear my uniform to help ease the entry onto the school grounds. I was a full colonel at the time, equivalent to a Navy Captain.

At the right time, I arrived at the academy and was swiftly allowed to enter. After parking my car, I began looking for the dormitory Steve was housed in. I soon ran into the same problem I had encountered at the University of Virginia. I encountered dozens, if not hundreds, of students in uniform and so the salute parade began.

After the 20th or 30th salute, I was asked if I needed help finding a particular building. I said, "Yes!" and I gave the young man the name of the dormitory. We soon arrived and I called Steve. He answered and quickly joined me in the lobby.

After several minutes of conversation, Steve said that he would go up to his room and change into his dress uniform. I asked him, "Why go formal?" and he replied that, as a "plebe," he was not allowed to go off base unless he was wearing the proper uniform. When he returned, we ate at a pizza place off base.

When we got back, he asked me if I would like to see his room. I said, "Sure, let's take a look."

We got into the elevator and he pushed the button for his floor. The elevator opened and we entered a hallway where an enlisted navy sailor sat behind a desk. This sailor, upon seeing the eagles on my shoulder, immediately jumped up and shouted, "All hands on deck!"

Doors to the rooms began to fly open and dozens of students lined up at attention, while Steve tried to suppress a big smile.

Steve then proceeded to take me down the hall to his room, where the door had not flown open. Steve pulled a key out of his pocket and opened the door. There I am, looking at Steve's roommate, who was reading a text book, sitting in a chair which was tipped back. He had his feet on the desk in front of him and when he saw me, a panic struck him. He attempted to jump up to attention but only managed to crash over backwards.

At this point, Steve broke into a full belly laugh.

With the Army Reserve, there have been a number of other opportunities of which I have been able to take advantage, or opportunities I have passed on to my unit. I don't have enough space to cover all of the annual trainings that I or my units have experienced, so I have selected some that I remember best.

We have attended or supported training in Panama; Korea; Germany; Honduras; Fort Hood, Texas; Fort Sheridan, Illinois; San Luis Obispo, California; Washington, DC, and many other locations.

On Sunday, October 31, 1993 at 8:30 a.m., my executive officer, Dana McCue, and I left Port Columbus for Chicago O'Hare Airport, the first stop on an all-day trip. We were one half of the first increment of the Ninth Military Law Center bound for two weeks of training in the Republic of Panama. Our mission was to assist the Staff Judge Advocate for the United States Army South. In accordance with the provisions of the treaty with Panama, we were traveling in civilian clothing. Our destination was Fort Clayton Army Base, Panama City, Panama. Fort Clayton

MILITARY SERVICE

was one of a number of military bases the United States maintained in Panama in the 1990s.

*A photograph of me as a Colonel
At Panama '93 and '94*

In 1903, the Hay-Bunau-Varilla Treaty was signed between Panama and the United States. It created the Panama Canal Zone as a US-governed region and allowed the US to build the Panama Canal. In 1977, the Panama Canal Treaty was signed by the Commander of Panama's Nation

Guard and US President Jimmy Carter. Over time, it would replace the 1903 treaty.

On October 1, 1979, the Panama Canal Zone was abolished and all unused areas were returned to Panama. Between 1979 and December 31, 1999, the US transferred all military areas and constructions to Panama. In total, 95,293 acres with 5,237 buildings were handed over. Their estimated value was $4 billion (USD)! In 1993, the US Army was still active in Panama and was the location of the headquarters of Southern Command (SOUTHCOM), which was responsible for US Army operations throughout much of Central and South America.

Photograph of the Panama Canal Locks. A Trip to Ocuá

On our first tour in Panama, the local Staff Judge Advocate (the senior officer in the law office) asked me to assign members of my unit to five duty sections based on the current needs of the office and the individual's skills.

MILITARY SERVICE

In addition to the Staff Judge Advocate and his staff, the following divisions were part of the SJA office: administration, operations law, international law, civil law, claims, and trial prosecution and defense.

The criminal trial law division had many of the same types of duties found at any active post. They helped process adverse administrative actions, assisted commanders and defendants with non-judicial punishment, and they tried court martials.

The operations law division was responsible for advising Joint Task Force Panama and the Southern Command regarding all legal aspects of military exercises conducted in that area of operations.

The international law division dealt with the U.S. army's relations to the host country and other nations in our sphere of operations which included most of Central and South America.

The civil law division was where the legal assistance office was. This group provided legal advice to all military personnel of any branch of the United States military and to their dependents.

The last office, which my unit provided assistance to, was the claims division. This office had the responsibility to investigate, pay, or, if necessary, litigate claims for and against the government.

Claims investigations sometimes required a helicopter ride to a different part of the country for an inspection of damaged property or to take part in a conference with Panamanian nationals. On Monday of my second week, I was invited to participate in a claims mission that involved a 1-hour Blackhawk helicopter ride to a small village called Ocu.

While we were there, we examined a building that the villagers said had been damaged by wind when an Army helicopter flew over. The chief investigator for our office was a civilian who had to write a recommendation to the approving authorities. She had lived in Panama for almost 20 years and was fluent in Spanish.

The damaged shed was an old structure with a tin roof, wood beams and open sides. It was located in a fairground and was owned by the local government district. After our inspection, we concluded that there was a preexisting structural weakness that contributed to the collapse. Despite this, we offered to supply materials if they would perform the labor. This was agreed to and everyone was happy.

The trip to Ocu was interesting and informative, but it was the trip back to Fort Clayton that I will never forget. We boarded our Black Hawk helicopter with six passengers and a crew of three.

There were only four sets of earphones, so I was the only non-crew member listening to the cockpit conversation. This was the rainy season in Panama and it was common for heavy rains to swoop in and drench different areas practically every afternoon. As we left Ocu and gained altitude, we could see that storm clouds were forming ahead of us. The pilot announced that he was going to set the Black Hawk down on a beach so we could button up the cabin to keep it dry if it rained.

We landed on the beach, buttoned up, and took off into the rain clouds. The copilot reached over and turned on the windshield wipers since it had begun to rain rather significantly. As we continued to fly, I could not see very far forward at all. The pilot asked the copilot if the wipers could go any faster, and the copilot responded, "That's a negative!"

The pilot then looked back at me and said, "I don't like flying blind. I'm going to try to find an opening." He swung left and went up. Within seconds, we emerged from the cloud bank, and the crew and I gasped! A small mountain was 75 to 100 yards in the direction from which we had just changed. If we had continued forward for a few seconds more, we would have smashed into the side of the mountain! We then took a different route, avoiding the clouds whenever possible.

The next day, I had a visit scheduled at the Atlantic side of the Panama Canal and the transportation was a helicopter. My unit's members were looking forward to the trip but the only way they could take the flight was if a Colonel (me) accompanied them. Despite my real concern, I went on the visit and we made it safely to our destination.

MILITARY SERVICE

To this day, some 30 years later, I get goose bumps when I think about how close we were to death and how life is so fragile.

In a helicopter while traveling to Ocu

LET ME TELL YOU MY STORY

HOW I AVOIDED TROUBLE IN A PANAMANIAN BAR

While my unit was performing active-duty training in Panama, we had opportunities to assimilate to the culture and to interact with the Panamanian people. One of the fulltime civilians who was working in our office told us about a bar and grill in Panama City which had fantastic Latin American sandwiches. My deputy and I decided to check it out.

When the workday ended, we caught a taxi at the gate and settled back for the 10-to-15-minute ride into Panama City. During this ride, the lieutenant colonel expressed his disappointment that he did not speak Spanish. I pointed out that my Spanish was very limited and that there were many Panamanians, especially in the city, who could speak English. This didn't satisfy him and he asked me to teach him how to order a beer in Spanish. Since that was a rather simple phrase, I told him I would. I instructed him to say, "Me gustaria una cerveza fria, por favor."

The lieutenant colonel began to excitedly repeat the phrase with several mistakes or omissions. I repeated the phrase in Spanish and when the taxi driver turned around his head and indicated that he didn't have any beers, I told my friend not to speak. We reached the restaurant and got out of the taxi. As I was paying the driver, I could hear my friend repeating a phrase in Spanish.

We turned to go into the restaurant and the lieutenant colonel said, "Me gusta una cabeza fria, por favor!" I stopped him and said, "Let's stick to English." When he asked me why, I told him that he had, more or less, just said, "I would like a cold head please."

We spoke English and enjoyed our sandwiches and beers.

MILITARY SERVICE

AN ANGRY TAXI DRIVER

In 1993, I was the commander of the Ninth Military Law Center located in Columbus, Ohio. We had small units attached to us which were scattered throughout Ohio. My headquarters was ordered to perform two weeks of annual training in Panama in Central America. This was a training opportunity as well as a support mission to the Southern Command. As we always did before going to a foreign country, we studied the recent history of the country and we received a threat assessment from the Army.

Because of the location of the Panama Canal, the United States had a presence in Panama for many years. During President Jimmy Carter's presidency, the U.S. agreed to shut down all its military bases in Panama over a period of time.

In 1989, the United States had invaded Panama and jailed the de facto leader of the country, General Manuel Noriega. This invasion had been precipitated by a number of incidents during the 1980s.

In 1983, Noriega had assumed power not as president but as the leader of the army. He began to assist various U.S. agencies in monitoring and suppressing drug dealers and potential adversaries. However, after two rigged elections, he tripled the size of the Panamanian army and began to import significant numbers of military weapons.

He also began to assist or even participate in money laundering and drug dealing. He was also accused of murdering several of his opponents. The U.S. began to crack down on Noriega and he turned hostile.

On December 15, 1989, he declared war on the United States. A few days later, four United States military personnel were stopped at a roadblock by Panamanian soldiers and one of the U.S. troops was shot and killed.

The next day, on December 20, 1989, the United States invaded Panama. The invasion force consisted of 27,000 Soldier Marines and Sailors as well as 300 aircraft. As a result of the invasion, Noriega was captured and eventually sentenced to 40 years in prison. During the invasion the U.S. suffered 23 dead and 324 wounded. The Panamanian defense force had 300 to 800 killed and possibly up to 500 civilians were also killed.

After the takeover, the rule of the country was returned to the Panamanians and the majority of the citizens were generally sympathetic to the U.S. for disposing of Noriega. However, understandably there were bitter feelings from those who lost loved ones due to the invasion.

A little more than 3 years later, my soldiers and I were going to a country which still had some undercurrents of resentment among some of its citizens. When we arrived "in country," we were stationed on a U.S. Army base and spent most of our time there while performing our mission. The Panamanians who worked on base were very friendly and made us feel welcome.

During our off-duty hours, we were allowed to go into Panama City or into the country nearby. When we went anywhere, it was suggested that we not go alone and most of the time we traveled in groups.

One day, members of my unit were going to a restaurant in the city and I was going to join them. I was delayed by a meeting and told the group to go ahead and I would catch a taxi as soon as I could. When my meeting ended and I went to the gate to get a taxi.

When the cab pulled up, I got into the front seat next to the driver, a man in his 50s, and we started off. We had not gone more than a couple of miles when the driver, in an angry voice, said, "I AM MAD AT YOUR COUNTRY!" I began to regret traveling alone.

I asked the man why he was mad at the United States and he replied that he had two reasons for being upset. "First, you send millions of dollars to Panama each year and it goes right into the pockets of the politicians!"

I told him that such actions upset me also. I added that if it was used for humanitarian purposes I would not be upset. I then asked, "What was the second reason you were mad?" I held my breath expecting the invasion to become the topic.

He turned toward me and said, "They are making you soldiers leave the country." I suspected that he had a concern that he feared the loss of business when we left and I said to him, "You don't want a foreign army in your country, do you?" He replied, "We trust you more than we do our government!"

Fortunately, we had reached the restaurant and no further political discussion was possible.

A QUIET WEEKEND OFF-DUTY

On yet another two-week tour of duty in Panama, I had two days free during the middle weekend. I did not want to stay in Panama City and visit bars, so I contacted a fishing guide and made arrangements to go fishing. When the guide picked me up at the base, he was pulling a boat on a trailer and he was wearing a pistol on his belt. I asked him why he carried a gun, and he replied, "This is Panama, you never know."

I got into the truck and we were on our way. The guide told me that he had chosen an exciting area to try our luck. It was on a river which flowed into the Atlantic Ocean and was very near the country of Columbia.

We drove into the tropical rain forest, and, after a number of miles, we came to a boat launching area. I hadn't eaten breakfast and there was a shack there selling coffee and pastries. As I approached the shack and greeted the lady behind the counter. I discovered that she only spoke Spanish! I ordered coffee and a pastry in very basic Spanish and she acknowledged that she understood.

While I waited for my order, I heard a sound coming from nearby which sounded like, "Bak Bak Bak." My grandmother had raised chickens and this cry certainly sounded like a chicken. I asked the lady, "Donde esta el pollo?" (Where is the chicken?) She indicated that there were no chickens here. I then heard the same sound and asked her again. She smiled and pointed up at a nearby tree. There sat a parrot who was doing the best imitation of a chicken that I had ever heard!

Food shop in Panama, the upper left tree is where the "chicken" was

Having satisfied my appetite and gained a new appreciation for parrots, I headed to the launch area. There was the guide with the boat already in the water. There was a large slab of concrete extending from the edge of the bank into the water and the guide said that "Because of the nearness of the ocean, the river would rise and fall around 19 feet with the tide."

This phenomenon created a condition where, at high tide, the river would rush upstream. When the tide was about to recede, the river was calm, almost like a lake. And, when the low tide began, the river would rush downstream. As we moved into the river, I noticed that strong currents were carrying sticks and chunks of dirt swiftly past our boat. In addition, there were small whirlpools nearby.

As we began our trip upriver, I could hear screeching noises coming from the forest. The guide told me that these noises were coming from Holler monkeys. We soon saw alligator-like creatures called Caiman which were about 6 to 8 feet long along the river banks and an ox-like creature on the shore. The guide also revealed that jaguars and ocelots could be lurking in the rain forest as well as a variety of snakes.

We began to fish, and several things happened. I caught a four-foot-long Garfish which had a snout at least 10 inches long. The guide had a fish which was putting up a huge fight until his line went slack. It turned out that his lure had been bitten in half! It was at this point that I resolved to not put my hand in the water.

We then had several fish on our lines which got away. We turned and went down river where we came up on a boat of native Panamanians who were fishing. We remained at a distance but we stopped to watch. They did not have rods and reels but were fishing with hand lines. As we watched they caught several big fish and the guide decided that we should move along.

In an attempt to locate more fish, the guide steered the boat into a tributary river which had its headwaters in Colombia. As we headed up the river, the guide, in a low voice, suddenly said, "Get down on the floor!" He then sharply turned the boat around and accelerated the motor. As I dropped to the bottom of the boat, I asked, "What's the problem?"

He replied, "See those logs lashed together? They are cedar trees and, they are being illegally forested by smugglers who will shoot us if we don't get out of here now!" We sped out of the tributary and back to the main river. I breathed a sigh of relief when no shots rang out.

We decided that we had experienced enough excitement for one day, and we headed for the boat landing. The next time I was in Panama I went fishing again but it was on the canal near Panama City and the most exciting thing that happened was catching peacock bass.

In Panama with a Garfish

KOREA

When I was commander of the Ninth Military Law Detachment, members of my unit were selected to participate in the War Games training exercise in South Korea. As a senior officer, I would not take part directly, but I would help coordinate the planning for my unit's participation as directed by commanding officer of the Korean theater. I was asked to fly to Seoul, Korea for a series of meetings with the regular army officers who were conducting the training.

I was given twelve days of notice before my departure date. During this time, I was given a briefing as well as a series of shots. I then boarded a commercial 747 aircraft and, approximately sixteen hours later, I was in Seoul.

The time change was troubling. I tended to wake up at 2:00 a.m. local time and feel very sleepy in the afternoon, but the magnitude of what I was experiencing kept me going full speed.

I was soon caught up in a whirlwind of military meetings and an exotic environment. The planning sessions were very professional and conducted with a sense of urgency. These meetings concentrated on how the planners could best use my soldiers in the exercise.

I spent only five days in Korea, and during off-duty hours, the local JAG officers took me to the shopping district and also made arrangements for a visit to the DMZ. I couldn't wait! I was going to get to see North Korea!

The day of my visit to the border soon arrived and I was ready to go. Then I was called into the SJA office and told that there was some incident in "the zone" and all scheduled visits had been canceled.

My hosts knew that I was disappointed and tried to make up for that by taking me out for an authentic Korean meal. We had spicy pork, garlic cloves, kimchi, and the biggest bottle of beer I had ever seen.

I believe that my trip to South Korea and my unit's participation in a major active-duty training exercise was a validation of our unit's value to our nation's defense.

As I got ready to leave, I reflected on the dangerous situation faced by our troops stationed on the Korean peninsula. We had about 25,000 troop in Korea. The North Korean military numbered over 1,000,000 strong. The distance from the DMZ to Seoul (population close to 10,000,000) was about thirty-five miles, well within artillery distance!

I ask that everyone who reads this would reflect on the serious nature of what happens in Korea. The US Armed Forces who are stationed in or near Korea are dedicated, well-trained, and disciplined.

The military is controlled by our elected officials. That is how it should be, but those elected officials need to listen and take seriously what our senior military leaders say before any action is taken.

GERMANY

For many years, Europe was the focus of our armed forces. The Russians had occupied certain portions after World War II and tensions ran high. If the Communist Bloc took an aggressive position and attempted to expand their holdings, NATO and the US would be the only deterrent. In order to prepare for the defense of Europe, the United States Army had comprehensive plans to meet and defeat the invading armies.

As is true in Korea today, the number of soldiers in Europe was not sufficient to be successful in this defense. That meant that there needed to be a rapid influx of reinforcements. This plan of defense required the participation of active duty and reserve forces.

The army's plans called for a coordinated call-up of troops, including the 115th Area Support Group from the California National Guard and a number of units subordinate to the 115th, including the Ninth MLC. As a result of these war plans, I was tasked with going to Germany along with my sergeant major to prepare a "battle book," which would be used if our unit was called up.

A battle book was a document I compiled to be used in decision-making during time of war. Its purpose was to familiarize me with the area in which we would be deployed.

This annual training might appear to have all the earmarks of a vacation. We were going to Germany, where we would rent a car and travel around the country in civilian clothes. But there was a very serious undertone that could not be ignored. We would be the eyes and ears of our unit to ensure our success, and therefore our lives, in the event that we had to respond to crisis.

This mission required that we take notes and pictures of every important landmark along the way with the following reasoning: If we needed to get from Frankfurt to Stuttgart, what would we do if certain bridges were destroyed before we got there? Who would we contact in the local populace for assistance? What resources were there that might be commandeered to complete the mission?

At the beginning and the conclusion of our self-guided trip, we met with active duty and reserve troops who were charged with the defense of this area. These meetings were helpful in understanding how the overall response was planned.

Several years after our assignment, the Berlin Wall fell and the immediate threat of invasion was diminished. This caused the Army to readjust its focus, and a whole new set of priorities were developed. I don't think that this meant that the plan for the defense of Europe was a waste of time. Whenever the objective of a plan is to prevent war, it is a good thing when that is what happens.

HONDURAS

I personally have never been in the country of Honduras, but there have been many times that my units have supported the missions going on in this country. The United States military forces are not meant to exclusively fight wars and defeat the enemy.

Over the past fifty years, the Army has responded to requests for assistance from many Central and South American countries regarding humanitarian projects. These missions are not meant to benefit just the foreign country. If the construction of a road, a school, a dental clinic, or other project gives our engineers an opportunity for valuable training, then the JAG may recommend that funding be approved. A number of these projects are done in conjunction with the State Department. Many of the troops participating in these humanitarian endeavors are National Guard or Army Reserve units.

When there is extensive activity in a country, there are probably going to be legal issues that arise. That is when we Army Reserve lawyers jump into action. The legal issues can get rather interesting. How much of a claim is paid if an army truck hits a Honduran and kills him? How much is paid if it is a water buffalo instead of a human? I will not get into the answers here, but you might be surprised.

FORT HOOD

Not every annual training is conducted outside of this country. My unit went to Fort Hood, Texas one year, and we were confronted with many interesting challenges.

I met with the SJA to introduce myself and find out his expectations for our two-week training period. He mentioned that they had an ongoing environmental issue and I advised him that our unit had an environmental law specialist. He was thrilled! He also commented on the need to better prepare his young legal assistance attorneys to advise on probate matters. It just so happened that we had a probate court magistrate in our unit.

After placing my unit members in the area where I felt that they were best suited, I still had a Captain Mastrangelo whose experience was primarily criminal prosecution.

The base SJA asked me if I would like to have anyone participate in a field exercise concentrating on handling prisoners of war. I immediately suggested the young captain and he was assigned to the officer in charge.

The exercise involved 500 soldiers who were designated as prisoners of war, and a significant number of military police to process and control them. My captain was initially reluctant to participate since he had no prior experience in the area.

After three days in the field, where it rained constantly, the captain returned, muddy uniform and all. I asked him for an after-action report and he just glowed as he recounted his experiences in a realistic setting. The military police commander kept our captain right by his side throughout the exercise, seeking his advice whenever a legal issue arose.

Captain Mastrangelo said that, for the first time in his Army experience, he felt that he was actually an Army officer involved in a wartime setting.

FORT SHERIDAN

One of the AT's that held a special place in my experience was Fort Sheridan in Illinois. There was not a lot going on when we got there, but when we asked how we could help, the SJA indicated that they had experienced several spousal abuse cases recently and, if we were interested, they would like some guidance on drafting a policy statement.

I accepted the challenge and began a review of the problem. I realized that there were no guidelines in place regarding the issue and that the entire spectrum needed to be addressed. I talked to the other professionals who were concerned with this issue and we drafted a command policy letter that would be sent out to all units within the command.

I then helped to establish a spousal abuse committee to deal with future incidents. We were not able to follow up because of the short time we were there, but I believe that we put in place a program that would address the problem and provide a platform for future action.

Unfortunately, the military is not exempt from this horrible problem, but there are serious attempts to properly deal with it.

LET ME TELL YOU MY STORY

SAN LUIS OBISPO

I have previously mentioned that the Ninth MLC was a subordinate unit to the 115th Area Support Group, a California National Guard unit. As such, the Ninth was given an opportunity to perform AT with the 115th in a massive training exercise in California involving many units from across the United States.

As this time, I was the executive officer of the Ninth and I was going to be in charge of my unit during these exercises. In our communications with the 115th, we were told that we would be providing legal support along with the JAG officers embedded within the 115th.

I contacted the lieutenant colonel in charge of the SJA section of the 115th and suggested that we get together and decide what part we would play in the important exercise. His response was that we should keep a low profile and just interact between us "lawyers."

I replied that we did not feel that it was worth our time to fly to California to keep a low profile. He insisted that our participation should be limited to thinking up legal problems and then submitting them to each other to be solved. I disagreed.

As soon as we got to California, I went to the commander of the 115th and suggested that we would provide him with legal play problems, which would then be presented to various unit commanders to see if they could identify them as legal problems and ask us for help. He agreed and suggested that we have a Ninth MLC representative sit in on the command post briefings and monitor the exercises. The ensuing weeks of training proved valuable to our unit and hopefully to the 115th.

Because of the sensitive nature of this training exercise, security was very important. One incident brought home how important training and evaluation is to future success. The headquarters was surrounded by a fence and the gate was patrolled by military police. One day, a pickup truck pulled up to the gate. It had post identification decals on it and the driver identified herself as the wife of a sergeant who was participating in the training.

The guards talked to her for a while, probably because of the skimpy sundress she was wearing. Lots of leg was shown. When she begged to get an important computer to her husband, they did not ask for ID beyond her driver's license, and they did not open or search the boxes in the back of the trunk.

During the post-exercise evaluation, it was revealed that she had been planted to move the truck with simulated explosives into the compound and park it next to headquarter. If she had been a real terrorist, the majority of the staff would have been killed in the explosion.

To some readers, it might seem like a gross mistake that could not be forgiven. Certainly, carelessness by our soldiers must be eliminated. This demonstrates why realistic training must be conducted and taken very seriously by all who participate in it.

THE COURT OF MILITARY APPEALS

I have previously told you about Judge Everett, who had been appointed by the president to serve as the Chief Judge of the Court of Military Appeals (now known as the United States Court of Appeals for the Armed Forces). One year, when I was the SJA for Eighty-Third ARCOM, I was trying to decide what I could do to fulfill my annual training requirement. I called up Judge Everett and asked him if he know of any opportunities in Washington DC.

He enthusiastically replied that he could use some help, and why didn't I come to the court for two weeks. I was thrilled and so was my boss, the ARCOM commander. I arranged the details and arrived excited about the opportunity I would be experiencing.

Judge Everett handed me several folders and explained that the court was being asked to decide whether the results of a polygraph test should be allowed to be introduced in a court-martial. This was an important issue, and as with all cases, the three judges would make the decision. My job was to supplement the research and case precedent that had already been done by the attorneys representing the parties. I would also have an opportunity, based on my research and the arguments of counsel, to suggest what I would decide if I were one of the judges.

The two weeks in Washington flew by, and I was honored when Judge Everett thanked me and asked if I could come back the next year. I told him that I would no longer be the SJA, but I would see to it that another officer, one even more learned, was assigned to assist the court.

The very next year, Professor Greg Travalio clerked for the court and was involved in assisting Judge Everett in a major decision that was eventually reviewed by the United States Supreme Court.

Our unit continued to provide assistance to the court until Judge Everett left the bench. We were privileged to be the only Army Reserve JAGs in the United States to serve in this capacity!

SUMMARY

As I look back on my time in the military, I realize that prior to my 30th birthday, I never thought that I would spend 30 years in the United States Army and retire as a full colonel.

I never thought that I would be trained in combat arms and air defense. I didn't think I would be the legal representative of a two-star general or be the commander of units of military lawyers.

I never could imagine that I would be appointed to assist the Judge Advocate General of the Army or be appointed to the list of candidates eligible to be considered for becoming a general in the JAG Corps.

MILITARY SERVICE

In the Army I learned a great deal about how to succeed in life. When you are put in a position of responsibility, you must determine who is the most knowledgeable in accomplishing your objectives.

Once you have surrounded yourself with experts, ask for their input, listen to them, and then act on your best intelligence. It is not important that you get credit for success, but it is vital that you succeed.

MY MILITARY RANKS

ACTIVE ARMY
August – October, 1968 Basic Training (Private) E-1
October – December, 1968 Advanced Individual Training (Private) E-2
January, 1969 Missile Training (Private First Class)
February – March, 1969 Direct Commission to JAG (Captain)
May 1968 – February 1973, Trial Lawyer & Legal Assistance (Captain)

ARMY RESERVE 1973 – 1998
148th Legal Detachment (Captain)
Deputy Staff Judge Advocate 83rd ARCOM (Major)
9th Military Law Center Training Officer (Major)
9th Military Law Center Executive Officer (Lieutenant Colonel)
Staff Judge Advocate 83rd ARCOM (Colonel)
Commander 9th Military Law Center (Colonel)
Individual Mobilization Augmentee (TJAGS)
General's List (Considered for Promotion)
Retired

Chapter 7

LEGAL PROFESSION

IN NOVEMBER OF 1968, I was sworn into a select body of professionals by the Chief Justice of the Ohio Supreme Court. I was now officially an attorney at law! The dream that was inspired in the 1950s by the TV series Perry Mason and doggedly pursued from the eighth grade on, had come true even though it was against all odds!

Why would this accomplishment seem unobtainable to me? I was the first college graduate from my extended family. I was then the first post-graduate student from my family and, when I got to law school, I discovered that 1/3 of my fellow first year students would not move on to the second year. That meant that approximately 70 of the 200 first-year students would quit or would flunk out!

In addition to all these negative indicators, and even though I was working while I was in college and law school, I did not have enough money for all three years of tuition.

Despite the odds, I did get the LSAT (Law School Admission Test) scores to get into law school. (I scored in the 99th percentile.) I also managed to survive the first-year slaughter and, thanks to my grandma, I had enough money to stay in school until I graduated.

The last hurdle I had to clear to become an attorney was passing the three-day bar exam. This was not an easy task under the best circumstances. To do well, you needed to focus your mind on what you had learned over the three years of law school, and you needed to approach the test with confidence and a sense of calm.

A PRISON RIOT

During the summers, as I worked my way through law school, I was able to get a job with the Columbus City Prosecutor's office. My job was to review complaints filed by citizens regarding alleged crimes. I would then determine whether to issue an arrest warrant or not.

If I believed that the complaint was more of a dispute between neighbors rather than a crime, I would send a letter to the involved people and request that they come into the office to discuss the matter.

I was so employed when an event occurred that was out of the ordinary. I was in my office when the City Attorney walked in and asked, "Who wants to go to a prison riot?"

Being young and foolish, I raised my hand, as did several other legal assistants, and he said, "Come on, let's go!" As we walked the 4 to 5 blocks to the Ohio State Penitentiary, the prosecutor filled us in on what was happening. Less than 30 minutes before, some prisoners housed in the maximum-security prison had overcome several guards and were holding hostages in an area within the walls fronting on the main street outside of the prison. The call went out that a major event was unfolding and that all available law enforcement officers were needed now!

LEGAL PROFESSION

As we hustled to the prison, sirens were blaring. Police from all over Central Ohio began rushing to the scene. As we neared the prison, we could see heavily armed and grim-faced men and women in uniforms. There was Columbus city police, sheriff's deputies, highway patrol, and prison guards. They were starting to form a circle around the very large prison.

There were hundreds of hardened criminals in this prison, and it once held over 5,000 prisoners. This ancient relic of a structure was built in 1834 and demolished in 1984. Prison conditions were described as primitive.

We were stopped by a heavily armed policeman and my boss showed him identification and said to us "Let's go." The policeman did not try to stop us. As we began moving closer, we were again stopped, this time by a highway patrol lieutenant.

The patrol had assumed command since all state property was in their jurisdiction. The prosecutor then identified himself and asked if the prisoners were armed. He was advised that, other than homemade knives and some scissors, they did not believe that there were any weapons such as firearms.

We were about to move closer, when a gunshot rang out behind us. We all dropped to the ground and the highway patrol commander ran in the direction of the shot. He soon returned and advised us that a deputy sheriff from an outlying county was removing a shotgun from his trunk when it went off. It appeared that the only thing shot was his cruiser.

The commander then moved us closer and we could hear the prisoners shouting threats to kill the hostages if anyone tried to get into the prison. We were now about 25 to 30 yards from the prisoners!

Over the next hour or so there was a mixture of planning and confusion. The mayor of Columbus arrived and then flew away in a city police helicopter. The prisoners got quieter and the highway patrol commander was communicating with the guards who still controlled a majority of the prison. Soon fire trucks arrived and the prosecutor indicated that it was time to go.

As evening drew near, the prisoners had still refused to surrender. That night the National Guard placed explosives on the roof and blew a hole in the ceiling right above the prisoners. A SWAT team then dropped into the room and shot one of the prisoners who charged at them. The rest immediately gave up and none of the hostages were hurt.

THE NEXT PHASE

Less than three months before I was scheduled to take the exam, the United States Army notified me that I had been drafted. I was supposed to report for duty approximately three weeks before the bar exam was to be administered. So much for calm and clear thinking!

I got an extension on the reporting date, I got my new wife prepared for my departure, and I passed the bar exam. I then got on a bus and headed for Fort Dix, New Jersey to begin my first fulltime job. I was trained as a lawyer and now I would be retrained as a light weapons infantryman and as a missileman.

Since I am sharing my Army experience in another section of this book, I will just summarize the next five years of my life. After training for combat, I applied for, and was accepted into the Army Judge Advocate General's Corps (army lawyers).

I received further training at the Judge Advocate General's School on the campus of the University of Virginia and then sent to Fort Devens, Massachusetts. I was assigned to the criminal defense team whose mission was to advise and defend soldiers if they were facing adverse actions by the army.

Over the next 18 months, I represented 168 soldiers in Court Martial proceedings. These cases included Army specific crimes such as Absent

Without Leave (AWOL) and criminal charges found in civilian courts such as assault, drugs, and theft.

I also had some more unique cases. One was a traffic manslaughter case where two young girls were killed by a soldier who was driving while intoxicated. I also represented a young man for desertion who was part of the Chicago Seven at the 1960 Democratic Convention in Chicago.

After averaging 9 trials per month for a year and a half, I was burned out! I asked for a transfer to legal assistance where I would draft wills, powers of attorney, and give legal advice regarding civil law matters.

This was also an active practice and I completed my four-year commitment to the Army, having learned a great deal about the practice of law.

Since I was discharged from the active-duty Army in February of 1973, I sent resumes to a number of law firms in Columbus, Ohio. I also sent a few to Delaware, Ohio which was just north of Columbus. Delaware had a university as well as several nice parks.

After hearing from several law firms in Columbus, I began to set up interviews. Then I got a phone call from an attorney who said he was a partner in a two-person law firm in Marysville, Ohio. I had never been to Marysville which is 30 miles from downtown Columbus, and I had not sent a resume to this firm.

The attorney went on to say that a Delaware law firm had forwarded my resume since they knew the Marysville firm was planning to hire an associate attorney. He then told me that he had been an Army JAG Officer also and he felt that I would be well qualified. I told him when I would be in central Ohio and we set up a date and time for me to interview with them.

The time came for my trip back to Ohio. I did not take Karen on this trip since she had gone to school there and was somewhat familiar to the area.

After several interviews in Columbus, I got in my car and headed for Marysville. As I was driving and looking at a map (pre-GPS), I thought to myself that I was wasting my time with this interview. I felt good about the possibilities of getting a job in the "big city" state capital. But I had an obligation to see this through.

I arrived in Marysville and pulled into the law firm's parking lot. The office was in an older house. It looked well kept, but it did not give off the same aura as the modern settings of the Columbus firms in their tall buildings surrounded by a bustling city.

Oh well, this was the county seat of Union County and there, next to the law firm's office, was a beautiful, majestic courthouse, which had been built in 1890 and had been well preserved over the last 83 years.

I entered the office and was ushered into a conference room. I was soon joined by the two partners. The senior partner was in his mid-50's and the other attorney was in his 30's.

I discovered that this firm and its predecessors had a rich history in the practice of law in central Ohio. The list of businesses that they represented was impressive and included O.M. Scott's Company who is the nation's leading lawn and garden provider and whose world headquarters was in this quiet little town.

The Common Pleas Judge had been the senior partner of this firm for many years prior to ascending to the bench. And, while none of us knew it then, the current senior partner would be elected to that important position six years after this job interview.

We had a very nice extended conversation about many things, including my opportunity, if I joined the firm, for direct client contact and early partnership opportunities. As we were ending our talk, they asked if I would wait for them in the waiting room and then they would like to take me to visit the Judge.

I became a bit lost in my thoughts as I waited for them. I didn't know if I stood a chance at the position, but the meeting had gone well. I couldn't wait to tell Karen about the unexpected opportunity I might have to be part of an active practice in a small-town setting.

LEGAL PROFESSION

When the partners came to get me, they shocked me by asking if I was ready to commit to the position now. I told them I would have to talk it over with my wife. They said they understood this and they would be happy to fly both Karen and me out to Ohio and put us up in a hotel so she and I could get to see the community.

Karen and I followed up on this interview trip by accepting the firm's offer to fly us out to Ohio. After we rented a car and headed northwest towards Marysville, Karen remarked that she was enjoying the sights of Metropolitan Columbus once again. It had been three years since she graduated from OSU and joined me at Fort Devens in Massachusetts.

As we turned off interstate 270 onto route 33, which would take us to Marysville, she commented that we were passing a lot of farmers' fields which would soon be planted with corn or soy beans. After about ten minutes she again looked out at more fields and asked, "Where are all of the cities?"

Remember, Karen was raised in a town in New York that was close to the city with millions of people. Concerned that she might be forming an adverse opinion before we even got to Marysville, I told her that she would soon see the beautiful little town with a commercial center filled with late 1800's buildings.

We arrived and checked into the modest hotel which had been booked for us. Soon, we made arrangements to meet with the partners for a tour of the city and parts of the nearby county.

Both of the partners seemed genuinely happy to see us and I soon sensed that Karen was making a good impression on both of them. As we toured the town, we noticed an impressive hospital campus which, we were advised, was owned and operated by the county and was a source of pride for the community. We also saw numerous churches, which prompted our inquiry as to whether there were any Lutheran churches in Union County.

They advised us that there were two within the city limits, one on the edge of town, and two others to the south of the county. Neither Karen or I had ever been in an area so filled with German Lutherans.

My potential employers again extended an offer to me and, although I had several possible offers pending in Columbus, I decided that I needed to decide one way or another on the position in Marysville.

When we were alone, Karen and I talked about the positives and negatives. Then, Karen looked at me and said, "I think that this type of practice would be perfect for you – for us!" I agreed and we accepted the offer.

MY PRACTICE OF LAW IN THE CIVILIAN WORLD

In 1973, I had completed almost four years as an attorney in the United States Army.

I received wonderful experience in the practice of law. I had more trial experience than most licensed attorneys and I spent three years as a civil legal assistance attorney.

I then entered a more standard legal practice in Ohio. Even this course was not typical as I was the primary defense counsel on three first degree murder trials.

After I opened my own practice, I no longer took criminal or domestic relations cases. I spent the next forty years practicing in a wide variety of areas, including estate planning and probate, real estate, both planning and zoning, and civil trial work including personal injury and wrongful death, and corporate work. I spent nine years in my first firm, after which I went on my own and eventually became the senior partner of a six-attorney law firm.

LEGAL PROFESSION

When I was in my mid-seventies I began to prepare for retirement. I could have stayed active, but the demands on my time were too great to enjoy the practice as much as I did when I was younger.

My firm was, in my opinion, the best firm in the county.

My long-time law partner Faye had accepted the position as managing partner and was very capable of overseeing and providing excellent legal services to our clients.

I had spent 30 years in the United States Army and over 50 years practicing law. It was time to take my leisure time more serious.

TIME TO ACT

As an attorney in the general practice of law, my firm did trial work and also transactional law such as real estate. One day, I was in the county recorder's office searching the public records, as was often the case.

Even though Marysville was the county seat, neither the city nor the county was populous. That allowed for an easy friendship with many of the people who worked in the courthouse including county office holders.

While I searched the records, I was carrying on a conversation with the Union County Recorder who was standing behind me. Suddenly, I heard a thud and turned around to find the Recorder laying on the floor. He did not appear to be conscious, and he had relieved himself. Upon checking, I could not detect a pulse. Panic broke out among the Recorder's office staff.

As a former army infantryman, I had been taught basic first aid and I believed that the Recorder had suffered a heart attack. I didn't consider myself an expert, but immediate action appeared to be needed and there were no medically trained individuals in the room.

I hollered to the clerk to call the squad and I then knelt over the Recorder to recheck his pulse, his respiration, and his airway. At that time, the prescribed first aid for a heart attack was mouth to mouth resuscitation. This involved holding his nose, blowing into his mouth, and performing chest compressions. Even though I knew what to do, I had never actually tried it on a human being and I had uncertainty as to whether I could do a proper job.

There was no time to question my ability, I had to do what I was trained to do. After ensuring that his throat was clear, I began to aid him. There was another person in the room and I called him over to help. I gave him a 10 second instruction on how to do chest compression and we began to assist his heart. I knew that it was important that I not hyperventilate and that the individual doing chest compressions could keep the heart beating while not cracking a rib.

The Chief Clerk shouted that the 911 call had been made and the squad was on its way. The fire department was located just a block away from the recorder's office but it took them 7 minutes to get there. It seemed more like an eternity.

After they arrived, the squad took over and transported the Recorder to the hospital where it was confirmed that he had suffered a heart attack.

The recorder survived and after a period of convalescence returned to work. I knew that legal work in the courtroom could be exciting but I never expected that real estate work would have such drama.

I learned that preparing yourself for life emergencies is important and you can accomplish more than you realize if you just try. I guess the Army training was more than just teaching me how to kill!

THE DEFENDANT PLEADS NOT GUILTY
(Representing Three Killers)

I had only been in Marysville for about nine weeks when I received a phone call from the Common Pleas Judge's bailiff. She said that the judge wanted to see me right away. I hurried over to the courthouse and was ushered into the judge's chambers. A young female attorney named Charlotte was already seated in front of the judge's desk.

The judge got right to the point. "There has been a double homicide in Union County and the police have taken a suspect into custody. This individual has already admitted that he killed two people! I am appointing the two of you to represent him."

There was no public defender's office in the county and therefore, the judge would select an attorney or attorneys to represent any indigent accused of a crime. Unless you had a conflict of interest or your training and experience made you incapable of serving, you had no choice. When the judge spoke, you listened!

I had tried 168 courts martial in the United States Army, all of them as a defense attorney. However, I had never tried a murder case. Charlotte was new to the profession and had never had a jury trial. She has since proven her skill as a lawyer and a judge of the probate and juvenile divisions. There were no other attorneys in the county who had tried a murder case.

We met with our client and he was somewhat incoherent. He did, however, admit to the facts that the judge had told us about. He had allegedly stabbed his sister and brother-in-law to death with a butcher knife. He had been suffering from mental illness for years, but had not shown violent tendencies in the past.

Approximately one month before the killings, he had admitted himself to a mental health hospital in Columbus. He was experiencing paranoid and schizophrenic thoughts and was disturbed by them. After five days, the hospital released him and told him to go to a local mental health facility. He did not know where to go, so he went to his sister's house in Richwood, Ohio. She agreed to take him in and he lived with his siter and her husband for approximately one month. As time passed, his actions became more and more bizarre. Finally, his sister expressed to her husband that she couldn't put up with her brother anymore and that they had to "get rid of him." The sister and her husband did not know that our client had overheard this conversation and was disturbed by it.

That day at lunch, the sister served her brother Cranapple juice which he had never tasted before. He swallowed some of the juice and it tasted bitter. He believed that she was trying to poison him and he ran to the sink to spit out the juice. This upset his sister, and she and her husband admonished him before heading to their bedroom to take a nap.

At this point, our client was certain that his sister and brother-in-law were trying to kill him. He went to the knife drawer in the kitchen and picked up a large butcher knife. He then went into their bedroom and stabbed them to death.

Since our client had admitted to killing the victims, our most viable defense was "insanity." To prove that, we needed testimony from a psychiatrist that, at the time of the killings, our client was mentally ill and out of touch with reality. Charlotte and I went to The Ohio State University College of Medicine to find a psychiatrist who would agree to examine our client and assess what his mental condition. If he or she found that our client did suffer from this rare condition, could they convince a jury of small-town conservative citizens to find him not guilty by reason of insanity?

One professor of psychiatry came highly recommended by a professor at the law school. However, when we talked to this psychiatrist, he told us that, in his opinion, most of the pleas of "not guilty by reason of insanity" were bogus. He admitted that a very small percentage of people charged with a serious crime are probably "legally out of touch with reality."

We assured him that we were seeking an honest medical opinion regarding our client's mental condition. He finally agreed to interview our client and, if he believed that there was merit in our claim, he would consider helping us out. He went on to say that he had two conditions before he would examine our client. First, he wanted this to be a learning experience for his students and second, he would not accept ANY payment from us or the county for his services.

LEGAL PROFESSION

We agreed to student participation when we found out that the students were all doctors working on the advanced specialty of psychiatry. They would be covered by the doctor/patient confidentiality rule.

We tried to talk him into accepting remuneration for his services. We told him that the county would pay him, although it would not be much. (Charlotte and I each received $1,500—which worked out to be about $5.00/hour!) He again told us forcefully that he would not take ANY money, including reimbursement for gasoline expenses.

We and the psychiatrist agreed to terms and an interview of our client was arranged. About a week later, I received a phone call from him which began with a loud declaration, "You're not going to believe this, this guy is nuts!" We were not surprised by this but, both Charlotte and I hoped that his testimony at trial would be a little more professional.

At trial, he was brilliant. He mesmerized the jury with a detailed yet understandable explanation of temporary insanity. He used real life examples to demonstrate how a susceptible person could move from a diminished mental state to a psychotic state without realizing it himself. He helped all the jurors understand how they, or a family member, could be susceptible to this terrible condition. He told them that the Defendant needed to be in a hospital, not a prison.

The prosecutor was not impressed by our expert's report and he refused to offer us a reduced plea agreement. After a lot of preparation and a five-day trial our client was found not guilty by reason of insanity. According to the judge, this was the first murder case in the county that actually went to trial. The judge also told us that he had been a visiting judge in a nearby city with a much larger population, and it was the first time that he had seen a successful insanity defense.

Our client was then sent to a psychiatric hospital where he was to remain until found by a judge and two doctors that he had been restored to reason and was no longer a threat to himself or society.

The next few years were not as exciting on the criminal defense front and then, I received a phone call from a person who had been arrested for murder. He said that he shot his girlfriend in the chest. He claimed that it was an accident. He admitted that he had gone to her house with a loaded pistol but he explained that he needed it for protection since he had received death threats. This was the 1970's and he was a black man who was dating a white woman. The prosecutor filed an indictment for first degree murder and said that the defendant had shot her on purpose because she was threatening to leave him.

Since the intent to kill was a crucial element, I spoke to the OSU psychiatrist we had used on the previous case and explained what we knew about the circumstances regarding the night the girlfriend was shot. After quizzing me about the defendant, the psychiatrist said that there did not appear to be any mental illness defense. However, since our client was confused in his recitation of what happened that night and he had been drinking when she was shot, the doctor had an idea of how to get a more accurate picture of the events leading up to and culminating in her death.

He said that, if my client agreed, he could administer a test using sodium amytal (which had been called "truth serum"). The doctor could not guarantee that the test was 100% accurate, but it might help us better understand our client's actions. He went on to explain that the drug can have side effects which he, as a doctor, would have to explain to my client in great detail. After discussing the test with me and the doctor, our client, who was facing a life sentence, agreed to take the test.

We knew that the test would not be admissible in a trial unless the prosecutor agreed to let it in but, we wanted to know what happened that night. The test took place at The Ohio State University hospital. The psychiatrist was in charge and he was assisted by 7 or 8 student doctors.

My client was asked to lay down on an operating bed and he was hooked up to an IV. He soon lost consciousness and the doctors, who were assisting, took turns holding my client's head in place so he would not asphyxiate. After about 45 minutes my client began to speak slowly in a "drunken" sounding speech.

The psychiatrist went to the next room and returned with a nurse. She had been given instructions on what to say and she began to talk to my client in a manner meant to portray the victim. In fact, she said, "Jerry, this is Jenny." She asked him if he wanted another beer. He replied that he did. She asked him to take her to Kroger, to which he firmly replied, "No! I told you I am going home." The nurse then said, "Where are you going? Why do you have your gun out? Give me the gun." At that point, the psychiatrist clapped his hands near my client's ear and the nurse screamed!

The psychiatrist pointed at me and I began talking to my client. I asked him, "Jerry, what's happening?" He replied, "Oh my God, I shot her!" I continued to question him about what was going on. With tears streaming down his cheeks, he launched into a narrative about running to his girlfriend's teen-aged daughter's room and telling her that he had shot her mother and she should call the sheriff!

He then said that he ran back to his girlfriend, at which point we could not interpret his words. Later, when we reviewed the video which was recording the entire procedure, we realized that he was trying to administer "mouth to mouth resuscitation!"

We offered to share the video with the prosecutor, but he refused to look at it and he also refused to reduce the charge from first degree murder. The case went to trial and, after five days of tearful testimony, the jury deliberated for fifteen hours. They came back at 4:30am with a verdict of second-degree murder.

We appealed the case on numerous grounds to the Court of Appeals and they ruled that a new trial was warranted. At that point, the prosecutor offered to reduce the charge to manslaughter, since our client was intoxicated, had a loaded gun in his possession, and had acted in a reckless manner. Our client accepted the reduced charge.

After preparing for and trying two first degree murder cases, I hoped that I would never have to try another one. I was not to be that lucky!

Once again, I received a phone call from the judge and when I got to the courthouse, there was my friend and co-counsel, Charlotte. The judge then advised us that there had been another killing and that a suspect was in the county jail.

Our client this time was in his early twenties. The victim, we discovered to our horror, was a 20-month-old child. Charlotte and I both reacted in the same way. We asked . . . no, pleaded with the judge to appoint someone else. We told him that we felt we had done our part in representing previous murder clients.

The judge told us that he understood our concerns, but that we were the most experienced attorneys in this type of case. Truth be told, we were the only attorneys in the county who had defended a murder case. We really didn't have any choice in the matter; it was our professional responsibility to represent this client to the best of our abilities.

Charlotte and I visited our client in the jail. He told us that his girlfriend asked him to babysit her daughter. While he was watching the little girl she began to cry and he didn't know what to do. His response was to hit her in the stomach. He did this at least several times and as a result the child died.

In our conversations with the accused, we also learned that he was a drug addict, with his drug of choice being LSD. This mind-altering drug had profound consequences which were unpredictable since they sometimes heightened the user's senses to sounds, colors, and images. They were especially frightening because, in the mind of the user, the hallucinations that occurred presented a direct threat.

In our trial preparation, Charlotte and I determined that our client had not been under the influence of drugs at the time of the incident. We also knew that drug usage was not a defense in Ohio. Once again, we contacted the Ohio State University professor and relayed the details of the murder to him. He indicated that he would have to look at medical records and interview our client, but he was pretty certain that our client was not mentally ill as defined by the law.

Over the months that followed, Charlotte and I spent a significant amount of time with our client. He had not had access to any drugs during this time since he was in jail. However, he had what are known as flashbacks. Basically, a flashback is seeing someone or something in an unreal manner, and in the medical community it may be called a Hallucinogen Persisting Perception Disorder (HPPD). The cause of HPPD is not fully known. It only occurs in someone who has previously ingested a hallucinogen, such as LSD (acid), but it is not caused by the retention of the drug in the body. Flashbacks can happen days, weeks, months, or even years after taking the drug.

As our client sat on his bunk in jail, he would suddenly believe that he was being attacked by an animal which he described as a groundhog. Several other times, he would look at the front of his cell and believe that the bars were not there. He would then walk into them, injuring himself. Our psychiatrist did his research and advised us that, while our client had severe anger issues and he was a drug addict, he was not, and had not been, mentally ill as described under the law.

Given that insanity was not an available defense, and since our client admitted that he intentionally hit her, our best hope was to argue to the jury that, while he intended to hit the little girl, he did not intend to kill her. We asked the prosecutor to reduce the charge to second-degree murder, but he refused. We went to trial and the jury found him guilty of second-degree murder.

WHY DO WE NEED TRIALS?

My mother was not very happy that I was being made to defend "these people" and she said that I should just tell the judge that I didn't want to represent any more murderers. I tried to explain to her that everyone was guaranteed a competent attorney to help them if they were charged with a crime such as murder. Her reply was, "Why bother? All three of your clients admitted that they had murdered someone!"

I explained that all three of my clients admitted that they had killed someone but not necessarily murdered them; there was a difference. This did not satisfy her and she said, "If you kill someone, it is murder and you should be hung."

I replied, "If you are sleeping in your bed and a man with a knife comes into your bedroom and says that he is going to kill you, is it murder if you reach into your nightstand, pull out a gun, and shoot him dead?"

"Of course not. That is self-defense!" Mom would answer.

"If Dad is in the Army and he shoots an enemy soldier, is he guilty of murder?" I asked.

"No, that's self-defense again," she'd say.

"I am cleaning my rifle, I don't realize that it is loaded, and I shoot my sister?" I suggest.

"Well, that would be an accident, but you should have been more careful."

"I've been drinking and I drop my loaded gun, it fires, and my neighbor is shot?" I ask.

"I guess that is an accident, but you shouldn't be drinking!"

"I truly believe that someone is trying to kill me and so, I kill them first?" I say.

"Why did you believe that they were going to kill you? Was that true?"

"I get into a fight and I punch someone who falls, hits his head on the curb and dies."

"You shouldn't be fighting, but if the other guy started it, I guess you didn't know that he would hit his head on the curb."

"The common fact in all six incidents is that someone killed another person! The state needs to determine what level of responsibility each of

LEGAL PROFESSION

the killers had and the jury needs to decide whether the prosecutor was right." I am not sure that she changed her mind about me representing "those people," but she did realize why a trial might be necessary.

After I had this conversation with my mother, I began to think that she might be right about what was best for me. My civil practice was busy and the criminal defense practice was physically and emotionally exhausting. The main problem I had in deciding whether to continue defense cases was, how to tell the judge that I can't take a case he wants to assign to me? In today's world, there are a lot of public defender offices that are established to handle these cases. The answer to my dilemma came with another phone call from the judge.

At this point in my legal career, I was serving in the United States Army Reserve as a JAG officer (Army lawyer). I had been asked to teach a class at the Judge Advocate General School in Charlottesville, Virginia and was there preparing to teach when, my wife called to tell me that our county sheriff had been shot and killed by a burglar!

Although I had been a criminal defense attorney, the sheriff and I had been good friends. I was very upset and I called the county prosecutor to get the details. He told me that they did not have anyone in custody yet, but they expected to make an arrest soon.

I asked the prosecutor if there was anything I could do. He told me no, but if I got appointed to represent the suspect, we could talk. Suddenly, I had inspiration. I said, "No, Larry, I want to help YOU on this one." He replied, "If I gave you something to do, that would be a conflict . . . . Ohhhh, I see! Well, maybe you could do some legal research on an issue that might come up." I replied, "Done."

I got back from Virginia, the suspect was caught, and the judge called me up. I explained that I was helping the prosecutor on this one. He wasn't happy, but he knew that I was not available. My career as a prosecutor was brief, but it served its purpose!

LET ME TELL YOU MY STORY

RBG AND THE UNITED STATES SUPREME COURT

For an attorney, the most prestigious government entity is usually the United States Supreme Court. In order to practice before this court, you need to submit an application, you must meet certain requirements, and you must be sworn in. The admission certificates may be obtained by a formal motion to the court or by appearing before the Court for an in-person ceremony.

Some years ago, our county bar association arranged for an in-person ceremony for any of the attorneys in the county who were qualified to apply. We were given a date and time to be there. A number of us then traveled to Washington DC for the swearing in ceremony.

Prior to the court opening, we were ushered into a room where they had coffee, tea, and water. As we waited, an assistant clerk entered the room and asked if we had any questions. I asked her if William Suter was still the clerk of the Supreme Court. She said that he was and asked if I knew him. I told her that I had met him on several occasions when he was the Judge Advocate General of the Army and I was a colonel in the Army JAG Corps.

The clerk left the room, but soon returned with a surprise visitor. She was accompanied by Justice Ruth Bader Ginsburg! Justice Ginsburg had been appointed to the Supreme Court in August of 1993. At this time, she was the most recent appointment to the Court.

I had the opportunity to talk informally with Justice Ginsburg along with several members of my law firm. It was a very interesting conversation. I am not sure whether or not we discussed law at all! We were all in awe of her taking the time to speak with us. She was about to begin hearing cases which she and the other justices would have to rule on. Their decisions could impact more than 300,000,000 Americans.

After Justice Ginsburg left, we were ushered into the courtroom where we sat in the front row seats. Within 10 to 15 minutes a man

LEGAL PROFESSION

walked in dressed in a 1700's style suit and a wig. I recognized him as Major General William Suter, the former Judge Advocate General of the Army. He hurried around the court room making sure that everything was ready for the entrance of the judges.

Suddenly, he turned toward our group and came over saying, "Dennis, how are you? It is good to see you again!" We shook hands and exchanged small talk. My associates were amazed, and quite frankly so was I! It had been a few years since I had talked to the General. I suspect that the assistant clerk pointed me out to him.

He then turned to the bench where the Justices were about to sit and he began the proceedings.

"The honorable Chief Justice and the Associate Justices of the Supreme Court of the United States, OYEZ! OYEZ! OYEZ!

All persons having business before the honorable Supreme Court of the United States are admonished to draw near and give their attention, for the Court is now sitting. God save the United States and this Honorable Court."

That day was one of the highlights of my professional career!

Our surprise visitor; Justice Ruth Bader Ginsburg

LET ME TELL YOU MY STORY

A STOLEN CAR IN A POLICE CHASE

One day my law partner, Faye and I had gone to lunch at a local Chinese restaurant. We were returning to the office and I was driving on a main street in town. It was a three-lane road for traffic east to west and west to east with a parking lane to the right of my lane.

I was in the eastbound lane and I was approaching a car that was traveling in the westbound lane. I was traveling about 30-35 miles per hour and the westbound car was approaching at a similar or even slower speed.

Suddenly, another westbound car that was traveling 50-60 miles per hour came into our lane in an attempt to pass the car in front of him. At that moment, I was facing a head on collision, so I swung my steering wheel sharply to the right, into the parking lane. Fortunately, there was no one parked in that lane at that location.

The approaching car turned partially back into its proper lane, and in doing so, it struck the driver's side of the car that it was trying to pass! Significant contact was made with the left side of the other vehicle. The collision caused the air bags to deploy and disabled both the errant car and the car in the other lane. The speeding car had missed colliding with the front of my car by only inches.

Just as the collision occurred between the other vehicles, a police car sped up to the scene with its lights on. It turned out that the speeding car was stolen and was being pursued by a sheriff's deputy!

In the moment of fear when we were facing a head-on collision, my partner and I had a quick realization that life can change in an instant. Maybe some of our perceived problems are minor and need to be placed into proper prospective so we can better enjoy life.

LEGAL PROFESSION

SUMMARY

The practice of law is a diverse profession. The underlying job description is to help your clients by solving problems they are facing or by preparing them to avoid problems arising in the future.

It can be very satisfying when you are able to solve a client's problem, but it can be disheartening when you fail to do so. You can't win every time unless your name is Perry Mason.

Each day you take on the problems of others. This can wear on you, but if you don't feel disappointed, you may not have the proper empathy to be a lawyer.

I practiced this profession for over fifty years. There were days when I wished I had become a teacher and there were days, weeks, months, and years when I was joyful that I had the opportunity to do what I spent much of my life doing, helping others.

Dennis in his role as a boy scout leader

Chapter 8

SERVICE TO OTHERS

WHAT IS THE ESSENCE of life? According to the Greek philosopher Aristotle, it is to "Serve others and do good."

In my opinion, this declaration by Aristotle, which was made more than 2500 years ago, is still the profound truth. If we would all shape our lives around this philosophy, the world would be a better place for everyone. As Mahatma Gandhi put it, "The best way to find yourself is to lose yourself in the service of others."

For nearly 50 years I have lived and worked in a small town. In that environment, a natural part of life was to give back the community. The desire to serve arose for different reasons. In my case, my parents had lived a life filled with serving others. My church emphasized that a Christian is expected to serve others. But another important reason was that it was possible to make a real contribution to the community we had chosen to live in.

I have included a list of many of my civic endeavors at the end of this section and broken them down into what area of service was addressed. I would just like to emphasize, I always gained more in my life's satisfactions when I was helping others as they traveled through their life than when I became self-centered on my own, as we all do at times.

COMMUNITY DEVELOPMENT

Over the past 50 years, my hometown of Marysville has evolved from a small sleepy town to a vibrant, active community. Union County ranks second in the growth rate for the state. There are 88 counties in Ohio. This can be an exciting and positive change or it can negatively impact the hometown atmosphere we were first attracted to.

When Honda of America Manufacturing announced in the late 1970s that they would be locating a manufacturing plant eight miles outside of Marysville, there was a sense of excitement and, for some, a sense of dread. The plant would provide many employment opportunities but, it would also present many problems which needed to be addressed.

If the local governments did not properly plan and implement the guidelines necessary for orderly growth, the county and the city could suffer. Honda was not the only large manufacturing facility to be located in Marysville. The O M Scotts company, the world's largest manufacturer of lawn care products, has its world headquarters located here as well.

I decided to get involved in some of the organizations that would study and make recommendations to the governing officials. I was initially appointed to the Economic Development Action Plan committee which took a broad-based view of the challenges which we would probably be facing and then explored the sources of funding which would be needed to prepare for the change. Our findings were then shared with the local government officials and interested members of the public.

I also served on the Marysville Comprehensive Plan Committee which made specific recommendations to the City Council regarding planning and zoning.

I was active on the Marysville Housing Council which evaluated and approved or disapproved tax abatements for new construction. I was the only non-government member of the committee.

The core of our county is "Uptown" Marysville. I served on the Chamber of Commerce group called Uptown Revitalization Team. Our mission was to preserve and strengthen the uptown area, which had initially been built in the late 1800s.

The Union County Chamber of Commerce and the Economic Development arm of the Chamber were instrumental in organizing and implementing many of these working groups. There are currently over 500 members of the Union County Chamber. I was on the governing board of the Chamber and served as its president. In 2017 I was named by the UCCC as the Union County Businessman of the Year.

CHURCH ACTIVITIES

I will cover my volunteering with my church in more depth in the chapter on religion, but Karen and I have attended the Trinity Lutheran Church in Marysville, Ohio for over 50 years.

Karen has given of her time in many activities and currently serves as a Stephen Minister. In that capacity she is paired with someone who has requested support in building their faith. The objective is to strengthen the care receiver in order that, through God, they will be better able to deal with life.

I have served on Church Council and two call committees. I also organized and conducted a Bible study class for nine years. I have served as a communion assistant and I man the visitor/help desk on Sunday mornings.

I have also participated in church plays and skits.

LEADERSHIP INSTITUTE

In order to integrate into community service, it was important to learn more about the history of Union County and about the current organizations which were actively engaged in public service.

In 2004, a friend of mine was working for the Union County Chamber of Commerce and was asked to organize a Leadership Institute. This group was tasked with choosing 20 community leaders who would meet once a week for eight weeks to learn about the local government, the school system, the law enforcement, and judicial system amongst other aspects of life in Union County.

While immersing themselves in these learning experiences, they got to know each other and learn about the organizations which each participant worked for. I was thrilled when I was asked to be a member of the initial Institute and I believe that I learned a great deal about the community I lived in. I also made many friends and business contacts.

The Leadership Institute has had a new class almost every year since and I know that Union County has benefitted because of these efforts. There are now hundreds of men and women who hold important jobs in the community and who have a better appreciation for the community in which they live and work.

SERVICE TO OTHERS

SOCIAL SERVICES

A community grows by building houses, factories, and infrastructure. It thrives if its people are, in large part, more important than the physical structure. That means that the community provides adequate physical and mental health services to everyone.

Marysville has a very good regional hospital which is owned by the county. In addition to its own staff and a number of board-certified physicians, the hospital also has a partnership with Ohio State University. I had a small part in this important entity by serving on the development council, and Karen and I supported the hospital in some of its building drives and fundraisers.

My main interest in social services was in the mental health area. I was appointed by the county commissioners to serve on the Mental Health Board for a total of eight years. I was president of the board for three of these years.

Some of the major challenges which we faced when I was the board president included establishing a working relationship with the county hospital administration, establishing and staffing half-way houses, and providing inpatient facilities for those suffering from mental illness.

After leaving the Union County Mental Health Board, I continued to act as the hearings attorney for the local mental health agency. In this capacity I would represent Union County when an involuntary hospitalization was thought to be necessary. I was also asked to serve on the Mary Haven Mental Health Board in the state capital of Columbus. This non-profit organization is one of the largest mental health and addiction agencies in Ohio.

GUARDIANSHIP SERVICES

Within the last 10 years, the Union County Probate Judge and I collaborated on establishing a board to provide guardians to those people who needed one but did not have a relative who could perform the services. Also, it served to ensure that county agencies were providing services which their wards needed.

The Union County Guardianship Services Board now has a membership of individuals representing most of the social service agencies in the county. This organization is designed to find and serve the most vulnerable individuals in the county. Often, there are mental health issues and there may be problems with alienation from the family. One of the objectives is to address the needs of these wards prior to the intervention of the police or the courts.

We now have professionals in place to act as guardians and the inclusive nature of the Board provides for a smooth provision of services to the client. A large portion of the funding for this is from local charitable donations.

CHILDREN

Just as those who are aged or infirm, the youth of a community need someone to work with their parents to provide guidance and activities which will support individual and community well-being.

BOY SCOUTS

When we moved to Marysville, the demands on my time were significant. I was the trial lawyer for a busy law firm. I was a husband and father of a two-year-old, with another child soon on the way. Still, I knew I wanted to become involved in the community and Karen and I were meeting and spending time with many new friends.

One of these friends was John Eufinger, the husband of my co-council for my murder cases. One day, when John, Charlotte, Karen, and I were grilling some bratwursts, we started talking about our experiences as youth in the Boy Scouts. We decided to look into helping out a local troop, perhaps by being merit badge counselors or helping out the scoutmaster on camping trips.

It turned out that one of the local troops needed a scoutmaster and they asked if we would take on that position. We said we were rather limited on our free time, but we would come to a meeting to see if we could help in some way.

We walked into the meeting and were introduced to everyone as the new scoutmasters. We cautioned that we had not decided to take on the leadership role yet but, by the end of that evening, the enthusiasm and the pleas for help led us to agree to serve as co-scoutmasters.

John and I instituted a number of changes, including introducing the troop to Camp Tuscazoar, which had been the primary camping area that I had spent my youth in some thirty years earlier. In fact, this was the camp my dad went to as a youth in the 1930's!

After a few years, I couldn't justify the time it took and John became the scoutmaster. He became one of the best leaders in central Ohio and his service to the troop has lasted for decades.

YMCA

In the 1970's, Union County was affiliated with the Columbus YMCA. We did not have a building to conduct our activities and we often used local schools or other government buildings.

As the population of the county grew, so did the demand for a real YMCA. People wanted a pool and a gymnasium and, it turned out that there was also a desire among local businesses and industry. Not only was there interest, there was a willingness to donate significant funds.

I had been asked to serve on the YMCA Board and was eventually elected President. We began planning and fundraising and soon we realized our dream could come true.

Although I was no longer on the board when the construction of the new building was completed, I was thrilled to help bring it into being and to see that it had two pools (one therapeutic), a gymnasium, locker rooms, and racket ball courts!

BALLOON RALLY

One aspect of practicing law in a small town was the expectation that you could and would be an active participant in many of the community activities. As my family and my law practice grew, I joined the local community theater group and volunteered to act and sing in the fundraising events sponsored by the hospital and the YMCA.

A major event which was conducted annually was the balloon rally. Local businesses sponsored 30-35 hot air balloons which attracted thousands of spectators.

SERVICE TO OTHERS

For seven years, my law office sponsored a balloonist and his balloon. In return, our name was prominently displayed on the basket of the balloon and my wife, children, partners, and some staff got to ride in the balloon and to work on the launch, tracking, and return of the balloon.

I am not totally fearless when encountering heights and my first ascension found me tightly grasping the edge of the basket. Surprisingly, I found the ride to be smooth and fun. Unfortunately, the wind can make the landing a bit bumpy!

After the first year, I came to enjoy the balloon experience, but I always enjoyed helping to support the local charities which benefitted from this event.

PARTNERSHIP IN EDUCATION (P.I.E.)

In order to have a healthy, vibrant community, you have to have a healthy, vibrant school system. The school systems of Union County are first-rate but, like many other school systems in this country, the voters sometimes do not want to pay taxes to keep its operation up to what it should be.

When I was president of the Chamber of Commerce, the Marysville School District had failed to gain approval in three straight bond issues. This was creating a financial crisis and the district was looking at cuts to staff and faculty. There seemed to be a disconnect between the district and the public.

In my role as president for the Chamber, I approached a number of community residents and asked them a single question, "If you were to vote against the school levy, why would you do so?"

A significant number of them said that they had questions about the business decisions that were being made by the School Board. They knew that a school system was unique but, it still had to spend the money it was given in a wise, businesslike manner.

Since the Chamber of Commerce was primarily a group of businesses, I decided to get the Chamber involved by assessing how well the administration was employing good business decision and fiscal responsibility.

I first went to a high-ranking officer at Honda of America and explained my plan. He agreed with the plan, but cautioned that the School Board would probably be sensitive to any criticisms that might become public during the inquiries.

I sat down with professional facilitators from Honda and met with a high-ranking individual who was being loaned to us to co-chair the inquiry group we would put together.

We then approached the Superintendent of Schools and advised him of our plan. We emphasized that we would present our findings in the most favorable way, which was consistent with the truth. He was not opposed to a committee being formed, but when I explained that the committee would not include representation by the school system, including any appointments by them, he said that he did not believe that the School Board or the Teacher's Union would agree to cooperate unless they were represented.

SERVICE TO OTHERS

After further discussions with our industrial partners, all of the school representatives agreed to provide us with the information we needed.

Eleven months later, we published a report which was paid for by Honda and the O.M. Scott Company. This report covered our findings in the areas of Finances, Faculty, Facilities, Curriculum, and Community Relations. The school administration began to adopt many of our recommendations. The report also answered voters' questions regarding spending, and the newspaper helped with its wide distribution.

The next three levies were successfully passed. People have a right to know if their tax dollars are being spent wisely.

VISUAL & PERFORMING ARTS

The arts are a very important part of any community! Plays, musical performances, dance, and movies stoke the imagination of people of all ages, provide them with entertainment, and, at times, an escape from a troubled world.

I have been fortunate to participate in several arts activities such as community theater, charity variety shows, and working to bring professional acts to the community.

COMMUNITY CONCERTS BOARD

Living in Marysville, which is about 30 miles from Columbus, has the advantage of access to many restaurants, theaters, and other venues which offer food and entertainment to central Ohio. On the other hand, it is nice to have the entertainment come to our little town instead of us driving in Columbus.

I was privileged to be part of the board of Union County Community Concerts. This organization would book professional singers, dancers, or musicians and make them available to the members for a very reasonable cost. Most of the expense was paid by corporate and individual sponsors. I served as president of the board for three years and Karen and I continue to attend concerts decades later.

THE AVALON THEATRE
(A 1930's Movie Theater)

In 1936, the United States was still feeling the effects of the Great Depression with an unemployment rate of nearly 17%. Franklin Roosevelt was elected for his second term as President, and The New Deal was beginning to work.

In Germany, the summer Olympics were held in Berlin and Jesse Owens, a young black Ohio State student, won four gold medals with

Hitler in the stadium. Margaret Mitchell published her book "Gone with The Wind" and Life Magazine was created. Meanwhile, in Marysville Ohio, the Avalon Movie Theater opened its doors to the public.

In the mid-1930s, economic hardship was occurring around the world, and people needed a diversion to escape from reality. The answer for many was a trip to the local movie theater. There, they could laugh at the Marx brothers or Laurel and Hardy, or they could marvel at the acting of Bette Davis or Clark Gable. If dancing was your love, Fred Astaire and Ginger Rodgers were right there on the silver screen for your entertainment.

Realizing that people were enduring hard times, the federal government was subsidizing the construction of movie theaters. The cost of an average movie ticket was twenty-five cents. If you go to YouTube and search Avalon Theatre in Marysville, Ohio, you will see how popular movies were in these times.

An old movie lineup for the Avalon in 1951

The Avalon Theatre was the focal point for movies in Union County Ohio for decades. Unfortunately, television replaced movies as the most popular entertainment medium and the theater doors closed in 2009. The building was vacant for years and continued to deteriorate.

A local bank held the mortgage on the theater and, since it was in default, they foreclosed. Soon, the bank's president contacted us and asked if we would like to buy the theater for $60,000. Knowing that the building would require major renovations, we explained that we were not trying to make any money, we simply wanted to improve the Uptown area. The bank president again approached us and offered to sell the property for $60,000, but simultaneously donate $100,000 to the renovation project. So, a group of six private investors purchased the building.

The immediately needed repairs used just about all of the $40,000 we had netted from the contribution, including shoring up the foundation of the building.

We initially formed a nonprofit corporation called Marysville Uptown Theater with a mission to renovate and operate the Avalon Theatre. The next good fortune to descend upon us was a $350,000 capital improvement grant awarded to us from the State of Ohio. We hired an architectural firm as well as a remediator expert and a structural engineer to assess the cost and the viability of the project.

These experts then worked with a central Ohio construction company and we were advised that the estimated cost of rebuilding the building to serve as a theater and performing arts center was 2.8 million dollars!

We have spent more than ten years and hundreds of hours on this project. We've worked on fundraising, construction, programing, and public relations. Today, the theater is run by an executive director and a Board of Directors representing diverse sections of the community.

The dream is that the quality of life in Union County will improve by providing cultural arts experiences that will entertain, educate, and enrich the lives of its citizens. It is the goal of Marysville Uptown Theatre to

SERVICE TO OTHERS

provide the Union County community with a cultural arts center, paying homage to its 1930's art deco style. To this end, the front wall replicates the original theater façade.

The Avalon has a 240-seat movie theater auditorium as well as a 50-seat small screen viewing area. In addition, the County has begun talks with the Avalon Board to operate the Veteran's Memorial Auditorium which will seat nearly 500 people.

The Avalon is more than just a movie theater. It hosts live entertainment, both professional and local talent. It presents opportunities for business meetings and private parties. It has also begun to book speakers on many areas of interest.

If you have driven on South Main Street in Marysville, Ohio lately, you will see that construction has been completed. Marysville Uptown Theater worked closely with architects, contractors, and engineers to develop a concept that fits the mission and honors the historic integrity of the theater.

To get where they are today, the Board established a capital fundraising goal of $3.2 million. Over the past several years, the theater has received pledges of more than $3 million. The public campaign to cover programming costs is ongoing, but the theater itself is completed, open, and running.

Every day each of us does a self-evaluation of our quality of life. This involves many different factors. Our health and our family and friends' well- being are often in the forefront. I cannot make a great difference on all these individual needs, but I can work with others to make resources available in our community which will help its citizens to better enjoy life wherever they choose to live.

Community service not only helps others feel better, but it can have a major effect on our own well-being. Ask yourself, "What have I done to make this world a better place to live?" Remember, little things add up to big things.

The Avalon Theater in Marysville, OH during the final stages of its renovation

SERVICE TO LEGAL PROFESSION

REAL ESTATE CERTIFICATION COMMITTEE

In Ohio, an attorney cannot hold himself/herself out to be a certified specialist in a particular area of law unless you meet certain requirements set forth by the Ohio State Bar Association (OSBA) and it is approved by the Ohio Supreme Court (OSC).

You must have measurable involvement in the specialty area, fulfillment of ongoing education requirements, and an evaluation by other attorneys and judges familiar with your work.

In addition, you must pass a written examination which is composed and conducted by a select committee established by the OSBA and approved by the OSC. I was asked to serve on this committee in order to create a comprehensive examination to verify that those attorneys applying for real estate certification were qualified to bear the title of a certified specialist.

UNION COUNTY BAR ASSOCIATION

In Ohio there are various forms of bar associations. There is a state bar association which is established to address the concerns unique to Ohio attorneys and the Ohio public as it interacts with the legal system. I was a member of this association for almost fifty years and I participated in many of its activities.

Many Ohio counties have local bar associations and, my home county (Union County) has always had an active association. I served as president of our bar and for the last several years have served as the chairman of the Professionalism Committee. This committee oversees any complaints by or against attorneys in Union County. The committee is charged with gathering information and forwarding this information to the Ohio Supreme Court if requested to do so or if we believe it should be investigated even if not requested to do so.

Federal Bar Association

This group is located in Columbus, Ohio and limits its activities to matters involving federal courts and matters involving federal law. I was a member of this bar association for a period of time and served as its President for a year.

PUBLIC DEFENDERS

I served on the Public Defenders Committee on appointment by our Common Pleas Judge. In that capacity, we discussed the conduct of the local Public Defenders' group with the Public Defenders, the County Prosecutors, the Common Pleas Judge, and the County Commissioners. We would annually make a recommendation to the Commissioners regarding how much money the county should allocate for representation of indigents.

OHIO CRIMINAL JUSTICE SERVICES ADVISORY BOARD

I was appointed by the state to serve on the Ohio Criminal Justice Services Advisory Board (OCJS). This board oversaw the allocation and use of State and Federal grants in the administration of criminal justice services. I was honored to be asked to serve, however, I only served for a couple of years since I did not enjoy the politics involved in money matters at the state level.

MENTORING YOUNG ATTORNEYS

As the senior attorney in my law firm, I was always mentoring young attorneys regarding the practice of law. The Ohio Supreme Court established a formal mentoring requirement which all new attorneys were required to participate in.

Shortly after the inception of this program, The Ohio State University reached out to me and asked if I would agree to be a mentor. I agreed and they sent me the required course materials and a written confirmation that I was approved as an instructor for the program.

SERVICE TO OTHERS

The title of this required course was Lawyer to Lawyer Mentoring Program and it was set up to pair one experienced and certified attorney with a newly admitted attorney. These two would then meet at least six times over the course of a year and discuss the practice of law.

The mentors' kit included a predetermined list of subjects to be discussed. The new lawyer was allowed to ask relevant legal questions which were not listed in the agenda. When the new attorney had successfully completed these sessions, the mentoring attorney would certify such completion to the Ohio Supreme Court and the new attorney would be given credit.

I enjoyed serving as a mentor although I spent many more hours than the minimum required by the course.

SERVICE TO COMMUNITY BOARDS

As an attorney, I was constantly being approached by someone out of the office who had a quick legal question. (Something along the lines of: If you wouldn't mind . . . it's probably a simple answer . . . if necessary, I could come into the office . . .) I would usually acquiesce and, if it really was simple, I would answer without a charge.

In Union County there were several boards who had a number of legal questions arise rather frequently and I seemed to be the one to be asked. I found it easier to make myself available to the group as their official counsel. It made the asking and answering easier and, sometimes, it led to actual paying representation.

The local mental health agencies, the local Board of Realtors, and the local Builders' Association considered me their lawyer and they felt free to ask legal questions without a guilty conscience.

As the attorney of the Board of Realtors, I planned and conducted continuing education classes which were certified by the State for required credits. I did this for over 20 years, until the state Board of Realtors established their own courses.

TEACHING THE LAW

Over the years in Union County, I have been asked to teach various legal subjects to community members and local lawyers. I've taught estate planning, land use, litigation techniques, legal ethics, real estate transfers, and real estate title.

When I was a Major, I taught at the U.S. Army Judge Advocate General's School in Charlottesville, Virginia. I taught there for five years during two-week annual training periods. The 200+ students were attorneys from all over the United States.

The fulltime faculty and staff of the JAG School oversaw and evaluated my instruction, and the courses were often attended by the Judge Advocate General of the Army.

SERVICE TO OTHERS

DENNIS A. SCHULZE
18606 Boerger Road, Marysville, Ohio 43040
dennisschulze555@gmail.com

FAMILY

- My wife, Karen, and I have been married for more than 50 years.
- We have a daughter, a son, and four grandchildren

EDUCATION

- Graduate of Alliance High School, Alliance, Ohio – 1961
- Graduate of Mount Union College – Bachelor of Arts – 1965
- Graduate of Ohio State University, College of Law, Juris Doctorate – 1968
- Graduate of Judge Advocate General School, U.S. Army – 1969

SERVICE TO PROFESSION

- Senior Partner of Schulze, Howard, and Cox Law Firm; now Schulze, Cox, and Will
- Admitted to practice before United State Supreme Court and U.S. District Court Southern Ohio
- Admitted to practice before Ohio Supreme Court and U.S. Court of Military Appeals
- Founder of Midland Title Agency of Union County & Midland Development Services, Ltd.
- Former member of Real Estate Certification Committee, Ohio State Bar Association

- Member and former president of the Union County Bar Association
- Former member of Union County Public Defender Committee – County appointment
- Former member of the Ohio Criminal Justice Services Advisory Board – State appointment
- Mentor for young attorneys – Supreme Court appointment
- Legal advisor for Mental Health Agencies, Board of Realtors and Builders' Association
- Taught real estate, estate planning, and land use courses to clients and other professionals
- Served as guest instructor at Judge Advocate General School, University of Virginia

SERVICE TO COMMUNITY

- Project Manager and Chairman of the Board of Trustees for Avalon Uptown Theatre Revitalization
- Member of Marysville Housing Council & Economic Development Action Plan Committee
- Member Marysville Comprehensive Plan Committee
- Former Board member of Ohio Veterans Hall of Fame Foundation
- Former Board member and President of Union County Chamber of Commerce
- Active member of Trinity Lutheran Church
- Former member and President of Union County Community Concerts Board
- Former member and Chairman of Union County Mental Health Board

SERVICE TO OTHERS

- Former member and President of Union County YMCA Board
- Former Boy Scout Leader and Cub Master
- Founder of Partnership in Education (PIE) project
- Former Board member of Maryhaven Recovery Services
- Charter member of Union County Leadership Institute
- Co-founder and Member Emeritus of Union County Guardianship Services
- Retired Colonel in the United States Army
- Former Commander 9th Military Law Center
- Former Staff Judge Advocate, 83rd Army Reserve Command
- Author of "Welcome to the Army," now available on Amazon and Apple

Chapter 9

LEISURE TIME

A NUMBER OF CHAPTERS in this book deal with giving of your time to help others. Time is precious and you must be sure to save a lot of time for your family.

While you are at it, the way to make and keep friends is to spend quality time with them and let them know that you do care about them.

When you evaluate the time that you have given others, don't forget a very important person who needs some of that time you are allocating. YOU!

Most of us have many interests. Some are shared with others and some may be unique to your circle of friends. Whatever your interests, they should give you a sense of joy and fulfillment. They should not be counter-productive. (NO SMOKING ALLOWED!)

Okay, I have a confession to make. When I was in law school, and for a few years after, I enjoyed fussing with my pipe and, on special occasions, puffing on a fine cigar. I justified this by saying it relaxed me. I know that adverse risks are high and I hope you don't follow my wayward action. (I'm sure you will find other parts of this book where I strayed from good decisions!)

I have chosen a few of my favorite pastimes to share with you. (Reading, Theater & Movies, Sports, and Travel.)

There are obviously many other pastimes you might enjoy, including quality time with your spouse, playing games with your children, meditation . . . the list goes on and on.

Here is how I unwind.

READING

Reading has always been important to me. Naturally, I had to do extensive reading in college and law school. And, when I practiced law, the need increased my reading extensively.

What interested me most? Those were the books which I read for entertainment rather than from necessity. When I look at my bookshelves and couple that with my use of electronic books, I realize why reading has been important to me. It stimulates my mind and provides me the opportunity to not only learn new things but also to be immersed in other worlds. It helps me to smile or even LOL. Sometimes it spurs me into action or helps me to clarify my beliefs.

Although I love to read books, I am not the world's greatest reader. My wife probably reads twice as many books as I do and she is currently in two book clubs. My choice of reading may not inspire anyone, but for purposes of explaining who I am, here is a summary of many of the books I have collected, and which currently occupy bookshelves in my house:

- I have hundreds of paperback mysteries and action books. Not counting the many hundreds that I have given away to charity.
- I have a number of hardbacks; fiction and nonfiction.
- I have 25 Hardy Boys mysteries as well as Tom Swift and Tom Quest. (Popular in the 50's.)
- I have books about words, puzzles, trivia, and quotations.
- I have Peanuts cartoon books.
- I have books about the law and the Constitution.
- I have books about former presidents and other historically significant people.
- I have many travel books.
- I have Army books, including "Welcome to the Army," which I wrote prior to this book.
- I have at least 10 versions of the Bible or Bible study books, as well as one copy of the Koran.
- I have classics, including 20,000 Leagues Under the Sea, Swiss Family Robinson, and Treasure Island.
- I have a couple of Spanish textbooks and 20 Spanish CD's.

LEISURE TIME

- I have sports books related to The Ohio State University.
- I have self-help books.
- I have some schoolbooks.

When my son was in high school, I had a book called Quiz Time which was 2 inches thick and filled with questions and answers. I would ask my son to name a page and he would give me a number. I would go to that page, select a question, and he would attempt to answer it. If he didn't know the answer, I would disclose it and we would discuss that subject. Both of us were gaining knowledge and, as a bonus, we were spending time together.

I still enjoy reading and I get very good advice on what books to read from Karen.

THEATER AND MOVIES

One of the things that Karen and I enjoy is live theater. A local university nearby has an excellent reputation for producing plays and musicals. In fact, some of their graduates go on to perform on Broadway.

Another source of entertainment which we have utilized over the years is the Broadway Series which consists of professional members who light up the Ohio Theater in Columbus. This theater seats 2,791 people and was built in 1928. Its interior is lavishly decorated in the Spanish Baroque style and has a large chandelier which hangs over the audience.

Once, in 2018, when we were attending a showing at this theater of the movie "Gone with the Wind," the battle scenes had progressed to the attack on Atlanta. During this scene there were numerous cannon blasts and other explosions. As we sat transfixed, audience members began pointing at the chandelier which had begun to shake and gently sway!

How could they add to the cinematic effect by literally shaking the theater? It turns out that they didn't. As I discovered when I left my seat to ask a theater staff person what was going on, it turned out that a 1.5 earthquake had struck Ohio at the very time that Atlanta was being demolished!

Fortunately, no one in the theater, and I assume no one in the movie, was injured.

SPORTS

Sports have always been an important part of my life. My physical development did not allow me to reach the pinnacle of success in any sport, but that did not diminish my interest.

I was in my teens when I first experienced competitive sports. At my high school graduation, I was 5'8" tall and weighed 120 pounds. I was not a very fast runner; however, my coordination skills and my deep desire to compete allowed me to experience the thrill of victory and the agony of defeat.

My first competitive team sport was Little League baseball. I was an infielder who had a decent batting average. I actually made the "traveling team," although I spent most of the time on the bench.

My most vivid memory of Little League was a tournament game against a nearby city's team. It was the seventh inning with runners on base and two out. The opposing team's pitcher had to be at least 6 feet tall and he had a fastball that was probably over 80 miles an hour. The coach looked down the bench and signaled me to pinch hit.

Shocked, I grabbed a bat and walked out to home plate. I spent as much time as the home plate umpire would allow and I stepped up to the plate. I looked out at this giant who was about to throw a missile near me and I crouched down to reduce the strike zone.

LEISURE TIME

He went into his stretch, rocked back, and threw the ball at a speed I could not see or counter. Strike one!

He then prepared for and threw strike two!

The first two pitches were in the zone, but I didn't swing. The last pitch was about to be thrown and I was determined to hit it out of the park.

He stretched, he pitched, and I swung. I missed. Strike three!

Shortly after this momentous occasion, I decided I should try out football.

As a seventh grader entering junior high school, I had a choice to make. Would I continue to play the saxophone and try to work myself up to first chair in the band, or would I try out for the football team? To my parents' dismay, I chose football.

When I reported to the first practice for seventh grade football, I didn't know what the coaches thought of my decision. Looking back, I don't imagine that they viewed me as the savior of the team.

I wasn't.

The coaches decided to have me play wide receiver. This may have been to keep me as far out of the way as possible. I know it wasn't because of my blazing speed.

I was on the team for all three years of junior high school and I played whenever the victory was assured or the defeat was inevitable, but I was on the team. I will get to my high school career soon.

Basketball was probably my best potential sport. Oh sure, I probably needed to grow another 6 to 7 inches and bulk up a bit. I never tried out for the school basketball team, but I played a lot of sand lot games against some pretty good players and I held my own unless they were 6'5" or above.

*Future NFL players from Alliance High School,
Charles King & Jim Davidson*

A STATE FOOTBALL CHAMPIONSHIP

In Ohio, football (American style) is very important. (Ok, so is football world style, but let's talk about the American style that I played.) There are two professional teams and many college and high school programs that are supported by millions of Buckeyes!

My introduction to the sport was on the junior high and high school level. The 1958-59 football season was a special one for me and the Alliance High School Aviators. We had fielded a good football team for a while now and in my sophomore year we were in the race to be crowned state champions. In fact, we finished high in the state rankings all three years that I attended AHS.

LEISURE TIME

My school was located in Stark County, Ohio which had a national reputation for excellent football teams such as Massillon and Canton McKinley. The Aviators played their games on the campus of a small college called Mount Union. There were more than 10,000 seats in the stadium and, on game day, it was usually filled with cheering fans.

Our archrival Massillon had their own stadium with 21,000 seats. Canton McKinley played in a stadium located next to the Pro Football Hall of Fame. Each year, two NFL teams came to Canton to play an exhibition game prior to the regular season. It was obvious that this area of the country was a football hot bed!

When our team schedule was arranged, distance within the state was not a factor. When I was a junior, we traveled to the southern part of the state to play Cincinnati Elder and, as a senior, we traveled to western Ohio to play Springfield. The amazing thing was that these trips did not entail a long bus ride. We flew to them on a chartered airplane! There was a very active booster club.

The primary reason that my sophomore season was so special was that we won the state of Ohio High School Football Championship for large schools. There were no playoffs in those days. The newspaper and radio sportscasters voted each week and, when we finished the undefeated season with a big win, we knew that we would stay number one.

As we traveled by buses from the last game to home, we were met at the county line by police cars and fire trucks, all with their lights flashing and sirens blaring! When we got back into town, people lined the streets clapping and shouting! We were then treated to a fantastic meal. I'm not sure what they would have done with the meal if we had lost.

I would love to tell you that I was the star player who scored the winning touchdown but the truth of the matter was that I had been injured and didn't play a down that year. I did however get a state championship jacket which got a lot of use.

As a side note, as my injury healed, the coach pulled me aside and urged me to become the head manager. The coach pointed out that I probably would not make the travel team as a player but I would get to go to every game as the manager. I would be given a lot of responsibility as one of the coach's assistants.

Our team's chartered plane!

I was 5 foot 8 inches tall and weighed 120 pounds (½ of one of our defensive linemen) and I believe that he was concerned that I would get hurt again. I really wanted to play football but I realized the sensibility of the coach's suggestion. I wasn't very fast, but I could throw a football over

50 yards. The question was, would the pass be accurate? I agreed to be the team's head manager.

During my junior and senior years, we played evenly with both of our rivals Massillon and Canton McKinley, winning some and losing some, but we did not repeat as state champions. In my senior year, we played seven teams that had been in the top twenty the year before and we finished third in the state.

The proof of the skill on our team included the fact that we had a number of players who received scholarships from Division 1 colleges and we had three players in my graduating class who ended up playing in the National Football League!

These memories are precious to me.

DEPUTIZED FOR BASKETBALL
(My Law Enforcement Career)

When I first practiced law in Marysville, I knew and worked with the members of the Union County Sheriff's Department and the Marysville Police Department. One day, the Sheriff asked if the local Bar Association would like to form a basketball team to play games against the law enforcement teams. I checked and soon we were having a great time in our little league.

Then, the sheriff advised us that they had signed up to participate in a tournament in Columbus which featured police departments from all over the state of Ohio. He asked if the law partners (Frank and I) would like to play on their team.

I questioned him on how we would qualify to play since we were not members of law enforcement. "No problem!" he said. "I will deputize you!"

It sounded like fun so Frank and I said yes.

LET ME TELL YOU MY STORY

We attended a few practices and found out that Frank and I would be starting guards. We traveled to Columbus where we were told that it was a double-elimination tournament and we would be playing the Ohio State Highway Patrol in the first game. Then a few days later we would be playing against the Akron Police Department.

Game time was soon upon us and we trotted out of the locker room into a gymnasium which had quite a few spectators. The highway patrol team had not yet made an appearance, but when they did, it was spectacular.

In a very disciplined manner, they began to do layups. Then they started shooting long shots. Finally, they began dunking the ball.

I had never seen such shooting and I didn't realize there were such tall highway patrolmen. None were less than 6 feet tall and several were in the 6' 5" range.

It turned out that this team brought together men from all over the state of Ohio. They had just completed a tour of games against law enforcement teams throughout the southern states.

It was gametime and our coach called me aside and told me to guard against their fast breaks. As soon as the game began, they got the tip and scored on a layup.

Soon, a pattern developed. If we shot and missed, they would grab the rebound, turn in midair, and throw to a teammate streaking toward our basket.

Mindful of our coach's instructions, I would race to the other end of the court at the same time as the ball did. I had no choice but to let them score or foul the would-be shooter. So, I fouled the shooter once, then again, and again. I fouled out in the first half.

We lost the game!

Next was a game against the Akron Police Department. Our coach decided to change tactics and told me to drive to the basket. That way, if I missed the shot, we would have a better shot at a rebound or I would get fouled.

LEISURE TIME

We entered the gym and saw that Akron PD was warming up. Then, I saw him. Standing near the basket was an Akron player who was 6' 6" to 6' 8" and he had to weigh 300 pounds. He was not fat, he was burly. I immediately sought out our coach and told him that I did not think the plan to attack the basket was going to work.

We lost our second game, but we had fun!

With Greg and Christina at an OSU game

SUITE SEATS

My love for college football is very strong. The Ohio State University is my favorite team, but I will watch any game that is televised.

Given the choice of watching a Hallmark movie or a football game, there is no contest. This is true even if the game is between two Division 3 teams or if the game was recorded in a previous year.

Karen realizes this fact and will often acquiesce in sending me to my man cave in the basement. Her surrender is now memorialized by a sign she bought at a craft show. It reads – This marriage is paused for football season.

Archie Griffin is the only college football player in history to win the Heisman trophy twice (1974 and 1975). He spent seven years in the National Football League and, after retiring from professional football, he became the president of the Ohio State Alumni Association. He also served as an assistant athletic director at Ohio State and used to make pregame talks to the football team before every game.

In the 1990s, I was at an OSU football game and it was pouring down rain. The game went on and so did the halftime events. I was wearing a thin plastic poncho that didn't completely cover my legs. I was miserable in the rain, so I was very happy when it briefly stopped.

Mr. Griffin was at midfield giving an award to someone and then he left the field and headed down to one of the end zones where I happened to be sitting. As he began to climb the stairs, he stopped to watch what was happening on the field. Despite the fact that there are about 100,000 seats in the stadium, he was standing right next to me. As he finished watching, I said, "Hey Archie, do you want to trade seats for the second half?" He laughed and replied that he would love to have these wonderful seats but they expected him back up in the trustee's box.

A few years later, I got lucky. As a lawyer I had represented many real estate developers. One of the companies I represented had a partner who was chairman of the Board of Trustees for The Ohio State University. One day he asked me if I would like two tickets to an upcoming game. He told me that they were not the best seats, but I knew that they would be better than any that I would have been able to buy. He then said, "Why don't

LEISURE TIME

you and your wife come and sit in the trustee's box?" I was shocked and immediately accepted his offer.

On the day of the game, we met my client at an elevator which went up to the suite level. He took us past the security people and we entered the suite. There were 20 to 30 people inside and a large table of food and drink sat in the middle of the room. Two large screen televisions were showing pregame activities and there, in front of us, was the window viewing area. It was open and stretched from about the 40-yard line to the other 40-yard line. I went over to the windows, which were open but could be closed in inclement weather, and I looked down on the field at the 50-yard line!

Dennis with a friend and the Governor of Ohio

This was going to be an awesome experience! I then looked around the room. I did not recognize most of the people, but I did see the president of The Ohio State University chatting with someone. As I looked further, I saw Archie Griffin! I guess I wouldn't have to worry about trading seats with him on that day.

I had been in my own little world and hadn't noticed that my wife had wandered off. I looked around the suite again and spotted her talking to some man. They seemed to be deep in conversation and I wondered who he was. Then, I looked again and recognized him as the governor of the state of Ohio!

I didn't interrupt and, when she rejoined me 5 to 10 minutes later, I asked her what they were talking about. She said, "Oh, I was telling him all about the Head Start program. He seemed very interested."

LEBRON JAMES – THE KING

I have talked about my love of football and I have to be honest; I am not a big NBA fan. I will watch an All-Star game, the championship game, or a Cleveland Cavaliers' game if Lebron James is playing.

A client of mine, whose corporate headquarters was in Cleveland Ohio, asked me if I would like a couple of tickets to a regular season game of the Cavaliers. I figured that they would be decent seats and I said yes.

My wife didn't want to go since it was a 2 ½ hour drive to Cleveland. I asked my friend Len if he would like to go. He is not an NBA fan either but he said, "Sure, I'll go."

I received the tickets on the day before the game and didn't pay much attention to where they were, since I didn't know anything about the Cleveland Coliseum. My friend and I didn't get an early start and I calculated that we would get there close to game-time. We arrived in Cleveland with about 15 to 20 minutes to spare and walked over from the parking garage to the game site.

I pulled out the tickets and approached an usher. I asked him where we should go and he replied, "Down the hall to the elevator and then go

LEISURE TIME

down one floor." As we were about to leave, he handed us back the tickets and said, "Who's your daddy?" I must have looked confused, and he added, "Where did you get the tickets?" I told him and he indicated that made sense.

Len and I went down the hall, got on the elevator and pushed the button for the first floor. As the elevator doors opened, we were greeted by security people who inspected the tickets and then said, "Over there is a complimentary bar and next to that are the appetizers. The game is about to start. The court is that way." He pointed down a hall ahead of us and said, "When you get to the next hall, turn left." We skipped the food and drink and headed down the hall.

As we turned left, we found ourselves directly behind the referees and the Cavaliers' cheerleaders who were standing with their hands over their hearts. More security people hurried over and, as soon as the national anthem ended, the referees and cheerleaders ran onto the floor.

Our tickets were checked once again. The security person nodded his approval and told us to walk behind the nearby basket and look for our seats behind the bench and timekeeper. The crowd was cheering loudly (I don't think it was for us) and we began to follow instructions. We just passed the basket when we realized we were within 15 feet of Lebron James! We did not say hello, and he did not even look at us.

We turned the corner and started looking for the box number. We found it and we were seated in the second row of a box which had its own waiter! Throughout the game, we could hear many of the conversations coming from the bench.

I wondered how much these tickets had cost my client. I don't know how accurate it was but, on each ticket, it said $800. I wouldn't say that this one game made me a fan of the sport, but it did give Len and I something to talk about.

LET ME TELL YOU MY STORY

THE DEEP BLUE SEA

This life incident is about the sport of fishing. It is a well-known fact that fishermen tend to exaggerate their accomplishments. I can assure you that there are no exaggerations in this story beyond the usual fisherman's tale.

Karen, our daughter Christina, and I were on vacation in South Carolina with a couple of our friends. A good friend named Len and I decided to go deep sea fishing. Len was not a fisherman, but he said that it would be interesting to watch Christina and me fish.

We boarded the charter boat and headed for an area where the captain said we could catch what he called sand sharks. These fish averaged about 3 to 4 foot long and put up a decent fight. My daughter and I caught several sharks and I asked Len if he would like to try it. He said that he would like to give it a try.

The first mate baited the hook with a big chunk of meat and then threw the line into the water. It wasn't long after the pole was placed in the holder that it began to bend. The mate set the hook and handed the pole to Len.

The fish pulled stronger and Len began to slide toward the back of the boat. The mate and I grabbed him and strapped him into a chair. With advice from the mate, Len pulled up on the rod while reeling in the line. Each time Len was able to reel in line, it seemed that he was getting nowhere. It was obvious that the fish was not going to give up

This went on for at least 15 to 20 minutes and speculation was growing over what Len had on the line. After a grueling dual a black shadow started to emerge at the back of the boat. "It's a ray!" shouted the captain, as Len tried to finish the struggle. The captain then shouted, "I don't want that damn thing in this boat with us." Len and I looked at each other and said, "Neither do we."

The mate reached over and took control of the reel. He told us that the Manta Ray we had at the back of the boat was a female about five feet wide. The mate then released the hook and the giant ray swim out of sight. Len, who does not profess to be a fisherman, now had bragging rights that would put many real fishermen to shame!

After catching sharks and a huge manta ray, we still had a little time left to see if we could catch something else. We told the captain that we would like to continue to fish. The mate baited the hook and threw it out behind us as the captain was picking up speed. The chunk of meat was bouncing on the water when, all of a sudden, a pelican swooped down and grabbed the meat and the hook!

I don't believe that I have ever seen a more epic battle. (This was an even more epic one than we had with the Manta Ray!) The captain advised us that they couldn't just cut the line because the pelican would die. So, the mate slowly reeled in the bird who fought him every inch of the way.

When they got him up close to the boat, the captain grabbed the bird by the neck so that he wouldn't get pecked, but the bird started to pummel him with his wings. The captain reached around him with his right hand and turned him so that he could do a bear hug on the wings. The mate then removed the hook and the captain released the bird.

The captain got clipped by both wings and he was not happy. Judging from the squawks coming from the water, neither was the pelican! He did, however, fly away.

Just a couple more facts regarding that ray, the one which Len caught was just a little bigger than 5 feet wide. The confirmed world record for a manta is 25 feet wide and weighed 5,070 pounds! The fact that Len's ray was caught off of South Carolina is out of the ordinary since manta generally like tropical or sub-tropical waters.

TRAVEL

Travel has always been an important part of my life. When I was young, my family did not venture far. About the farthest that I can remember going was to Florida to attend my uncle's wedding.

I did get to go to Washington D.C. with the school patrol and with my family we visited friends or family members in states nearby such as Pennsylvania, Wisconsin, and Indiana.

For family fun we would go to a State Park, Lake Erie, Amish country, and once, to the state's capitol, Columbus. On special vacations my family would travel to Canada to go fishing or to visit Niagara Falls.

As I graduated from college my worldly experiences were limited. Then, I began law school at Ohio State and my travel options were even more limited. Most of my time was spent in Ohio and, although I love Ohio, I was beginning to have a desire to see other parts of the U.S. as well as other parts of the world.

The United States government decided to help me out. I was drafted (then joined) the Army. When I was on active duty, we were fortunate to be about 30 miles out of Boston. If we went northwest, we would reach the mountains of New Hampshire and Vermont. The hiking was great.

If we went east, we would pass through history in Lexington, Concord, and Waldon Pond. Boston was an easy drive (until you got into the city) and offered many amenities such as dining, plays, and sporting events.

North was Maine with spectacular coastlines along the Atlantic Ocean. Karen had relatives in Massachusetts and Maine who introduced us to clambakes and fresh boiled lobster.

After joining the Army, I spent the next five years in New Jersey, Texas, New Mexico, Georgia, Virginia, Massachusetts, New Hampshire, Vermont, and New York.

LEISURE TIME

When I separated from the active Army, we returned to central Ohio and settled in a small town near Columbus, Ohio where we both had gone to school.

We loved New England where we had lived for the last four years and we knew that there were a lot of great cities to settle in. However, we wanted to stay in a family-friendly area which was slow paced, but also near major action. Columbus fit that criterion with more than a million people in the metropolitan area.

When we settled in Marysville there were about 22,000 people in the city and 50,000 in Union County which bordered on Franklin County and Columbus.

Our travels within the U.S. and Canada eventually expanded into 38 states and then to more than 25 foreign countries. When I was serving in the U.S. Army Reserve I traveled to Panama, Mexico, Germany, Japan, and Korea, as well as many U.S. States including Hawaii.

We had vowed that when our children were old enough, we would introduce them to a variety of cities in various parts of the eastern United States.

We fulfilled that promise by taking the children to Boston, New York, Washington DC, South Carolina's shoreline, Atlanta, Northern Florida, Tennessee, Chicago, and other places of interest including Texas, Los Angeles, Seattle, and San Francisco. We also traveled into Canada to visit Toronto, Montreal, and Quebec.

Karen and I have been to numerous islands in the Caribbean as well as Croatia, Slovenia, Spain, Germany, England, Austria, and Italy.

We visited our son and his wife in Chile where he was attending graduate school for his MBA. We also visited him in Singapore where he lived for five years while working for Expedia. We also spent New Year's in Cambodia where we experienced the most spectacular entertainment for this holiday.

Each of these travel experiences provided my wife and me an opportunity to experience different places, people, and cultures in addition to giving us so many wonderful memories.

In Hawaii with sea urchin

In Minnesota with a pike I caught

Karen and I at the Grand Canyon

Karen and I in Hawaii

Our 40th Anniversary in Aruba

LEISURE TIME

ANTIGUA

Over the years, Karen and I took a number of cruises in the Caribbean and also flew into some of the islands to spend a week on shore. For instance, we spent our 33rd and 35th anniversaries on Aruba.

On one occasion our son and daughter-in-law treated us to a cruise to Antigua. There, we experienced one of the most memorable experiences when Karen decided she wanted to go swim with the sting rays!

Now, I have visited the Columbus Ohio Zoo and had an opportunity to "pet" sting rays which were small and had been de-barbed. This challenge was different since these creatures were wild sting rays who lived in the ocean and had not been surgically modified.

We signed up for the experience and were soon on our way to a bay just off the island. Our boat pulled up to a man-made dock and we were fascinated by the large black circles moving slowly through the waters.

The tour guide told us that we would be entering the waters and we should move slowly, shuffling our feet because we didn't want to step on any rays!

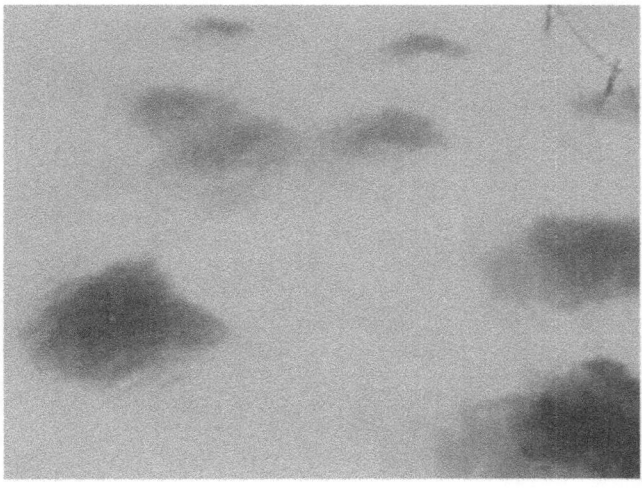

LET ME TELL YOU MY STORY

STINGRAYS IN ANTIGUA

Karen said she would take pictures of me swimming (shuffling) with the sting rays. I firmly told her that this was her idea and she was going in the water with me!

She finally agreed and told me that she was going to be right behind me. The guide finally said, "Everyone in the water," and I happened to be one if not the first in the water.

The guide handed me a plastic cup with small dead fish in it and proceeded to give me instructions on how to feed the rays.

Since I was the only one dumb enough to have the "bait," I was soon the center of attention. I pulled out a fish and a rather large sting ray swam right up to my chest and I fed him. (Her?) I was soon out of fish.

No one else had begun to feed the rays, so I was the center of their attention. The next thing I knew was that my first ray decided she wanted more and she approached me and head-butted me.

I held her to my chest until the guide began to give fish to the others and I was able to return to the boat.

I have a hungry friend

LEISURE TIME

I MEET A STAR
(A Stranger in Paradise)

In the 1980s an opportunity came along which I could never have imagined. My Uncle George and his wife Donna had moved to Hawaii some years before. They now planned to take a cruise for their vacation. They were going to be gone for about 30 days and needed someone to "house sit" for them. They owned a modest home on the north part of the Island of Kauai.

They asked if Karen and I could help them out. A month in Hawaii, going to the beach, picking fruit off the trees, and living in tropical splendor?! We thought it over for about five minutes and then said "YES!" We were given the dates that they would be gone, and reality began to set in. Could I afford to be gone from my office for 30 days? What about our children who were 14 and 17. Could we afford the cost of four flights? We talked over all the reasons why we shouldn't go then we realized that this was something that we might never get to do again.

We knew that this should be a family experience and Christina and Greg were going to go with us! The decision was made but we needed to work out the details. I determined that I could not take more than two weeks off from my job.

We decided that we could fly separately and save some money. I was a member of the Army Reserve and one of the perks was the ability to fly for free on a military aircraft. I checked with the Wright Patterson Air Force Base Flight Section and found that, with a little maneuvering and a lot of luck, I could get to Hawaii for free. Karen and Greg would follow me on a commercial flight, and, because of her job, Christina would leave two weeks later. So, Karen and Greg would have to be the primary house sitters for 30 days, while I would need to return home after 15 days. Christina would join Karen and Greg for the last two weeks.

On the day that I was to leave, I drove to Wright Patterson and signed in. I was required to wear my dress green uniform and I was told that there could be a five hour wait until my ride took off. I was supposed to ride in a cargo plane with web seats and no frills.

The first stage of my trip would be from WPAFB to St. Louis. I would then take a shuttle to a commercial airport where I would catch a military charter flight to Oakland California. After that I would catch a flight to the Hawaiian Island of Oahu. My aunt and uncle lived on Kauai and there were no military flights from Oahu to Kauai so I would need to pay for a commercial flight on Hawaiian Airlines.

As I sat in the waiting room at WPAFB time seemed to be dragging. After 2 hours, a man in a flight suit with a pilot's helmet under his arm said, "Who is going to St. Louis?" I held up my hand and he said, "Come on, let's go!"

We walked through some doors and out onto the runway. The pilot pointed at a six passenger Lear jet and said, "That's your ride." It turned out that this plane had just brought a Navy Admiral from St. Louis to Ohio. On its return flight, the plane would be carrying a pilot, a copilot, and one flight attendant as well as one passenger, me!

The flight to St. Louis was swift and smooth. I caught the shuttle to the St. Louis airport and checked in at the assigned gate. There were hundreds of other military personnel milling around and I asked the clerk how many flights were going to leave from this gate? The response was that there would only be one plane leaving. That plane was going to Oakland.

My heart sank, because my priority for a free flight was less than that for an active-duty individual. I asked the clerk if there were going to be enough seats for me to get on this flight. She replied, "Yes there will be." and she pointed out the window at a 747 jumbo jet which holds more than 400 passengers. I had started my trip on a six-seat passenger jet and was about to board a 400-seat giant!

I made it onto the plane and caught my flight to Oakland. From there, it was across the Pacific Ocean to Oahu. That morning as we landed,

LEISURE TIME

I hurried to the Hawaiian Airlines terminal, secured my ticket, and got on the small interisland plane bound for Kauai.

As I boarded, there was a man sitting in what I guessed was first class. He looked familiar, but I couldn't think of who he might be. We landed on Kauai and I called my aunt and uncle. They told me that they would be at the airport in about 45 minutes.

As I stood by my luggage in my army uniform, I watched the guy from the plane who I thought I knew. He was walking rapidly to and from the baggage carousel followed by four or five Airport employees. Finally, the baggage handlers scurried off and he looked around, then looked at me.

The next thing I knew, the unknown man walked over to me and soon we were talking like we were old friends. He told me that his suitcases were missing and that had never happened to him before.

I asked him where he lived, and he said that he lived in Los Angeles, but that he spent a lot of time in Hawaii. For about 10 to 15 minutes, we talked about many things. However, I did not ask him who he was.

Then, I saw some bags streaming down the conveyor belt and directed his attention to what was happening. He said, "Oh thanks" and he rushed toward what he hoped would be his belongings.

As soon as he left, I grabbed a passing employee and asked him who I had been talking to. He replied, "That's Michael Landon." I was amazed that the star of many television shows including "Bonanza" and "Little House on the Prairie" was so modest that he didn't feel the need to make sure I knew who he was.

As the last bag came down the ramp, Mr. Landon shrugged his shoulders and headed back to me. We talked (I should say he talked) for another minute or two but I was tongue-tied now that I knew who he was.

Eventually, I heard my uncle honk his horn and I shook hands with Mr. Landon and said goodbye. I couldn't wait to tell my uncle who I had just met. But he just shook his head and said that a lot of stars lived on or played on Kauai. He had met Kareem Abdul-Jabbar, Sylvester Stallone, and Betty White, among other stars.

I could tell that this was going to be an interesting adventure.

Chapter 10

FAITH

RELIGION HAS ALWAYS BEEN an important part of my life. My faith in God has usually been strong, although my dedication to organized religion has ebbed and flowed at times. I am not, however, going to tell you how to worship God. God has done that. The observance of a belief in God is an individual practice as unique as we are.

When I was growing up, my family attended a Missouri Synod Lutheran Church in Alliance, Ohio. At an early age I was baptized and a bit later I was confirmed into the church.

Unlike many denominations today, which have contemporary services and praise bands, my parents' church was very traditional and structured. There were times to stand up and times to sit down. There were times to sing a hymn (organ music not guitars & often accompanied by a choir), times to hear the words of the Bible, times to pray, a time to listen to the sermon, a time for communion, and a time to share your bounty with others. There was an emphasis on repetition and order. We knew the words for each part of the service by heart.

Each service began with the lighting of the candles and, at the end of the service, the extinguishing of the candles. I was chosen as an altar boy and I learned to light the candles in a certain order and to reverse myself when it was the end of the service.

My family was faithful in attending church, but we did not go more than once each week and on occasion we missed a Sunday or two. If we did miss worship, we would often have a family service led by Mom and Dad. It was a simple service consisting primarily of prayers and songs.

As I grew older, I justified increased absences from church with the excuse that I was very busy with work and schooling. I don't believe I ever drifted too far away from God, just the organized recognition of my devotion.

When I was in college, my church attendance was even worse and I justified this by feeling overburdened by the intense study requirements while attending school and working in an industrial supply store.

In my senior year, I was dating a girl who expressed a desire to go church with me. I told her that I would like to go to church, the question was which one. I knew that she had been a devout Roman Catholic. In reality, my family church was very much like a Catholic Church with the exception of the administrative order.

We discussed the issue and she told me that she too had drifted away from her family's religious practices. She said that she would be willing to attend the Lutheran church with me. We began to attend services and found them very fulfilling.

After a period of time, for different reasons, we quit dating. I guess that you could say that, because of this friendship, I reverted to my childhood faithfulness and continued to attend church after we quit dating.

As college graduation neared, my thoughts and energy turned to getting into and staying in law school. Whatever excuse I may have made, I look back and realize that this was an important time to have a strong dedication to religion and I may have been lacking.

I made it into and through law school (again with little church attendance) and then, reality smacked me in the face. I was drafted into the United States Army and my life changed drastically! School studies morphed into other types of learning. I was now being trained in light weapons infantry and ground to air missile defense. I was going into the danger zone and I was learning to kill in order to stay alive.

This was the height of the Vietnam War which claimed over 58,000 lives of U.S. troops. There is a saying which existed in World War I and II, "There are no atheists in the trenches (foxholes)."

Some veterans may take exception with this philosophy; however, I found it to be true for me. Even as I trained thousands of miles from the war zone, I began to go to the base chapel and have some serious conversations with God! (Listen to the Elvis Presley version of "Crying in the Chapel.")

I soon realized that life was precious. It was also finite and it was more meaningful when I shared it with God. It helped to understand that He was there beside me. While I am not saying that there was any direct intervention to keep me safe, I did spend almost 5 years on active duty without being sent to Vietnam.

After I was trained as an infantryman and I transferred to the Judge Advocate General's Corp, Karen and I were stationed at Fort Devens, Massachusetts. It was a beautiful community and we enjoyed being there. However, there were not any Lutheran churches within an easy driving distance. We tried a lot of different churches but our church attendance during those four years was not good.

When we left the active Army and I was about to begin my civilian profession as an attorney in Marysville Ohio, we asked the partners of my law firm, "Are there any Lutheran churches in Marysville?" They told us there were three in Marysville and a total of five in the county. It was time for us to pay attention to what mattered. Our baby girl was now two and would soon be learning about how to live life.

The first church we attended in Marysville was just across the street from the house we were renting. It had a small but enthusiastic congregation and seemed super friendly. We had talked to the pastor before the first service we attended and we were shocked when, during the service, he said, "We have got some visitors with us today. Karen and Dennis stand up and say hello." At that point, everyone stood up and began clapping and I was thinking, I don't remember my childhood church being quite this informal!

The friendly reception we got that first Sunday was nice but the informality was not something we were used to. We decided that we would try a different church and, the next weekend, we went to a Missouri Synod church whose members were primarily farmers who had lived their entire lives in this small town. Many of their families had emigrated from

Germany and we discovered that it was not that long ago that one sermon per month was in German. Another recent change was the women no longer congregated on one side and the men on the other.

The deal breaker for continuing with this church was that there was no nursery and our two-year-old would be required to sit quietly with us. It wasn't going to happen! Two down and three to go.

The third Sunday, we went to the last Lutheran Church which was located in town rather than in the country. As we entered the sanctuary, there seemed to be a lot of gray-haired parishioners. There were lots of smiles and nods but no ovation during the service.

Not everything went smooth. At the beginning of the service, as we sat down in a pew, a lady came up to us and told us, "That is where my family sits!" We apologized and got up to move.

That could have been strike three except, as we were changing seats, another couple asked us to join them and then quietly said, "There are no assigned seats. If you want to sit there just tell her to get lost." It is now more than 50 years since we first visited our church but the memory still haunts me which is partly why I volunteer for the visitor center. I make sure to tell visitors that they can sit wherever they want to.

I was never anxious to get involved in the administration of the church. Whenever you have a significantly diverse congregation, there may be moments of disagreement. Within a couple of years of our attendance at this church, we discovered that the church had gone through a period of time when the people in the first service (traditional) and the people of the second service (contemporary) were questioning the need for the other service. They tried adding a third service which was a blend.

When that didn't solve all of the problems I was asked (probably because I was a lawyer) to serve on church council to help arbitrate the differences. I didn't want to be put in that position but I did serve and we had enough "cool heads" that it worked itself out. I turned down the suggestion that I run for subsequent terms on council.

As part of my service to the Church, I have provided free legal services. I have served on church council and two call committees. I have become a communion assistant. I taught Bible study for nine years. And, I have participated in plays.

THE LAST SUPPER, A PLAY

My church is an active one which presents a variety of options designed to teach the word of God. We have an early service that follows a traditional format. It features an organ and, at times, a choir. The middle service is "contemporary" and has a praise band and more upbeat music. The third service is somewhat of a blend.

In addition to the regular services, there are small groups such as Bible study, service circles, and social opportunities. There are also many community outreach programs such as the monthly food distributions to families who can't afford the store prices for fresh fruit and vegetables. Members of the congregation unpack, setup, and distribute a semi- truck full of fruits and vegetables to more than 200 people.

Every once in a while, a relevant play is presented and I have become part of those who perform. There are acting parts and once I was featured, offstage, as the voice of God.

One day, the director of the plays approached me about performing in one called "The Last Supper." The story took place in the days of Michael Angelo. He was commissioned to paint a picture of the Last Supper and he decided that he would rather pay live actors to inspire him rather than looking at prior paintings.

I agreed to take a part and the director handed me a script. I glanced at it and saw the name Jesus written on the cover page. I asked the director if that was the part I was to play and she said yes. I pointed out that I had just turned 50 and Jesus died much earlier than that. She assured me that age would not be a problem and that she knew I could handle the part.

We started rehearsing, and the play began to come alive to those 14 of us who were Michelangelo, Jesus, and the twelve disciples.

As each actor in the play was assigned a part and began to get into their character, Jesus (me) would talk to them and provide them with a greater understanding as to who they were and what their mission meant to the world. Each disciple began to learn that the character they were portraying was an important part of the growth of Christianity. This was even true of Judas!

The final scene was the Last Supper where Jesus broke bread and gave it to each disciple and then gave them wine with the admonition that this was his blood, shed for them. Each apostle then spoke directly to Jesus to share the love which he had found.

FAITH

The impact on me, and I believe on each of us, was profound! As each disciple spoke to Jesus to express their love for him, we became those men. We were transplanted out of our mundane world and found real meaning in the sacrifice God made for us.

After the play ended, the congregation was invited to come forward and receive communion. There were two receiving lines, and the senior pastor and I gave each member of the church the body of Christ.

I have never been so moved by a story. As I interacted with the chosen 12, I felt a resurgence of faith that has renewed me to this day.

While the play "Last Supper" may have impacted me the most, there have been many other opportunities to grow my faith.

I especially enjoyed teaching Bible study. Over the years, I prepared and presented a wide range of subject matter and methods. We did a yearlong session on the books of the Bible as set forth in the King James Version. We did a comparative timeline between Bible history and secular world history. We did many other in-depth studies of singular subjects and we also did a comparative religion course. For the comparative religion we asked a Catholic priest, a Jewish rabbi, a Mormon elder, and a Muslim Imam to attend and explain their religions to us.

I realize that when you are closer to "meeting your Maker" there may be more incentive to start showing up in church. However, I would like to think that our family's renewed interest in attending church resulted from a more meaningful coming together of like-minded people to learn about God.

As I reflect on my lifetime relationship with God, I realize the following truths:

- God gave me wonderful parents and a sister who were: <u>Supportive, loving, patient, positive, and filled with faith.</u>
- God gave me friends who were: <u>Caring, honest, giving, and who believed in God.</u>

- God gave me an opportunity to receive an education: <u>Both formal and informal which prepared me to live a comfortable life with many choices.</u>
- God gave me an opportunity to serve my country and community: <u>Which helped me to understand how fortunate I am and how I need to care about others.</u>
- God gave me an opportunity to work in a profession: <u>That allowed me to help others solve their problems.</u>
- God gave me an opportunity to live in a country where: <u>I am free to voice my opinion, travel where I choose, enjoy many pastimes, and practice my beliefs as set forth in the Bible.</u>
- God gave me an unbelievable spouse who has been: <u>My lifetime soulmate, my friend, my lover, my adviser, my counselor, my nurse, my advocate, and the mother of our children and grandchildren.</u>

God has given me all of this and He further has given me intelligence and strength to carry me through this life until we are together. For all of this God, I thank you and I pledge to you my faith.

SUMMARY

I HOPE THAT YOU ENJOYED reading this book and I hope that you will take some time to reflect on memorializing your own life. Don't ever think that no one will be interested in what you have to say. Every person's life is interesting.

As I started writing the first chapter about my early family, I gained a greater appreciation for how much my father, mother, and sister were positive influences on my life. They provided me with a desire to achieve, but they did not demand unreasonable results. They gave me a moral compass and, when I would occasionally deviate a bit, they would lovingly guide me back to our Christian roots. They also gave me a desire to succeed and an education to accomplish success.

As much as my early family lead me in the right direction, my friends played an important part in knowing right from wrong. They also taught me that before success there must be effort. I learned to listen to them as I began to trust their judgement and upbringing.

I learned more about life from teachers, mentors, and even from total strangers. Each of these interpersonal experiences helped shape me and gave me insight into how the world functioned and how I might best fit into it.

My wife, children, and grandchildren provided me with the most important part of my life and offered me the love, support, and understanding that I needed to live life to the fullest.

Beyond my family, I knew that for my life to be complete, I needed to give back part of myself to my country, my profession, and those who were in need.

God has blessed me in so many ways and I pledge to continue to give back as long as I am able. So, let's all celebrate life as we work to make our own even better.

THIS IS WHO I AM – CHAT TIME

This is an activity that is best done by 4 to 8 people. It might be completed in 10 minutes, or may take an hour, depending on how the participants enjoy it.

There are twenty questions posed on everyone's list and the manner of play is quite simple. The host/hostess chooses one of the twenty questions and answers it. The answer should take 3 to 5 minutes but should not exceed 5 minutes, unless the other participants are shouting, "MORE! MORE!" The speaker can also address any questions that the listeners might have.

Then, the play moves clockwise and the next player chooses one of the twenty questions to answer. The questions are NOT eliminated because someone has previously answered the same question. Remember, there are no wrong answers and you will be answering too, so be kind. This is not a competition; it is a sharing.

Spouses and close friends should not challenge any answer since it is the speaker's memory that is important, not the absolute truth!

The list of questions follows, but always feel free to add your own!

QUESTIONS ABOUT YOUR LIFE

- What is the first memory you have as a young child?
- What was your favorite subject in school? Why?
- What did you do on the first date with your spouse?
- What was a secret that you never told your parents about?
- Growing up, or as an adult, what was your favorite pet?
- What was the scariest moment you have ever experienced?

SUMMARY

- Who is the most famous person you have ever met?
- What is the dumbest thing you have ever done?
- Other than those present, who is/was your favorite friend?
- At this point of your life, what is your favorite pastime?
- What was the greatest honor you ever received?
- What is the best vacation you have ever taken?
- If you could start over, what job would you choose?
- What living person would you most like to talk to?
- What do you most admire about your spouse?
- What was the most interesting dream you ever had?
- If you could be any age, what would it be and why?
- What was the most dangerous thing you ever intentionally did?
- What was your best memory of high school?
- YOUR CHOICE – You may select any topic (be couth) and tell us something we don't know about you.

www.ingramcontent.com/pod-product-compliance
Lightning Source LLC
Chambersburg PA
CBHW020149090426
42734CB00008B/754